Diane Naughton

with John Peebles and Bob Hastings

PRE-INTERMEDIATE

Total English

Teacher's Resource Book

Contents

Syllabus outline

	UNIT	LESSON 1	LESSON 2	LESSON 3	COMMUNICATION
1	**24 hours** page 5	**Grammar:** likes and dislikes **Vocabulary:** daily routines and activities **Can do:** ask and talk about personal likes and dislikes **Skills:** **speaking:** do a quiz and talk about the results **reading:** read about two people's typical Saturday **speaking and writing:** tell other students what you are like; write about your typical Saturday	**Grammar:** Present Simple; adverbs of frequency **Vocabulary:** sleeping habits **Can do:** ask and answer questions about daily routines **Skills:** **speaking:** talk about your sleep habits; listen to other people talking about their sleep habits **Pronunciation:** /uː/, /ə/ and /ʌ/	**Grammar:** Present Continuous **Vocabulary:** shops and shopping **Can do:** write an informal email to update someone on your life **Skills:** **reading:** read about a famous department store **listening:** listen to a customer survey **writing:** write an email to a friend you haven't talked to for a long time (**Writing bank** page 145)	**Can do:** talk about your learning needs and ability **Lifelong learning:** ways to improve your English
		Film Bank: London (page 133) **Photocopiable materials:** Vocabulary, Grammar and Communication (Teacher's Resource Book page 99)			
2	**Music** page 15	**Grammar:** Past Simple **Vocabulary:** talking about biographies **Can do:** talk about personal events in the past **Skills:** **reading:** read about a real classic **listening:** listen to an interview with Robin Scott **speaking:** prepare and give an interview **Pronunciation:** /t/, /d/ and /id/	**Grammar:** *so* and *neither* **Vocabulary:** word families – nouns and adjectives **Can do:** say when you are the same as/different from, another person **Skills:** **reading:** read about how music affects your mood **Lifelong learning:** recording new vocabulary	**Grammar:** Present Perfect Simple (for experience) **Vocabulary:** verb/noun collocations about achievements **Can do:** talk about personal achievements and experiences **Skills:** **reading:** read about a child prodigy	**Can do:** explain why you like a piece of music
		Film Bank: Summer Holiday (page 134) **Photocopiable materials:** Vocabulary, Grammar and Communication (Teacher's Resource Book page 104)			
3	**Taste** page 25	**Grammar:** *going to* (future plans) **Vocabulary:** food and restaurants **Can do:** tell a friend about your future plans **Skills:** **reading:** read about a celebrity chef's new restaurant **speaking:** talk about your plans for the next two years	**Grammar:** defining relative clauses **Vocabulary:** talking about films **Can do:** write an informal letter to a friend **Skills:** **listening:** listen to a conversation about a film **pronunciation:** silent letters **writing:** write a letter to a friend giving news and inviting him/her to a party (**Writing bank** page 145)	**Grammar:** Present Continuous (for future arrangements) **Vocabulary:** adjectives; sense verbs **Can do:** make arrangements with a friend **Skills:** **reading:** read about a why we enjoy food **speaking:** make arrangements with different classmates	**Can do:** contribute to a simple discussion
		Film Bank: Jamie Oliver (page 135) **Photocopiable materials:** Vocabulary, Grammar and Communication (Teacher's Resource Book page 109) **Test 1:** Units 1–3 (Teacher's Resource Book page 189)			
4	**Survival** page 35	**Grammar:** comparatives **Vocabulary:** describing people **Can do:** compare people **Skills:** **reading:** read about two people and their achievements	**Grammar:** superlatives **Vocabulary:** survival skills **Can do:** write a thank-you note **Skills:** **listening:** listen to a talk by an instructor at a survival school **writing:** write a thank-you note **Pronunciation:** stressed words in sentences	**Grammar:** indirect questions **Vocabulary:** survival English **Can do:** ask polite questions **Skills:** **reading:** read about the English **listening:** listen to shopping dialogues **speaking:** do a market research survey **Lifelong learning:** Survival tips	**Can do:** agree on choices with a partner
		Film Bank: Surviving in the Sahara (page 136) **Photocopiable materials:** Vocabulary, Grammar and Communication (Teacher's Resource Book page 114)			

UNIT		LESSON 1	LESSON 2	LESSON 3	COMMUNICATION
5	**Stages** page 45	**Grammar:** *should, can, have to* **Vocabulary:** times of life **Can do:** exchange opinions with a friend **Skills:** **reading:** read about adolescents growing up **listening and speaking:** listen to people giving opinions **Pronunciation:** /t/ in *shouldn't* and *can't*	**Grammar:** Present Perfect with *for* and *since* **Vocabulary:** friendship **Can do:** write a personal profile **Skills:** **writing:** write a personal profile	**Grammar:** used to **Vocabulary:** habits **Can do:** describe yourself when you were younger **Skills:** **speaking and listening:** do a quiz and listen to the answers **Pronunciation:** *used to/ didn't use to*	**Can do:** make a simple informal presentation
		Film Bank: On Golden Pond (page 137) **Photocopiable materials:** Vocabulary, Grammar and Communication (Teacher's Resource Book page 119)			
6	**Places** page 55	**Grammar:** *will* **Vocabulary:** geographical features **Can do:** make general predictions about the future **Skills:** **listening:** listen to someone talking about New Zealand **reading:** read about *The Lord of the Rings* and New Zealand **Ponunciation:** *want* and *won't*	**Grammar:** *too, too much/ many, enough* **Vocabulary:** machines at home **Can do:** give explanations for choices **Skills:** **listening:** listen to two people talking about a TV programme **speaking:** choose 5 machines you can't live without	**Grammar:** uses of like **Vocabulary:** describing natural places **Can do:** describe a favourite place **Skills:** **reading:** read about a prison garden **writing:** write about your favourite natural place **Lifelong learning:** Brainstorm! **Pronunciation:** raising and falling intonation	**Can do:** explain your preference for a holiday destination
		Film Bank: Around the world (page 138) **Photocopiable materials:** Vocabulary, Grammar and Communication (Teacher's Resource Book page 124) **Test 2:** Units 4–6 (Teacher's Resource Book page 195)			
7	**Body** page 65	**Grammar:** First Conditional **Vocabulary:** appearance **Can do:** describe a person's physical appearance **Skills:** **reading and speaking:** read and speak about Reneé Zellweger in Bridget Jones's Diary	**Grammar:** gerunds and in.nitives **Vocabulary:** personality **Can do:** describe someone's personality **Skills:** **listening:** listen to someone reading their friend's palm **reading and speaking:** read about palm-reading and read someone's palm **Pronunciation:** word stress	**Grammar:** purpose/ reason/result **Vocabulary:** illness and injury **Can do:** talk about illness and give advice **Skills:** **listening:** listen to *Doctor, doctor* jokes **reading and speaking:** read and speak about alternative medicine **writing:** write a letter asking for advice	**Can do:** understand and talk about a magazine quiz
		Film Bank: Carry on Doctor (page 139) **Photocopiable materials:** Vocabulary, Grammar and Communication (Teacher's Resource Book page 129)			
8	**Speed** page 75	**Grammar:** Present Simple Passive **Vocabulary:** verbs about change **Can do:** describe simple changes **Skills:** **reading:** read about 'The Slow Movement' **speaking:** talk about changes in your country	**Grammar:** questions **Vocabulary:** phrasal verbs about relationships **Can do:** find out personal information **Skills:** **reading:** read about speed-dating **listening:** listen to four people speed-dating **speaking:** find out interesting information about people	**Grammar:** Past Continuous and Past Simple **Vocabulary:** talking about books **Can do:** ask and answer questions about past actions **Skills:** **reading:** read an extract from *The curious incident of the dog in the night* **speaking:** provide an alibi **writing:** story-writing (**Writing bank** page 147); write a story **Pronunciation:** *was/were*	**Can do:** talk for an extended period on a familiar topic
		Film Bank: Speed-dating (page 140) Photocopiable materials: Vocabulary, Grammar and Communication (Teacher's Resource Book page 134)			

	UNIT	LESSON 1	LESSON 2	LESSON 3	COMMUNICATION
9	**Work** page 85	**Vocabulary:** work **Can do:** respond to simple job interview questions **Skills:** **listening:** listen to people's stories about interviews **reading:** read about how to get a job **speaking:** act out an interview **Pronunciation:** word stress	**Grammar:** *can, could, be able to* **Vocabulary:** make/do **Can do:** talk about your abilities **Skills:** **reading:** read about a boy wonder **Lifelong learning:** Setting targets	**Grammar:** Past Simple Passive **Vocabulary:** crime **Can do:** write a short article **Skills:** **listening:** listen to a news story **writing:** write an article	**Can do:** take part in a simple negotiation
		Film Bank: The interview (page 141) **Photocopiable materials:** Vocabulary, Grammar and Communication (Teacher's Resource Book page 139) **Test 3:** Units 7–9 (Teacher's Resource Book page 201)			
10	**Wildlife** page 95	**Grammar:** phrasal verbs **Vocabulary:** phrasal verbs **Can do:** talk about people who influenced you **Skills:** **reading:** read about children raised by animals **listening and speaking:** listen to someone talking about people who influenced her; talk about who influenced you **Lifelong learning:** Keep a record (1) **Pronunciation:** word stress	**Grammar:** countable/ uncountable nouns **Vocabulary:** animals and zoos **Can do:** write a short contribution for a bulletin board **Skills:** **reading:** read about the advantages and disadvantages of keeping animals in zoos **writing:** start an 'online' bulletin board discussion	**Grammar:** the definite article (the) **Vocabulary:** verb + prepositions (1) **Can do:** speculate about sounds and pictures **Skills:** **reading and listening:** listen and read about a TV programme for pets **speaking:** say what things sound like	**Can do:** participate in reaching a group decision
		Film Bank: Wolves (page 142) **Photocopiable materials:** Vocabulary, Grammar and Communication (Teacher's Resource Book page 144)			
11	**Travel** page 105	**Grammar:** Present Perfect Simple with *just, yet* and *already* **Vocabulary:** holidays **Can do:** find out if someone would be a good travel companion **Skills:** **reading:** read a travel-diary **speaking and writing:** talk and write about travel companions **Lifelong learning:** Keep a record (2) **Pronunciation:** /dz/ and /j/	**Grammar:** verbs with two objects **Vocabulary:** greetings and presents **Can do:** make generalisations about customs **Skills:** **reading:** read some advice for UK business travellers **speaking:** talk about customs in your country	**Grammar:** Past Perfect Simple **Vocabulary:** travel writing **Can do:** write about a place you've travelled to **Skills:** **listening:** listen to an interview with a travel writer **writing:** write about a place you have visited **Pronunciation:** *had*	**Can do:** achieve your aim in a typical travel conversation
		Film Bank: Gill's wild world (page 143) **Photocopiable materials:** Vocabulary, Grammar and Communication (Teacher's Resource Book page 149)			
12	**Money** page 115	**Grammar:** Second Conditional **Vocabulary:** money **Can do:** say what you'd do in a hypothetical situation **Skills:** **reading:** read about 'honesty boxes'	**Grammar:** reported speech **Vocabulary:** education **Can do:** report what someone said to you **Skills:** **listening:** listen to a news item about a new program in a UK school **speaking:** respond to difficult questions **writing:** formal letters (**Writing bank** page 119); write a formal letter	**Grammar:** *both, neither, either* **Vocabulary:** verb + prepositions (2) **Can do:** describe similarities/differences **Skills:** **reading:** read about the $1million baseball **speaking:** find out what you have in common with other people **Lifelong learning:** Into the future **Pronunciation:** *both, either* and *neither*	**Can do:** make a simple complaint in a shop/ restaurant
		Film Bank: The Ladykillers (page 144) **Photocopiable materials:** Vocabulary, Grammar and Communication (Teacher's Resource Book page 154) **Test 4:** Units 10–12 (Teacher's Resource Book page 207)			

Introduction

Teaching and learning are unpredictable experiences. Learners can be dynamic and engaged one lesson and then demotivated, tired or even absent the next. The aim of *Total English* is two-fold: firstly to set new standards in terms of interest level, teachability and range of support materials; and secondly to address the reality of most people's unpredicatable teaching experience as it is, not as we hope it will be.

Research for *Total English* suggested three classroom 'realities' that need to be addressed in a coursebook: 1) learners often lack direction and purpose –they are often not sure about the relevance of what they are learning and where they are going with English; 2) learners need to be genuinely engaged in coursebook content just as they are in the newspapers, TV programmes and films that they see around them; 3) learners often miss lessons and this creates extra work for the teacher to make sure that no-one falls behind.

Finding direction and purpose

Learners need a clear sense of where they are going and how they are going to get there. They need to know what they are learning, why they are learning it and how it can be applied outside the classroom. Clear goals and objectives are crucial. *Total English* contains a clear grammar syllabus and plenty of practice. Each input lesson is organised on a double-page spread and has a grammar and *Can Do* learning objective clearly stated at the start. The *Can Do* objectives give a purpose and reason for learning and mean that students know why they are studying that lesson and how they can use the new language.

The learning objectives in Total English are derived from the *Can Do* statements in the Common European Framework which means teachers can feel confident that *Total English* covers the language areas their students need. The levels of *Total English* correlate to the Common European Framework in the following way:

Elementary	Covers A1 and goes towards A2
Pre-intermediate	Covers A2 and goes towards B1
Intermediate	Covers B1 and goes towards B1+
Upper Intermediate	Covers B1+ and B2
Advanced	Covers C1

Engaging learners' interest

Motivation through engagement is equally important for successful language learning. *Total English* lessons give a new twist to familiar topics – topics that reflect learners' needs and interests. This ensures that learners will always have something to say about the content of the lesson. There are frequent opportunities for learners to exchange ideas and opinions and engage with the material on a personal level. Activities have been designed to be as realistic as possible so that learners can see how the language they're learning can be applied outside the classroom.

In addition to the wide range of topics, texts and activities, each level of the *Total English* Students' Books has a DVD which adds an extra dimension to the course. Containing a range of authentic material from film and TV, the DVDs expose learners to a variety of different English media and give them a feel for how the language is used in real life. Each unit of the Students' Books has a corresponding DVD extract and the Film banks at the back of the Students' Books offer material to use in class or at home while watching the DVD.

Helping learners catch up

One of the most common problems that teachers face is irregular attendance. Learners often have busy lives with work, study or family commitments and attending English classes on a regular basis is not always possible. *Total English* recognises this problem and has been designed to help learners catch up easily if they miss lessons. In addition to the practice exercises in each lesson, there is a Reference page and a Review and practice page at the end of each unit. These provide an accessible summary of the main grammar and vocabulary covered.

The *Total English* Workbooks also have freestanding CD-ROMs that include interactive self-study 'catch-up' material to present and practise language from any lessons learners have missed. With this extensive range of animated presentations, interactive practice exercises and games, *Total English* ensures your students don't get left behind if they miss lessons.

The course package

Total English has five levels and takes learners from Elementary to Advanced. Each level consists of the following:

- **Students' Book**

The *Total English* Students' Books are divided into 10-12 units and contain approximately 80-120 hours of teaching material. Each unit contains a balanced mix of grammar, vocabulary, pronunciation and skills work including writing.

- **DVD**

The 'with DVD' version of the Students' Books has a freestanding DVD which provides additional listening practice linked to the topic areas in the Students' Books.

- **Video**

The DVD material is also available on video (PAL and NTSC).

- **Class Cassettes/CDs**

Total English Class Cassettes/CDs contain all the recorded material from the Students' Books.

- **Workbook**

The *Total English* Workbooks contain further practice of language areas covered in the corresponding units of the Students' Books.

- **Workbook 'Catch-up' CD-ROM**

The *Total English* Workbook CD-ROMs provide extra support for students who miss lessons. In addition to the recorded material from the Workbooks, the Workbook CD-ROMs feature 'catch-up' material related to the key grammar areas covered in the Students' Books.

- **Teacher's Resource Book**

The *Total English* Teacher's Resource Books provide all the support teachers need to get the most out of the course. The Teacher's Resource Books contain teaching notes, photocopiable worksheets, DVD worksheets and tests.

- **Website**

Total English has its own dedicated website. In addition to background information about the course and authors, the website features teaching tips, downloadable worksheets, links to other useful websites as well as special offers and competitions. Join us online at www.longman.com/totalenglish.

The Students' Book

Each unit of the *Total English* Students' Books follows the same structure making the material very easy to use:

- **Lead-in page**
  - acts as a springboard into the topic of the unit and engages students' interest.
  - introduces essential vocabulary related to the topic so that students start with the same basic grounding.
- **Input lessons**
  - three double-page input lessons, thematically linked, offer interesting angles on the unit topic.
  - each input lesson leads towards a *Can Do* learning objective in line with the Council of Europe's *Can Do* statements.
  - each 90-minute lesson focuses on a specific grammar area and includes vocabulary, pronunciation and skills work.
  - each unit contains at least two reading texts and a substantial listening element.
  - How to... boxes develop students' competence in using language, in line with the Common European Framework.
  - Lifelong learning boxes offer tips and strategies for developing students' study skills.
- **Communication page**
  - revises language taught in the previous three lessons in a freer, more communicative context.
  - each communication task practises a range of skills and has a measurable goal or outcome.
- **Reference page**
  - summarises the main grammar points covered in each unit and provides a list of key vocabulary.
  - helps learners to catch up if they miss lessons and is an essential revision tool.
- **Review and practice page**
  - provides a range of exercises to consolidate key grammar and vocabulary covered in the unit.
  - can be used to check progress, enabling teachers to identify areas that need further practice.
- **Film bank pages**
  - support the DVD which is attached to the back of the 'with DVD' version of the Students' Books.
  - feature a range of exercises designed to stimulate interest in each DVD extract and make the authentic material contained on the DVD accessible to students.

The Total English Students' Books also feature the following:

- **Do you know?**
  - an optional page to be covered before learners start the course which teaches basic language areas such as the alphabet, numbers and classroom language.
- **Writing bank**
  - provides models and tips on how to write emails, letters and postcards as well as guidance on different writing skills such as punctuation, spelling and paragraph construction.
- **Pronunciation bank**
  - provides a list of English phonemes, guidance on sound-spelling correspondences and weak forms.

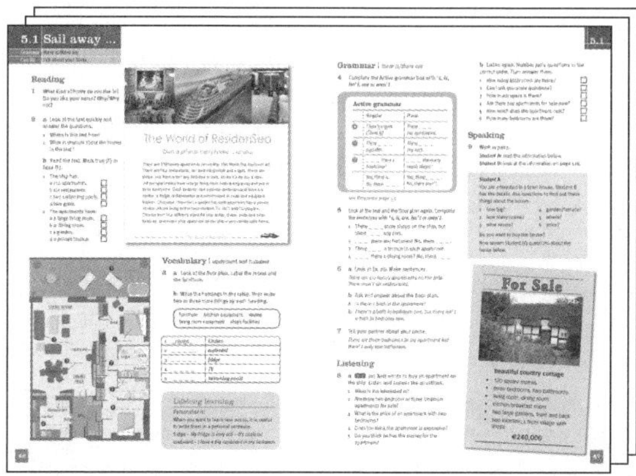

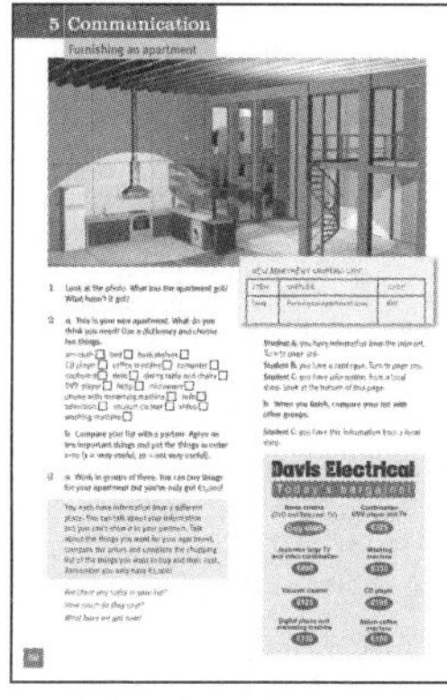

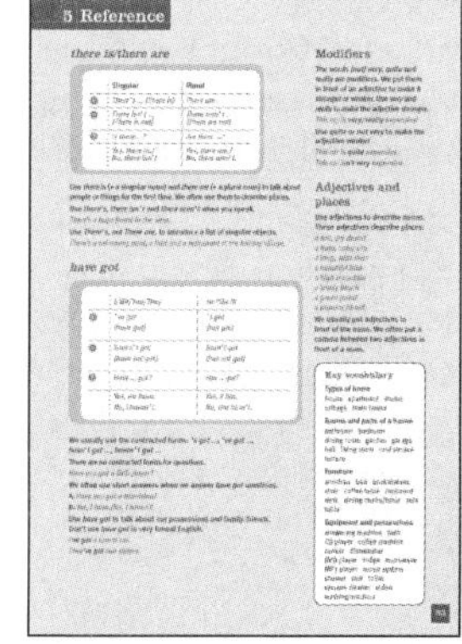

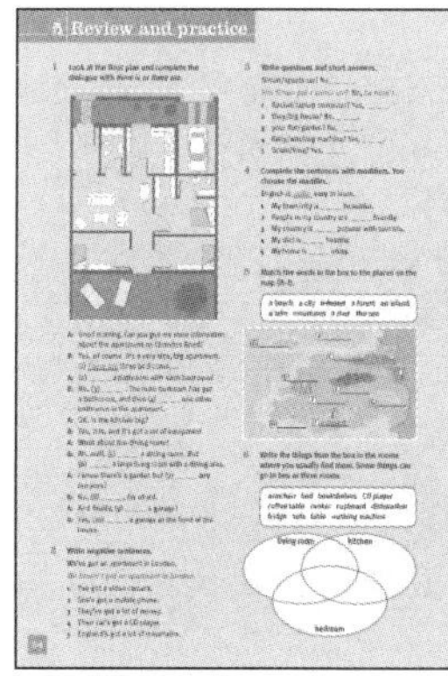

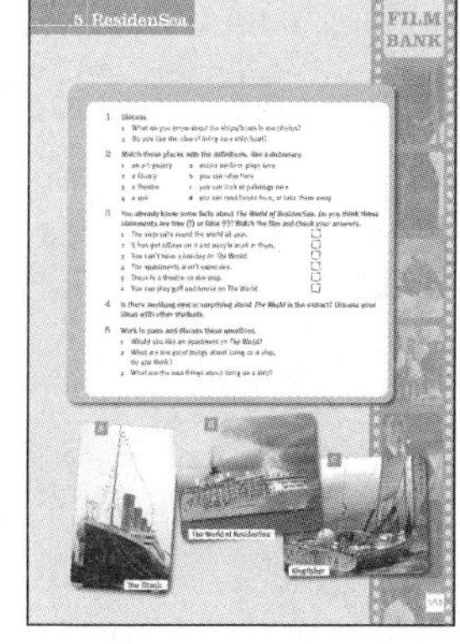

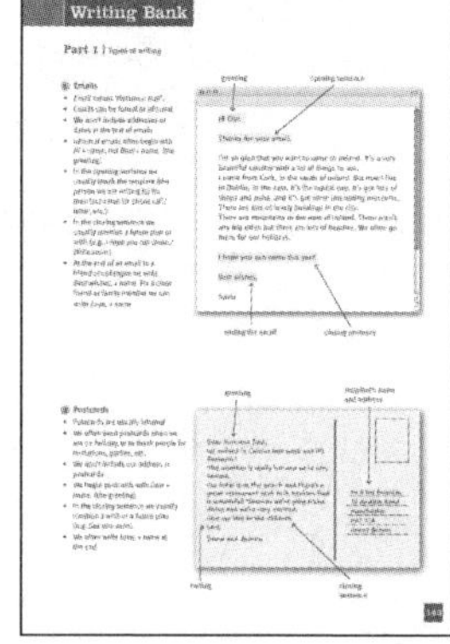

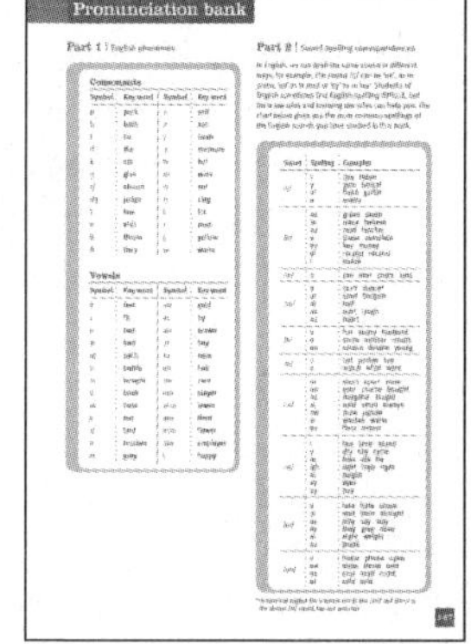

The Workbook

The *Total English* Workbooks contain 10-12 units which correspond to the Students' Book material. Each Workbook contains:

- **Additional practice material**
  Extra grammar, vocabulary, skills and pronunciation exercises practise language covered in the corresponding units of the Students' Books.
- **Review and consolidation sections**
  These occur after units 3, 6, 9 and 12 and contain cumulative practice of the grammar and vocabulary covered in the previous three units.
- **Vocabulary bank**
  This provides further practice in the key vocabulary areas covered in each unit of the Students' Books. Students can refer to this after studying a particular topic and record the new vocabulary they have learned. They can also add new items as they come across them.

The Workbook CD-ROM

In addition to the recorded material from the Workbook, the 'catch-up' section of the CD-Rom contains the following:

- **Grammar presentations**
  Simple, accessible grammar explanations summarise the target language of each unit in a succinct and memorable way.
- **Self-check practice exercises**
  A range of practice exercises (two for each grammar point) enable students to practise the target language.
- **'Can do' game**
  This provides communicative practice of the target language.

The Teacher's Resource Book

The Teacher's Resource Books are divided into the following sections:

- **Introduction**
  This explains the aims and rationale of the course and provides a complete description of the course package.
- **Teaching notes**
  These provide step by step instructions on how to exploit each unit as well as background notes and suggestions for warm-up, lead-in and extension activities.
- **Photocopiable resource banks**
  The photocopiable resource banks contain 60 photocopiable worksheets (5 worksheets for each unit of the Students' Books). The worksheets are designed to practise the grammar and vocabulary covered in the Students' Book units in a freer, less structured and enjoyable context. Detailed instructions on how to use each worksheet are also provided in the Teacher's Resource Book.
- **DVD worksheets**
  In addition to the Film bank pages in the Students' Books, the Teacher's Resource Books also have 12 DVD worksheets. Containing Before viewing, While viewing and Post viewing activities, the DVD worksheets provide more detailed exploitation of the DVD material. Instructions on how to use each worksheet including warm-up and extension activities are also provided.
- **Tests**
  Four photocopiable progress tests are included in the Teacher's Resource Books. Each test covers grammar, vocabulary, reading, listening and writing skills and is designed to be used after every third unit.

Teaching approaches

Grammar

Total English covers all the main language areas you would expect at each level and gives learners a thorough foundation in grammar based on the following principles:

- **Clear presentation/analysis**
  Each double-page lesson has a clear grammar aim which is stated at the top of the page. New language items are presented in context via reading and/or listening texts and grammar rules are then analysed and explained via the Active grammar boxes which are a key feature of each lesson.

Active grammar

I'm starting the course next month ...
Geoff is working in the US again in March ...

1. Which tense are the sentences?
2. Has Joanna decided to do the course?
3. Has Geoff organised his stay in the States?
4. Are the sentences describing an action in the present or in the future?

Total English takes a 'guided discovery' approach to grammar and learners are actively invited to think about grammar and work out the rules for themselves.

- **Varied, regular practice**
  Once learners have grasped the important rules, all new language is then practised in a variety of different ways so that learners are able to use the grammar with confidence. Practice activities include form-based exercises designed to help learners manipulate the new structures as well as more meaningful, personalised practice. Additional grammar practice exercises can be found in the Review and practice sections at the end of each unit as well as in the Workbooks and on the Workbook CD-ROMs. The Teacher's Resource Books also contain an extensive bank of photocopiable grammar activities which are designed to practise the language in freer, more communicative contexts.
- **Accessible reference material**
  In addition to the explanations contained in the Active Grammar boxes, there is a Reference section at the end of each unit which summarises the rules in greater detail and provides extra information and examples.

Vocabulary

Total English recognises the central role that vocabulary plays in successful communication. The emphasis is on providing learners with high-frequency, useful vocabulary which is regularly practised and revised. New vocabulary is presented and practised in a variety of different ways – via the Lead-in pages which provide a springboard into the topic of each unit enabling teachers to elicit vocabulary that learners already know as well as pre-teach essential vocabulary for the rest of the unit; via the reading and listening texts and related exercises; via special vocabulary sections in the main lessons. Additional vocabulary practice is provided in the Review and practice sections of the Students' Book, in the practice exercises in the Workbook and special vocabulary worksheets in the Teacher's Resource Book.

Speaking

The key aim for most learners is spoken fluency but low level learners cannot express themselves easily without support. *Total English* develops spoken fluency in a number of ways – by giving learners discussion topics they want to talk about; by setting up situations where they are motivated to communicate in order to complete a specific task; by providing clear models and examples of how to structure discourse and by encouraging them, wherever possible, to express their own ideas and opinions. All lessons feature some speaking practice and there are regular How to... boxes throughout the course which focus on the words and expressions learners need to carry out specific functions.

HOW TO ...

order in a fast food restaurant

Ask questions	______ *you have salads?*
Say what you want	*I'd ______ a cheese sandwich, please.*
Ask about prices	*How ______ is that?*

Communication pages at the end of each unit engage learners in a variety of problem-solving tasks and involve learners in a number of different skills – including speaking. The photocopiable activities in the Teacher's Resource Book are also specifically designed to promote speaking practice.

Listening

Listening is one of the most difficult skills to master and *Total English* pays particular emphasis to developing learners' confidence in this area. Listening texts include short dialogues as well as longer texts (conversations, interviews, stories and songs). There are lots of simple 'Listen and check your answer' exercises as well as more challenging activities where learners have to listen to longer extracts in order to find specific information. The recorded material features a variety of accents including British, American, Australian and some non-native speakers. There is additional listening practice in the Workbooks and the DVDs further enhance learners' confidence in understanding the spoken word.

Pronunciation

Total English pays particular attention to pronunciation which is integrated into all the lessons which present new language. The pronunciation syllabus includes word and sentence stress, weak forms, intonation and difficult sounds. The Pronunciation banks at the back of the Students' Books include a list of English phonemes, guidance on sound-spelling correspondences and weak forms. There is additional pronunciation practice in the Workbooks and on the Workbook CD-ROMs.

Reading

There is a wide variety of reading texts in *Total English* ranging from simple forms and advertisements to short texts from newspapers and magazines. Texts have been chosen for their intrinsic interest as well as for their usefulness in providing a vehicle for the particular grammar and vocabulary points in focus. Many all of the texts have been adapted from authentic, real-life sources (magazines, websites etc.) and related tasks have been carefully selected to develop learners' confidence in dealing with written texts. Activities include comprehension and vocabulary work as well as practice in dealing with different reading sub-skills such as reading for gist. There are a number of jigsaw readings where learners work together and share information. The length and complexity of the texts get more challenging as the course progresses.

Writing

With the growth of email, writing is becoming an increasingly important skill. *Total English* acknowledges this by including regular writing tasks in the Students' Books. These are carefully structured with exercises and examples designed to ensure that learners are actually able to carry out the tasks. Models of different types of writing – emails, postcards, formal and informal letters are provided in the Writing Bank at the back of the Students' Books as well as additional advice and guidance on different writing sub-skills such as punctuation, spelling and paragraph construction.

Revision and testing

There are plenty of opportunities for revision in *Total English* and language is constantly recycled throughout the course. At the end of every unit, there are special Review and practice pages which take the form of mini- progress checks enabling learners to identify areas where they might need further practice.

In addition to the Review and practice pages, there are four Review and consolidation sections in the accompanying Workbooks, and a whole range of additional practice material on the 'Catch-up' CD-ROMs. The Teacher's Resource Books include four photocopiable progress tests which are designed to be used after units 3, 6, 9 and 12.

Learner training

Total English places a strong emphasis on learner training and good study habits are encouraged and developed via the Lifelong learning boxes which are a featured in many lessons. The Lifelong learning boxes provide useful tips and suggestions on how to continue learning outside the classroom. In addition, the Vocabulary banks in the Workbooks not only encourage students to record vocabulary from particular lessons, but also to revisit and add further vocabulary items as they arise.

Lifelong learning

Personalise it!

When you want to learn new words, it is useful to write them in a personal sentence.

fridge – *My fridge is very old – it's useless!*

cupboard – *I have a big cupboard in my bedroom.*

Total English and exams

The table below shows how the different levels of Total English relate to the Common European Framework levels and the University of Cambridge ESOL main suite examinations in terms of the language taught and the topics covered. While *Total English* is not an examination preparation course, a student who has, for example, completed the Upper Intermediate level would have sufficient language to attempt the Cambridge ESOL FCE (First Certificate in English) examination. Many of the exercises in the *Total English* Students' Books, Workbooks and photocopiable tests are similar in format to those found in the Cambridge ESOL main suite examinations but specific training is required for all EFL examinations and we would strongly recommend this.

For further information on the University of Cambridge ESOL examinations, contact:

Cambridge ESOL
1 Hills Road
Cambridge
CB1 2EU

Tel. +44 (0) 1223 553355
Fax. +44 (0) 1223 460278
Email: ESOL@ucles.org.uk
www.CambridgeESOL.org

	CEF levels	Cambridge ESOL Exams	TOTAL ENGLISH LEVELS					
Proficient user	C2	CPE						
	C1	CAE						
Independent user	B2	FCE						
	B1+							
	B1	PET						
	A2	KET						
Basic user	A1							
			STARTER	ELEMENTARY	PRE-INTERMEDIATE	INTERMEDIATE	UPPER INTERMEDIATE	ADVANCED

Total English authors

Total English Elementary

Mark Foley has worked in English language teaching for over 23 years and has extensive experience in teaching (mostly in the UK and Spain), teacher training, examining and materials writing. He is the co-author of a number of publications, including the Longman ELT advanced titles, Distinction and Advanced Learner's Grammar. He is co-author, with Diane Hall, of *Total English* Elementary Students' Book and Workbook.

Diane Hall has worked in English language teaching for over 25 years and has extensive experience in teaching (mostly in the UK and Germany), publishing and materials writing. She is co-author of a number of publications, including the Longman ELT advanced titles, Distinction and Advanced Learners' Grammar. She is co-author, with Mark Foley, of *Total English* Elementary Students' Book and Workbook.

Total English Pre-intermediate and Upper Intermediate

Richard Acklam lives in North London and has been involved in English Language teaching since 1982. He has taught and trained teachers in Egypt, France and the UK and has an M.A. (TEFL) from the University of Reading. His publications include components of the 'Gold 'series and he is co-author, with Araminta Crace, of *Total English* Pre-intermediate and Upper Intermediate Students' Books.

Araminta Crace lives in North London with her two young daughters, Petra and Lola. She has been involved in English Language teaching since 1984 and has taught and trained teachers in Brazil, Egypt, Portugal, Spain and the UK. Her ELT publications include Language to Go and Going for Gold. She is co-author, with Richard Acklam, of *Total English* Pre-intermediate and Upper Intermediate Students' Books.

Total English Intermediate and Advanced

Antonia Clare graduated from University College London in Psychology, and has enjoyed teaching (both adults and younger learners), and teacher training in Europe Asia and South Africa. She is now a full-time writer and freelance teacher trainer based in the UK. Her publications include Language to Go Upper Intermediate and she is co-author, with JJ Wilson, of *Total English* Upper Intermediate and Advanced Students' Books and Workbooks.

JJ Wilson trained at International House London and has taught in Egypt, Lesotho (where he ran a student theatre), Colombia, the UK, Italy and the U.S. His main interests in the field include vocabulary acquisition and the development of innovative methods and materials for the classroom. His short fiction is published by Penguin and Pulp Faction. He is co-author, with Antonia Clare, of *Total English* Upper Intermediate and Advanced Students' Books and Workbooks.

1 24 hours

Overview

Lead-in	**Vocabulary:** 24 hours
1.1	**Grammar:** likes and dislikes **Can do:** ask and talk about personal likes and dislikes
1.2	**Grammar:** Present Simple; adverbs of frequency **Vocabulary:** sleeping habits **Can do:** ask and answer questions about daily routines
1.3	**Grammar:** Present Continuous **Vocabulary:** shops and shopping **Can do:** write an informal email to update someone on your life
Com. Focus	Wheel of English
Reference	
Practice	

Summary

Lesson 1: Ss do a quiz to find out if they are party animals and read a text which distinguishes between party animal, culture vulture and couch potato.

Lesson 2: Ss listen to a TV programme which talks about the different sleep habits of different species of animals and human beings at various stages of their lives. Then they talk about their own sleep habits.

Lesson 3: Ss read a text about Harrods, the most famous department store in the UK. Then they listen to a survey in which customers say where they are from and what they are doing in London and in Harrods.

Communication focus: Ss listen to a man talking about how important different aspects of English are to him and then Ss consider how important these different aspects are to them.

Film bank: London (4' 50")

A documentary film about London

This documentary shows us 24 hours in the life of London. Beginning with the market traders who are up at dawn, we follow the day right through to the nightlife in the evening. There are also introductions to some of London's most famous tourist attractions such as The London Eye, Tower Bridge and The Houses of Parliament.

Possible places to use this short film are:

▶ after Lesson 3 as a revision of Present Continuous and Present Simple

▶ at the end of the unit to round up the topic and language

For ways to use this short film in class, see Students' Book page 133 and Teacher's Book page 189.

Lead-in

▶ Do some general revision of numbers with Ss by playing the game 'Bucks Fizz'.

▶ Explain the rules of the game to the Ss. They have to count one by one around the class, but instead of saying 3 or a multiple of 3 they have to say *Bucks*, and instead of saying 5 or a multiple of 5 they have to say *Fizz*. If the number is a multiple of both 3 and 5, they say *Bucks Fizz*. E.g., 1, 2, Bucks, 4, Fizz, Bucks, 7, 8, Bucks, Fizz, 11, Bucks, 13, 14, Bucks Fizz. Ss who get it wrong are eliminated.

▶ Now revise the days of the week.

Q: What day is after Monday?
Q: What day is before Friday?
Q: When do you have English class?
Q: When do you go dancing?

▶ Write the following times on the board: 8a.m., 10.30a.m., 1p.m., 4.45p.m., 7.15p.m. Ask students to say the times in pairs. Now check the times with the whole class.

1▶ Ss discuss the two questions in pairs. Get feedback from the whole group, discussing their reasons for choosing certain times of the day or week.

2▶ Focus on the photos and tell Ss to look at the expressions given in the box and match an expression to each picture. Ss check answers in pairs.

▶ Ask different Ss to read out the rest of the activities, checking pronunciation and that all Ss understand the meaning of the verb phrases.

3a▶ Focus the Ss attention on the question and give some examples about yourself e.g., *I chat on the phone every day*. Now tell them to work individually, writing an appropriate letter next to each activity.

Answers: Pic 1: listen to the radio Pic 2: go clubbing Pic 3: check your emails

b▶ Give the Ss a couple of minutes in pairs to brainstorm other verbs that fit the two categories. When they have finished, get feedback from the whole class. Write the ideas on the blackboard. Tell the students to write down any new expressions, with an appropriate letter alongside (D, W, S or N).

c▶ Ss compare their lists with a partner (preferably a different one than before) to see what they have in common. Write an example on the board e.g., *I stay in bed late at weekends. What about you*? Remind Ss that *always/never* go before the main verb and *every day/at the weekend* go at the end of the sentence.

EXTEND THE LEAD-IN

Ss divide the activities from Ex. 2 into two columns according to whether they like doing this activity or not. Then they compare with a partner, giving their reasons. Get feedback from the whole class.

1.1 Are you a party animal?

Party animal is quite a modern-day expression, which people have been using recently in Britain to refer to somebody who likes going out and socialising a lot.

In this lesson Ss consider different activities that people do in their free time and do a quiz to find out whether they are party animals or not. Through this context they learn various ways of expressing likes and dislikes.

OPTIONAL WARMER

Brainstorm activities that people usually do in their free time and write them on the board. Ss talk to a partner about which of these activities they like and which they don't like. Get feedback from the whole class. If some of the Ss appear to be party animals, introduce the expression by saying: *I think X, X and X are party animals because they like ...* . If none of the Ss appear to be party animals, write the expression on the board and elicit the meaning.

Speaking

1a▶ Ss discuss with a partner what they can see in each picture. Encourage them to be as detailed as possible. Get feedback from a number of Ss.

b▶ Ss match the descriptions and the pictures. Point to the pictures one by one and choose a different student each time to read the corresponding sentence aloud.

Answers: 1 picture B 2 picture C 3 picture A

2a▶ Ss do the quiz in pairs, helping each other with any difficult expressions and making a note of their own answers. Alternatively, in order to give the Ss extra speaking and listening practice, student B closes his or her book while student A asks the questions and reads out the various options. Student B must listen and choose the option which best fits their behaviour. Student A makes a note of student B's answers. Then they swap roles with student B asking the questions while student A has his or her book closed.

▶ Ss then check their results. Elicit the meaning of *culture vulture* and *couch potato*.

Q: What do you think *culture vulture* and *couch potato* mean? *Culture vulture* and *couch potato* are colloquial expressions, the first meaning somebody who is very interested in all types of cultural activities, and the second referring to somebody who is a little lazy and likes to spend most of the time lying on the couch/sofa watching TV for example.

b▶ Ss tell their partner whether they agree with the results or not and why. Get feedback from a number of Ss.

Reading

3▶ Ss read through the text individually and decide what type of people Marek and Lola are. When they have finished, get feedback and ask the Ss if there are any expressions they don't understand. Elicit/teach the meaning of these expressions. Avoid going into too much detail about the various ways of expressing likes and dislikes at this point as this is covered in detail in Ex. 5.

4▶ Ss complete the sentences in pairs. Have different Ss read out the completed sentences for the whole class.

Answers: 1 Marek 2 Lola 3 Marek 4 Marek 5 Lola 6 Marek 7 Lola

Grammar

OPTIONAL GRAMMAR LEAD-IN

The Ss close their books and work in pairs to see if they can remember any of the expressions that were used in the text to express different degrees of liking or not liking. Get feedback and write the expressions on the board.

5▶ Focus on the Active grammar box and establish the fact that the faces represent different degrees of liking and not liking. Tell the Ss to work with a partner to complete the gaps by looking back at the expressions underlined in the text.

▶ Copy the chart onto the board and elicit the answers from the class.

Active Grammar

1 I absolutely love
2 I'm quite keen on
3 I don't mind
4 I'm not very keen on
5 I can't stand

▶ Draw Ss attention to the note at the bottom of the grammar box and write the following examples from the text on the board.

Noun: modern art Gerund: getting up early

▶ Ask Ss to find more examples of the gerund in the text (*having*, *going*, *doing*, *meeting*, *lying*, *checking*) and discuss with a partner the rules we use to make this form.

6▶ Ss work in pairs, writing sentences using the prompts. Get feedback from the whole class.

Answers: 1 I absolutely love my job. 2 I'm not very keen on/don't like doing crossword puzzles. 3 I really like beach holidays. 4 I can't stand/really hate being cold. 5 I don't mind dogs. 6 I quite like/I'm quite keen on going to the cinema. 7 ! can't stand/really hate talking on the phone in English. 8 I absolutely love going dancing on Friday evenings.

Person to person

7▶ The Ss change the sentences so that they are true for them. Then they cover the complete sentences and use the prompts from Ex. 6 in order to tell a partner their true sentences. Get feedback from various Ss.

OPTIONAL EXTENSION

Write the following nouns and phrases on the board: *play football, cats, jazz, travel, chocolate, watch tv, very hot weather, do homework, cook.*
Tell the Ss to talk in pairs about the words, saying how much they like or dislike each thing.

Speaking and writing

8▶ Put the Ss into small groups of three or four and have them talk about the type of person they are or aren't, giving reasons and using the expressions they have learnt. Go around the class monitoring the conversations. Finally, get feedback from various Ss.

9a▶ Ss write a paragraph about their typical Saturday, using the texts in Ex. 3 as a model. Go around the class monitoring the Ss' work and helping them to self-correct where possible.

b▶ Ss swap papers/notebooks and read each other's paragraphs. Ask various Ss what they have learnt about their partner.

OPTIONAL VARIATION

Ss work in pairs to tell each other about their typical Saturday. The listener can make brief notes about what their partner is saying. Finally, each student writes about their partner's typical Sunday in class or for homework.

1.2 Goodnight

Sleep research has developed greatly over the last twenty years and we now know all kinds of facts about sleep patterns and disorders.

In this lesson Ss listen to a TV programme about the sleeping habits of different species of animals and human beings at different ages. Through this context they revise the form and use of the Present Simple and learn adverbs of frequency.

OPTIONAL WARMER

Introduce Ss to the topic of sleep. Point out the bed on page 8 and elicit the other words from the Ss.
Tell them to brainstorm words related to bed with a partner. Give the Ss a couple of minutes and then elicit words from the whole class, writing them on the board e.g., *sleep*, *pillow*, *get up*, *awake*, *dream*, *alarm clock*, *pyjamas*.
Now add the word *goodnight*. Ask:
Q: When do people say *goodnight*? Just before going to bed.
Contrast this expression with *good evening*. Ask:
Q: When do people say *good evening*? In the evening and at night when we are not going to bed.

Speaking and listening

1a▶ Read the sentences aloud with the class and check everybody understands. Then Ss rewrite the sentences so that they are true for them. Get feedback from various Ss.

b▶ Tell the Ss they are going to listen to a TV programme about sleep habits. Focus their attention on the list of items that might be mentioned and read through them with the whole class. Play recording 1.1 and Ss tick the ones they hear.

Answers: cats, horses, fish, babies, children, adults

2▶ Tell the Ss to read through the questions with a partner and suggest answers for each one based on what they can remember from the recording. Play recording 1.1 again and Ss answer the questions. Tell them to check their answers with a partner and then as a whole class.

Answers: 1a fish 1b (newborn) babies 1c adults 2 They sleep standing up. 3 They don't close their eyes. 4 2,688 5 four or five

3▶ Ss discuss the questions in pairs or small groups. Get feedback from the whole class.

Vocabulary

4a▶ Ss work in pairs to match the questions and the answers.

b▶ Play recording 1.2 and Ss check their answers.

Answers: 1 c) 2 i) 3 j) 4 b) 5 e) 6 a) 7 d) 8 f) 9 h) 10 g)

c▶ Ss discuss the difference in meaning between the different expressions with a partner. If they find the concepts difficult to explain, then they can make example sentences that demonstrate the difference in meaning.

Answers: 1 *To wake up* refers to the moment when you stop sleeping and *to get up* refers to the moment when you physically leave the bed. 2 *To sleep* refers to the time that you are not awake, whereas *to fall asleep* refers to the moment in which you change from being awake to being asleep. 3 *To have a snack* means to eat a little, normally between meals, whereas *to have breakfast* is to have the first meal of the day.

5▶ Ss complete the text and check with a partner. Read the text aloud, eliciting the answers from the Ss.

Answers: 1 Have a snack 2 go to bed 3 have a nap 4 wake up 5 get up 6 have breakfast

6▶ Ss discuss the tips with a partner. Get feedback from various Ss and see if everybody agrees with the same tips.

Grammar

OPTIONAL GRAMMAR LEAD-IN

Say the following sentence: *You have a nap after lunch.* Ask the Ss to say this sentence in the negative and in the question form. Ss construct these sentences with a partner. Get feedback from various Ss. Repeat with the following sentences: *She goes to bed early*; *They get up at eight o' clock; We really like fish*; *He sleeps six hours a day.*

Now write *adverbs of frequency* on the board. Ask the Ss if they know what these are (they say how often we do something) and elicit as many as you can from the group, writing them on the board in a random order. Ss then put them in order.

7▶ Ss complete the Active grammar box. Copy the grammar box on the board and elicit the answers from the class.

▶ Pay attention to the use of the 's' in the 3rd person singular, asking Ss how they would have to change the first sentence if it began with *he*, *she* or *it*.

▶ Check carefully that all Ss have used the infinitive in the negative and interrogative sentences, pointing out that for this reason the 3rd person singular only takes the 's' in affirmative sentences.

Active Grammar

+ I usually go to bed about 10.30.

– They don't have a nap during the day.
He doesn't have a lie-in during the week.

? Do you wake up early?
Does she often have a snack before bed?

▶ Read through the note at the bottom of the box. Elicit examples from the Ss of things they do every day and things they do often using the Present Simple.

▶ Read through the adverbs of frequency with the whole class, checking pronunciation. Ask the Ss to look back at Ex. 4 to see what position adverbs of frequency take in a sentence. Elicit that normally they go before the main verb and teach the exception of the verb *to be*, where they go after the verb.

▶ Point out that we must use only affirmative sentences with *never* and *hardly ever* as we never use double negatives in English.

▶ Ss look at the reference section on page 13.

OPTIONAL EXTENSION

Dictate the following sentences to the Ss, who write them down including an adverb of frequency in the correct position so that the sentences are true for them. Get feedback from a number of Ss.
I eat meat; *I have a nap*; *I fall asleep watching TV.*

8▶ Ss choose the correct form. Check the answers with the whole class.

Answers: 1 Do 2 do 3 don't 4 go 5 Do 6 don't 7 gets 8 calls 9 Does 10 does 11 talks 12 doesn't

9▶ Focus Ss back on the questions in Ex. 8 and tell them to write true answers. Get feedback from several Ss.

Pronunciation

10a▶ Write the three phonetic symbols on the board and elicit the corresponding sound for each. Give an example of a word for each sound.

▶ Ss match the symbols to the underlined words.

b▶ Play recording 1.3 and have Ss check their answers. Ss practise the dialogue with a partner.

Answers: 1 b) 2 a) 3 c) 4 c)

Person to person

11▶ Focus Ss back on Ex. 4a and tell them to ask and answer the questions in pairs.

1.3 A day in the life

Department stores have become increasingly popular over the last fifty years in many countries, maybe because it's very convenient to be able to do all your shopping in one place, especially in Britain where it's often raining. Harrods is probably one of the most famous. It has a reputation for selling absolutely anything and it's probably one of the most important tourist attractions in London in spite of being quite expensive.

In this lesson Ss read about Harrods and listen to a survey in which customers say what they are doing there. Through this context Ss consider the use and form of the Present Continuous.

OPTIONAL WARMER

Write *department store* on the board and ask the Ss:
Q: What is it? A big shop where you can buy many different things in distinct departments.
Tell Ss to work with a partner to brainstorm twenty things they think you can normally buy in a department store. The first pair to get twenty items shout *stop* and all Ss stop writing. The winning pair read out their list and the rest of the class can add any extra items that they had thought of.
Ask the Ss:
Q: Do you know the name of any department stores in England? Elicit *Harrods* and ask where it is and if anybody has ever been.
Q: Why do you think it is so famous? Elicit ideas from the Ss.

Reading

1a ▶ Read through the words in the box and check that the Ss understand. Tell them to find these things in the photos with a partner. Get feedback from the whole class.

b ▶ Ss discuss the question with a partner. Get feedback from various Ss.

2a ▶ Ss read the text. Elicit reasons why Harrods is famous.

b ▶ Ss read through the text again and answer the questions in pairs. Elicit the correct answers.

Answers: 1 about 300,000 on special days 2 shop assistant, hairdresser, doctor, work in a bank, fire brigade/fire fighter, cleaner, doorman 3 All different kinds of people from all over the world can find anything they want at Harrods. 4 a baby elephant that someone bought as a present for Ronald Reagan 5 Because they are wearing the wrong kind of clothes. 6a) the age of Harrods b) the number of departments c) the number of people who work for Harrods d) the number of light bulbs on the outside of the building

3 ▶ Ss discuss the questions in pairs. Get feedback from various Ss.

Listening

4a ▶ Write *customer survey* on the board. Ask the Ss if they know what this is. Elicit or explain that it's a kind of questionnaire, which is normally used in market research. Ask the Ss if they can imagine what type of questions would be included in this type of survey. Get various suggestions from the class.

▶ Ss read the three headings with the whole class and tell the Ss that they have to complete the gaps. Play recording 1.4.

b ▶ After the recording, Ss compare with a partner and then play the recording again if you feel it is necessary. Elicit the answers from various Ss.

Answers: 1 Spain 2 just looking 3 Poland 4 on holiday 5 shopping (for clothes) for a wedding

Grammar

OPTIONAL GRAMMAR LEAD-IN

Q: Why did the woman say 'I'm shopping' and not 'I shop'? Allow the Ss time to talk about the question with a partner and then get feedback. Try to elicit the difference between the Present Simple and the Present Continuous.

5 ▶ Ss read the first two sentences from the Active grammar box and match them to the grammar rules. Check their answers.

Active Grammar

Actions happening at this moment: sentence 2
Temporary actions happening 'around' now but not at this moment: sentence 1

▶ Give the Ss some more examples by asking the following question:
Q: What are you doing now? Elicit *studying English*, *listening to the teacher* or *speaking in English* as examples of actions happening now.

▶ Now tell them about a book you are reading at the moment as an example of things happening around now. Ask:
Q: What book are you reading?

▶ Read the rule about state verbs with the whole class and contrast these verbs with other verbs such as *speak*, *dance* or *play* in order to explain the meaning of state. Explain that these verbs are not usually used in the Continuous tense.

▶ Have Ss look at the Reference page 13 and read through the other examples of state verbs.

6 ▶ Ss complete the sentences with a partner. Check the answers with the whole class.

Answers: 1 am waiting 2 are you doing 3 are sitting 4 aren't moving 5 am phoning 6 are you doing 7 are staying 8 is raining 9 aren't going

7▶ Ss choose the correct alternative with a partner. Check the answers with the whole class.

> **Answers:** 1 'm doing/starts 2 are you doing/Are you still studying 3 doesn't eat/doesn't like 4 do you usually do 5 often go

8▶ Play recording 1.5 and Ss listen to the sounds and write a sentence to describe what they have heard. Get feedback from the whole class.

> **Suggested answers:** 1 He/She's reading a newspaper. 2 He/She's making coffee. 3 He/She's falling asleep. 4 He/She's writing a text message. 5 He/She's having a shower. 6 He/She's running.

9▶ Student A looks at the illustration on page 11 and student B looks at the illustration on page 127. Allow the Ss a little time to look at their pictures and identify any problematic vocabulary items.

▶ Student A works with student B, but without looking at each other's picture. Tell them to ask each other questions, in order to find five more differences.

> **Answers:** 1 The shop assistant is chatting on the phone/taking the man's money. 2 A child is eating an ice-cream/a sandwich. 3 A woman is reading a magazine/looking at some shoes. 4 A baby in a pram is sleeping/crying. 5 An old woman is throwing a sweet paper/a broken umbrella in the bin.

OPTIONAL EXTENSION

Put the Ss in small groups and have one student from each group come to the front of the class. Tell them a sentence that they have to mime to the rest of their group. The Ss go back to their group and mime the sentence. The person who guesses then comes to the front of the class to get the next sentence to mime.

Possible sentences: You're making a cake; You're doing an exam; You're eating spaghetti; You're climbing a mountain; You're repairing a bicycle.

Writing

10▶ Ss read the email on page 138 with a partner and do the exercises.

> **1▶ Answers:** 1 A 2 C 3 C 4 B

> **2▶ Answers:** A 3 B 1 C 2

11▶ Ss write an email to a friend on a piece of paper. If you have computers you could have the Ss write emails to each other or to you.

Communication: Wheel of English

In this lesson Ss listen to a student of English talking about how important different language skills are to him, as represented in the diagram 'Wheel of English'. Ss then design their own wheel of English.

OPTIONAL WARMER

Ask Ss why English is important to them.
Q: Why are you studying English? Ss compare with a partner and then get feedback from the whole class. Explain that different aspects of English are more important to some people than to others, depending on your reasons for learning.

1▶ Ss work in pairs to write the words on the correct part of the wheel. Get feedback from various Ss.

> **Answers:** A listening (4) B grammar (3) C speaking and pronunciation (5) D writing (2) E vocabulary (4) F reading (3)

2▶ Play recording 1.6 and Ss listen and put a cross on the correct part of the wheel and then join the crosses. Check the answers together (see the numbers given above).

3▶ Play recording 1.6 again and Ss take notes about how good Antonio is at these different aspects of English. Let them compare with a partner and then get feedback from various Ss.

> **Answers:** Antonio is good at grammar but he isn't very good at remembering new words. He's quite good at reading and not very good at listening. He's quite good at speaking and pronunciation and writing.

4▶ Ss draw their own wheel of English. Put Ss in pairs or small groups. Focus their attention on the How to ... box and read through the different expressions they can use for this task. Tell the Ss to explain their wheel of English to their partner(s), using those expressions. Go around the class monitoring their conversations.

5▶ Ss read the Lifelong learning box and suggest one more way of improving each aspect.

6▶ Ss stand up and mingle, sharing their ideas. Get feedback from various Ss about which ideas they like the most.

OPTIONAL VARIATION

Draw three columns on the board with the headings: *I already do*; *I'm going to do*; *I'm not going to do*.
Ss copy the chart on a piece of paper and then mingle with other Ss, writing the ideas they hear in the columns.

Review and practice

1 ▶

Answers: 1 quite keen on 2 I can't stand 3 I really like 4 really hate 5 quite like pizza 6 absolutely love going 7 I don't mind 8 I'm/am not

2 ▶

Answers: 1 I get up 2 do you start 3 I go to bed 4 Do you go to bed 5 I fall asleep 6 Do you have a snack 7 I have dinner 8 Does he swim 9 He gets up 10 swims 11 he goes 12 Does he go 13 He doesn't go

3 ▶

Answers: 1 am sitting 2 am having 3 Is Jack watching 4 is checking 5 Are you and John doing 6 are walking 7 aren't getting

4 ▶

Answers: 1 is he speaking 2 doesn't rain 3 're working 4 Do you prefer 5 'm staying 6 does she want

5 ▶

Answers: 1 go 2 wake up 3 have 4 listen 5 do 6 fall 7 catch 8 chat

Notes for using the Common European Framework (CEF)

CEF References

1.1 Can do: ask and talk about personal likes and dislikes

CEF A2 descriptor: can say what he/she likes and dislikes (CEF page 76)

1.2 Can do: ask and answer questions about daily routines

CEF A2 descriptor: can ask and answer questions about habits and routines (CEF page 81)

1.3 Can do: write an informal email to update someone on your life

CEF A2 descriptor: can write very short, basic descriptions of events, past activities and personal experiences (CEF page 62)

CEF quick brief

The Common European Framework is a reference document for teachers. It is about 260 pages long. You can download it for free from www.coe.int. The CEF recommends that students use a 'Portfolio'. This is a document that aims to help students reflect on, record and demonstrate their language learning. There is a free downloadable 'Total English Portfolio'.

Portfolio task

Download the Total English Portfolio free from www.longman.com/totalenglish.

Objective: help learners to understand the purpose and value of the Portfolio.

This task can be done in Ss' L1.

Make sure that each student in your class has a copy of the Total English Portfolio.

1 ▶ Ask Ss to complete their personal details on the Portfolio and explain its purpose: to help Ss learn more effectively and demonstrate their language abilities and experiences to others.

2 ▶ Explain that you will ask them to update their Portfolio at regular intervals but you will not 'mark' their Portfolio – it is an aid to learning, not a focus for learning itself.

2 Music

Overview

Lead-in	**Vocabulary:** music
2.1	**Grammar:** Past simple **Can do:** talk about personal events in the past
2.2	**Grammar:** *so* and *neither* **Vocabulary:** word families – nouns and adjectives **Can do:** say when you are the same as/ different from, another person
2.3	**Grammar:** Present Perfect Simple (for experience) **Vocabulary:** verb/noun collocations about achievements **Can do:** talk about personal achievements and experiences
Com. Focus	My top three
Reference	
Practice	

Summary

Lesson 1: Ss read a text from 1979 about Robin Scott, lead singer of 'M', who became successful with the hit song *Pop Muzik*. Then they listen to a modern-day interview in which Robin talks about his past.

Lesson 2: Ss listen to some music by Mozart and read a text about the effect music can have on the way we feel and behave. Then they look at the formation of nouns from adjectives.

Lesson 3: Ss read a text about the singer Charlotte Church and answer questions about her life. They then consider her life experiences and achievements and discuss whether she has done too much, too soon.

Communication Focus: Ss listen to a radio programme about what music a person would choose if they were alone on a desert island and why. Then they choose their top three songs.

Film bank: Summer Holiday (2'42")

An extract from a classic British musical

Summer Holiday is one of the most famous musical films. It stars Cliff Richard and tells the story of a group of young people who take a London bus to France. This extract shows scenes of a typical British summer during the credits, followed by the song *Summer Holiday*.

Possible places to use this short film are:

▶ before Lesson 1 as an introduction to classic pop songs

▶ before Lesson 2 as an introduction to the topic of music and mood

▶ at the end of the unit to round up the topic and language

For ways to use this short film in class, see Students' Book page 134 and Teacher's Book page 189.

Lead-in

▶ Write the word *music* on the board. Ss brainstorm words related to music, in pairs. Give Ss a few minutes to do this, then ask each pair how many words they have.

▶ Have the pair with the fewest words read out their list and write the words on the board. Now ask other Ss to add more words. Check all Ss understand the final list.

▶ Give the Ss a few minutes to think of complete sentences using words from the list e.g., *Madonna is a singer*. Have different Ss read out one sentence each.

1 ▶ Ss look at the photos in pairs and name the instruments they can see.

Answers: Pic 1: trumpet Pic 2: guitar Pic 3: drums, keyboards, electric guitar Pic 4: violin

▶ Get feedback from the class. Then Ss think of more instruments in pairs and share their ideas with the class.

Possible answers: cello, clarinet, harmonica, harp, piano, saxophone, trombone.

2a ▶ Ss listen to recording 2.1 and match each extract to a type of music.

Answers: 1 pop 2 jazz 3 rock 4 classical 5 house 6 Latin

▶ Brainstorm other types of music e.g., *rap*, *salsa*, *reggae*, *blues*, etc.

b ▶ Ss ask and answer the questions in pairs. Encourage them to give complete answers e.g., *I like house when I go clubbing but I don't like it when I am at home.*

3a ▶ Focus on the words and phrases in the box and ask Ss if they understand all of them. Explain any they don't.

▶ Ss complete the sentences with the correct expression. Check in pairs and then with the whole class.

Answers: 1 favourite band 2 last concert 3 download 4 read music 5 compilation CDs 6 favourite record 7 lead singer 8 really into

b ▶ Ss tell a partner sentences about themselves using the words in the box. Get feedback from the whole class.

EXTEND THE LEAD-IN

Ss, in small groups, brainstorm song titles in English, checking the meaning of those titles with you or each other. Ss, paired from different groups play hangman with those titles. Alternatively, Ss from different groups draw pictures on the board as clues to the song titles. The rest of the class guess the title.

2.1 A real classic

In this lesson Ss read about Robin Scott, the lead singer of the pop group 'M', which topped the US and British charts in 1979 with the song *Pop Muzik*. It could be viewed as a 'real classic' due to its popularity and the fact that it was one of the first 'New Wave' (electronic) records released. It was also a one-hit wonder as M never had a single in the charts again.

Ss also listen to a modern-day interview with Robin Scott, and consider the use and form of the Past Simple through this context.

OPTIONAL WARMER

Write *a real classic* on the board. Ask: **Q: What do you think this expression usually refers to?** A song which was popular in the past but people still like today because it's thought to be particularly good.

Write a list of five real classics on the board without the name of the singer/band e.g., *Satisfaction* (The Rolling Stones), *Imagine* (John Lennon), *My Way* (Frank Sinatra), *I Will Survive* (Gloria Gaynor) and *Waterloo* (Abba)

Go through the list, one by one, and have Ss vote for those they think deserve to be called 'real classics'. If they don't know or don't like the song, they shouldn't vote. The winning song is the one with most votes.

Reading

1a▶ Ss look at the photo and discuss in pairs when they think that this pop star was famous. Get feedback from various Ss, encouraging them to give their reasons.

b▶ Ss read the text and complete the chart in pairs. Check the answers with the whole class. Then focus on any difficult vocabulary in the text e.g., *huge, lyrics*. Ask Ss to suggest the meaning of these words from the context.

Answers: Name of band: M Lead singer: Robin Scott Other singer: Brigit Novik Song: *Pop Muzik* Hit in: May 1979 Future for lead singer: certain to be a big star

Listening

2a▶ Ss close their books and listen to the interview with Robin Scott twenty-five years later. Play recording 2.2. Ask the class: **Q: Did he became a big star?** (No, he didn't.)

▶ Tell the Ss to discuss, in pairs, any other information they heard, and get feedback from the whole class.

b▶ Ss open their books and look at the questions. Read through the questions with the class, and then play recording 2.2 again. Ss answer the questions and compare with a partner. Elicit the answers from various Ss.

▶ If Ss mention *live shows* in question 8, point out the difference between the pronunciation and meaning of this adjective (/laɪv/ when the group is actually performing and not recorded) and the verb (/lɪv/).

Answers: 1 south London 2 art college 3 1969 4 Paris 5 It came from the M over the metro (underground) station in Paris. 6 *Pop Muzik* was released. 7 *Pop Muzik* was released again. 8 He's working with various artists and he wants to do some live shows with them.

3a▶ Ss discuss the questions in pairs. Get feedback from the class. You could write the list of student suggestions for question 2 on the board and vote for the best one as in the optional warmer activity.

b▶ Play recording 2.3. Ss listen to the song and give their opinion. Ask: **Q: Do you think this song is a real classic?**

Grammar

OPTIONAL GRAMMAR LEAD-IN

Write the following three sentences on the board but with the words in the wrong order e.g.,

1 *Robin Scott grew up in south London.* (Scott London up grew Robin in South)
2 *He did not become a famous pop star in the end.* (the become star end he not did famous pop in a)
3 *Did he study at art college?* (study he college art at did ?)

Ss put the words in the correct order in pairs. Elicit the answers. Ask: **Q: What tense is this?** Past Simple.

4a▶ Focus Ss on the Active grammar box and have them complete the gaps with a partner.

Active Grammar

\+ We formed a band with my brother.
I grew up in South London.
– I did not (didn't) feel very happy about my first record.
They did not (didn't) agree with me all the time.
? Where did it all start?
How did you think of the name M?

▶ Check the answers with the class. Explain they can use the complete form *did not* or the contracted form *didn't*, (more common in spoken English). Explain: We use this tense to refer to finished actions in the past.

b▶ Ss answer the question. Check the answers with the whole class and refer Ss to Reference page 23.

Answers: Regular verbs: form, agree, start
Irregular verbs: grow, feel, think

5a▶ Ss complete the sentences in pairs.

Answers: 1 went 2 wrote 3 played 4 was 5 made 6 taught 7 bought

b▶ Play recording 2.4 and Ss check their answers.

6▶ Ss complete the dialogue with a partner. Check the answers with the whole class. Ss then read the dialogue in pairs.

Answers: 1 did you grow up 2 was 3 lived 4 moved 5 didn't like 6 loved 7 Did you go 8 left 9 didn't go 10 got 11 saved 12 went

OPTIONAL EXTENSION

Tell Ss to look back at Ex. 5a with a partner and change the sentences, when appropriate, so that they are true for them e.g., *I watched TV last night.*

Pronunciation

7a▶ Play recording 2.5 and Ss repeat each word.

b▶ Ss put the verbs into the correct column, in pairs. Encourage them to pronounce the words together as they do this and discuss the pronunciation rules.

Answers: /t/ worked, finished, kissed (if the verb ends in an unvoiced consonant)
/d/ believed, moved, loved (if the verb ends in a voiced sound)
/id/ ended, wanted, waited (if the verb ends in -d or -t)

b▶ Ss work in pairs to add more verbs to each list.

Suggested answers: /t/ passed, walked /d/ seemed, played /id/ painted, visited

8a▶ Play recording 2.6 and the Ss write the sentences. Ss compare with a partner. Play the recording again.

Answers: 1 The concert finished at midnight. 2 I loved rock music when I was a teenager. 3 When I was a child, I wanted to be a pop star. 4 I worked in a CD shop last summer. 5 She moved her CD player into the living room. 6 I waited for three hours to see the lead singer.

Speaking

9a▶ Ss use the prompts to write questions in the Past Simple. Go around the class monitoring their work.

b▶ Focus Ss on the How to ... box. Read some of the expressions with the class. Give examples to show how to use them e.g., *I started teaching 3 years ago; I left school when I was 18 and after that I went to college.*

▶ Put the Ss in pairs so they can interview each other. Go around the class monitoring their conversations.

OPTIONAL VARIATION

Secretly write two numbers between 1 and 7 on a piece of paper. Then in pairs, student A interviews student B, using the prompts in Ex. 9a. Student B must answer truthfully, except when the question corresponds to the numbers on his/her paper. In this case, student B lies. Student A must guess which two answers were false. Then they change roles.

2.2 The Mozart effect

The Mozart Effect is the name of a book by Don Campbell, first published in 1997. It talks about the positive effects that different types of music can have on the mental and physical health of families and communities, helping everybody from children with learning disorders to adults with depression. Research on music therapy, carried out in France in the 1960s and later the USA, has shown that Mozart is particularly effective because it is structural and not over-emotional.

In this lesson Ss read about the 'Mozart effect' and develop vocabulary groups to express feelings. Then they look at the grammar of agreeing and disagreeing using *so* and *neither*.

OPTIONAL WARMER

Tell Ss you are thinking of a famous person (Mozart) and they have to guess who it is by asking questions. You answer only *yes/no* (If you don't know an answer, you can say I don't know). Give Ss a few minutes to think of possible questions in pairs before you begin. Ss ask questions until somebody guesses. If they ask all twenty questions and don't guess, give them clues by telling them some of the information below.

Mozart was born in Austria in 1756. He was both a musician and a composer. He married twice and lived in various countries. He was particularly influential in the music of the Germanic world, although he had a great impact on the whole world. His most well known works are *The Magic Flute*, *Requiem* and *Don Giovanni*.

Reading

1▶ Focus on the adjectives in the box. Ask a few Ss to read them aloud and check that everybody understands them all. Play recording 2.7 and Ss tell a partner how each piece makes them feel. Get feedback from the class.

2▶ Read through the headings with the whole class, checking that everybody understands. Ss read quickly through the text and choose a heading for each paragraph. Tell them not to worry about any words they don't understand at the moment. Ss check their answers with a partner then check with the whole class.

Answers: 1 d 2 a 3 c 4 b

3▶ Various Ss read the statements aloud and check that everybody understands. Ss read the text again and decide if those statements were true or false or if the text doesn't say (don't know). Ss check with a partner before the whole class check their answers together.

Answers: 1 T 2 ? 3 T 4 ? 5 F 6 F 7 ? 8 T

▶ Ask the Ss if there are any words from the text that they don't understand. Elicit from other Ss the meaning of these words, or explain them yourself.

4▶ Ss discuss the questions in pairs and then compare answers with another pair. Get feedback from the class.

Vocabulary

5a▶ Ss work with a partner to match the underlined words and the definitions. Various Ss read out the answers and the definitions for the whole class to check.

Answers: 1 intelligent 2 imaginative 3 energetic 4 relaxed 5 tired

b▶ Write an adjective on the board e.g., *beautiful*. Ask the Ss if they know the noun of this word. Elicit/teach *beauty*. Focus the Ss on the table and tell them to complete it, in pairs, using dictionaries if you have them.

Answers: See Ex. 6b.

OPTIONAL VARIATION

Write typical noun endings on the board before Ss do this exercise. Explain that many nouns end in *-ation*, *-ness*, *-ence* and *-y*. Ss then try to form the nouns, speculating over which sounds the best.

6a▶ Ss underline the stress with a partner. Encourage them to pronounce the words aloud as they do this.

b▶ Play recording 2.8. Ss listen and check their answers.

Answers: 1 relaxed = relaxation 2 tired = tiredness 3 energetic = energy 4 imaginative = imagination 5 intelligent = intelligence

▶ Ss answer the questions with a partner. Discuss the answers with the whole group.

Answers: 1 Those nouns finishing in *-ation* have the stress on the penultimate syllable. 2 intelligent/intelligence and tired/tiredness 3 relaxed/relaxation, energetic/energy and imaginative/imagination

▶ Read through the Lifelong learning box with the Ss. Divide the Ss into groups and give each group one of the words from the chart in Ex. 5b. Ss work out a way of recording this word, as in the example given for *relaxed*.

▶ Get feedback from the whole class, checking that Ss have used their words correctly in the examples given.

▶ Ask Ss if they can think of any other ways of recording vocabulary (e.g., by category, translating, with pictures etc.). Discuss the advantages and disadvantages of the different methods, allowing Ss to choose their own. Encourage Ss to make a vocabulary book in which they record all new vocabulary, and discuss ways in which they are going to try to learn this vocabulary.

7▶ Ss work in pairs to choose the correct answer. Check the answers with the whole class.

Answers: 1 energetic 2 intelligent 3 imaginative 4 tiredness 5 relaxation 6 imagination 7 intelligence 8 energy 9 tired 10 relaxed

8▶ Ss change the sentences in Ex. 7, where appropriate, so that they are true for them. Get feedback from various Ss.

Grammar

OPTIONAL GRAMMAR LEAD-IN

Say: *I think house music is really boring*. Ask which Ss agree with you and elicit/teach ways in English to say this:

Q: How do you say that you agree with me in English? *So do* I (If Ss say *me too*, tell them this is fine but that you want to concentrate on the 'so' expressions.)

Say: *I don't like rap music*. Ask:

Q: How do you say you agree with me in English? *Neither do I.*

Ask which Ss disagree with you and elicit/teach ways of disagreeing:

Q: How do you say you disagree with *I think house music is boring* in English? *I don't.*

Q: How do you say you disagree with *I don't like rap music*? *I do.*

▶ Tell the Ss to write a true sentence about their opinions on music. Chain around the class, with Ss reading out their sentences and the next person in the chain agreeing or disagreeing. Give Ss all the help they need at the beginning. By the end, they should be more confident but if not chain the other way around the class.

9a▶ Ss complete the Active grammar box and compare in pairs. Don't check answers yet as Ss will hear them in Ex. 9b.

Active Grammar

1 So do I. 2 So have I. 3 Neither am I. 4 Neither did I. 5 I don't. 6 I haven't. 7 I can. 8 I do.

b▶ Play recording 2.9 and Ss check their answers.

c▶ Ss cover part B in the Active grammar box and practise the conversations with a partner.

10▶ Ss write sentences with the stems provided. Tell them to look back at pages 15–17 if they need to remember vocabulary from those lessons.

Person to person

11▶ Ss read their sentences to a partner who agrees or disagrees. Alternatively, Ss mingle, saying each sentence to a different student.

12▶ Ss write a short composition about their musical tastes.

OPTIONAL VARIATION

If Ss have done Ex. 11 with one partner only, they could make notes of the things they have in common and the things they don't agree about. Then they write a paragraph about this.

2.3 Too much, too soon?

Too much, too soon is an expression used in English to refer to young people who have lived life too quickly, often with disastrous consequences.

In this lesson Ss read about Charlotte Church, a young British singer who is thought to be the world's most successful classical female artist. The public find her fascinating not only because she has 'the voice of an angel' but also because she has a slightly wild streak; hence the title *Too much, too soon*? Through a consideration of Charlotte's life, Ss examine uses of the Present Perfect.

OPTIONAL WARMER

Ask Ss to think of famous people who became very well known when they were still children. **Q: Can you think of examples of famous people who became stars when they were children?**

Ss work with a partner and then share their ideas with the class. Write the answers on the board. Possible answers include Macaulay Culkin (child star of the *Home Alone* films), Drew Barrymore (child star of *ET*), Michael Jackson (child singer with the Jackson Five) and Judy Garland (child star in *The Wizard of Oz*. **Q: What do you know about the lives of these stars? Do you think they were happy?** Ss talk to a partner. Get feedback from the whole class.

Reading

▶ Focus Ss on the photos and ask what they know about her: **Q: Who is this singer? What do you know about her? Have you ever listened to her music?** Get feedback from the class.

1a▶ Ss discuss the questions with a partner and then share their ideas with the rest of the class.

b▶ Ss read the introduction to the text individually. Ask Ss again why Charlotte is so famous and encourage them to comment on relevant parts of the text (Sony recording contract at age eleven, has sold millions of records, has sung for the American president, the Queen and the Pope).

2a▶ Divide the class into two groups, A and B. Ss A look at page 125 and Ss B look at page 127. Ss read the text about Charlotte Church with a partner, helping each other with any difficult words or expressions and answering questions 1–6 (student A) or 7–12 (student B).

Answers: 1 21st February 1986 2 She won a talent show on TV. 3 Yes, it was. 4 She argued with him and paid him £2 million to go. 5 her mother 6 She passed all of them, with 'A' grades. 7 when she was sixteen 8 Charlotte sacked her. 9 They said she went clubbing every night. 10 Yes, she does. 11 She feels they are very close and that her mother has always been supportive. 12 She's rich, happy and still loves making music.

b▶ Reorganise the class so that one student A is working with one student B. Ss tell each other about the text they have read, using the questions as guide.

3▶ Ss discuss the questions in pairs and then share their ideas with the rest of the class.

4a▶ Ss match phrases from column A with phrases from column B.

Answers: 1 g) 2 d) 3 a) 4 h) 5 b) 6 e) 7 c) 8 f)

b▶ Ask Ss to tell the story again, filling in any extra information they can remember. When they've finished, go around the class, having different Ss tell the various parts of the story.

Grammar

OPTIONAL GRAMMAR LEAD-IN

Ask Ss questions about the text using the Present Perfect and encourage them to give you complete answers, modelling if necessary.
Q: Who has Charlotte performed for? She's performed for the American president, the Queen and the Pope.
Q: Has she earned a lot of money? Yes, she's earned a huge amount.
Ask Ss if they know which tense you are using and write Present Perfect Simple on the board.

5a▶ Ss look back at the text and answer the questions with a partner. Get feedback.

Answers: 1 Past Simple. Yes, the action happened when she was eleven. 2 Present Perfect Simple. No, we don't know when the action happened.

b▶ Ss complete the rules with a partner. Check the answers with the whole class.

Answers: 1 Past Simple 2 Present Perfect Simple

6a▶ Ss complete the Active grammar box and discuss the question with a partner. Write the box on the board and elicit answers from various Ss.

Active Grammar

+	I've written a book.
	She *has* performed for the American president.
–	They haven't sold a lot of records.
	He *hasn't* seen the film.
?	*Have* you ever been on TV?
	Has she done too much, too soon?

The underlined verbs are examples of the past participle.

b▶ Ss look at the texts on pages 125 and 127 and find more examples of the Present Perfect Simple. Have various Ss read out the examples they've found. Draw the Ss' attention to the grammar Reference on page 23.

7▶ Ss work in pairs to complete the sentences. Get feedback from various Ss.

Answers: 1 met 2 played 3 been 4 worked 5 bought 6 studied 7 downloaded

8a▸ Ss work in pairs to complete the dialogues. Go around the class checking the Ss' answers and discussing reasons for mistaken tenses.

Answers: 1 Have you ever won 2 have 3 won 4 Did you watch 5 did 6 saw 7 Have you ever met 8 haven't 9 saw 10 Have you ever played 11 have 12 was

b▸ Play recording 2.10 and Ss check their answers.

Person to person

9▸ Ss work in pairs to ask the questions given in Ex. 8a, responding with true answers. When they have finished, ask various Ss to repeat one of the questions/answers for the rest of the class.

OPTIONAL VARIATION

Play a true/false game. Give each student a piece of paper with F (false) or T (true) written on it. Those Ss who have an F must lie when answering questions, and those who have a T must tell the truth. Ss stand up and mingle, asking the questions from Ex. 8a, and making a note of which Ss they think are lying. When they've finished, get feedback and tell the F Ss to reveal themselves.

Vocabulary

10a▸ Check that Ss understand *achievements* (we use it when we reach our objectives). Now they work in pairs to match a verb from column A with a phrase from column B. Get feedback from various Ss, checking that Ss understand the achievements clearly.

Answers: 1 b) 2 f) 3 d) 4 a) 5 c) 6 e)

b▸ Ss work in small groups to discuss their achievements. Tell them that the achievements don't have to be terribly important but could also be smaller things which they felt proud at having done.

OPTIONAL VARIATION

Ss think of a famous person they admire and make a list of achievements for this person. Then they tell the rest of the group and the others must guess the person.

Communication: My top three

This lesson is based on an idea taken from one of the longest-running BBC radio programmes, called *'Desert Island Discs'*. It first started in 1942 and interviews famous people who say what music they would take with them if they were stranded on a desert island.

1a▸ Ss look at the picture with a partner and predict the contents of the radio programme in pairs. Get feedback from the whole class.

b▸ Play recording 2.11 and the Ss comment on whether they were correct or not.

2a▸ Focus the Ss on the chart and tell them to complete it while listening to the rest of the programme. The reasons are quite extensive and Ss may have to use an extra piece of paper to make more complete notes. Play recording 2.12.

b▸ Ss compare answers with a partner and then check them with the rest of the class.

Answers: 3 *Dancing Queen*/Abba/reminds him of school, makes him feel happy and want to dance 2 *Symphony No. 5*/Mahler/great memories, made him cry, and it's very beautiful 1 *Angels*/Robbie Williams/ he's got a fantastic voice, heard it in Spain, and it's relaxing

3▸ Ss discuss the questions in pairs. Get feedback from the whole class.

4a▸ Focus Ss on the box and read through the expressions. Check they understand and discuss the difference between *remember* and *remind*, giving examples to clarify the difference (*to remember* is an internal action e.g., *I have to remember to post the letter*, whereas *to remind* is an external action e.g., *I've put a note on the fridge to remind me to post the letter*).

▸ Ss complete the sentences.

b▸ Play recording 2.13 and Ss check their answers.

Answers: 1 reminds me of 2 makes me 3 made me cry 4 remember listening

▸ Ss work together repeating the sentences.

5a▸ Ss complete the chart with their own choices of music.

b▸ Ss talk about their choices in small groups of three or four. Get feedback from the whole class.

OPTIONAL VARIATION

Ss work in pairs and role-play an interview like the one which they heard earlier. One person is the presenter and the other is the guest. Ss could then act out the role-play for the rest of the class.

Review and practice

1 ▶

Answers: 1 sold/bought 2 fell/broke 3 ate/drank 4 were/took 5 went/saw

2 ▶

Answers: 1 met 2 went 3 thought 4 didn't like 5 said 6 were you 7 lived 8 Did you like 9 hated 10 didn't like 11 stopped

3 ▶

Answers: 1 So did I. 2 I did. 3 So am I. 4 Neither do I. 5 I haven't. 6 So did I.

4 ▶

Answers: 1 haven't heard 2 Have you ever run 3 have been 4 Have you ever broken 5 hasn't ridden 6 Have you done 7 have worked 8 Have you ever downloaded

5 ▶

Answers: 1 Have you done 2 have 3 've had 4 worked 5 Were you 6 wasn't 7 was 8 's had

6 ▶

Answers: 1 energy 2 relaxation 3 won 4 intelligent 5 speech 6 imagination 7 classical 8 into

Notes for using the Common European Framework (CEF)

CEF References

2.1 Can do: talk about personal events in the past

CEF A2 descriptor: can ask and answer questions about pastimes and past activities (CEF page 81)

2.2 Can do: say when you are the same as/different from another person

CEF A2 descriptor: can describe his/her family, living conditions, educational background, present or most recent job (CEF page 59)

2.3 Can do: talk about personal achievements and experiences

CEF A2 descriptor: can give a short, rehearsed presentation on a topic pertinent to his/her everyday life, briefly give reasons and explanations for opinions, plans and actions (CEF page 60)

CEF quick brief

The Common European Framework is produced by the Council of Europe. The Council of Europe is concerned with issues like human rights, European identity, education and more. This identity is based on diversity and the Common European Framework gives equal importance to all languages of Council of Europe member nations.

Portfolio task

Download the Total English Portfolio free from www.longman.com/totalenglish.

Objective: help learners to use the Portfolio to assess their skills.

This task can be done in Ss' L1.

Portfolios are divided into three main sections. The first section is called the 'Passport'. The Passport is designed to summarise relevant language learning experiences and qualifications. This can be shown to others, for example new teachers, employers, etc. Firstly, however, it is helpful for learners to give their own assessment of their abilities in the different skills areas.

1 ▶ Help students to understand the self-assessment grids (there are many translations available as this is a standard document) for levels A1 to B1.

2 ▶ Ask students to assess their own abilities in the different skills areas (listening, reading, spoken interaction, spoken production, and writing). Students complete the language skills profile by shading in the relevant boxes.

3 ▶ Explain that students can update this profile as they progress and they can fill in profiles for other languages.

3 Taste

Overview

Lead-in	**Vocabulary:** food
3.1	**Grammar:** *going to* (future plans)
	Can do: tell a friend about your future plans
3.2	**Grammar:** defining relative clauses
	Can do: write an informal letter to a friend
3.3	**Grammar:** Present Continuous (for future arrangements)
	Vocabulary: adjectives, sense verbs
	Can do: make arrangements with a friend
Com. Focus:	Design a restaurant
Reference	
Practice	

Summary

Lesson 1: Ss read about Jamie Oliver, a popular celebrity chef in Great Britain. Then they listen to one of Jamie's trainee chefs talk about her plans for the future.

Lesson 2: Ss listen to a conversation about a film called *Big Night*, which is about two Italian brothers who own a restaurant in New York. Then they talk about films with a partner.

Lesson 3: Ss read about research that showed how the place in which you eat affects what you think of the food. Then they talk about what various things look, sound, smell, taste and feel like.

Communication Focus: Ss talk about restaurants and listen to a man describing his plans to set up a restaurant. Then they design their own restaurants.

Film bank: Jamie Oliver (4'46")

An extract from Jamie's TV cookery show

Jamie Oliver broke the mould for TV cookery shows and this extract illustrates why. We see Jamie's friends, lifestyle and also watch him cook salmon in newspaper (!) on the beach. The language level is high but the meaning is reinforced through action.

Possible places to use this short film are:

- ▶ before the Lead-in to introduce the topic of food
- ▶ after Lesson 1 to extend the topic of Jamie Oliver
- ▶ at the end of the unit to round up the topic and language

For ways to use this short film in class, see Students' Book page 135 and Teacher's Book page 190.

Lead-in

▶ Introduce Ss to the topic of taste.

Q: What does taste mean? It's a sense which we use to distinguish the flavour or quality of something e.g., It tastes sweet.

Write on the board: *Taste is a sense. We taste with our mouths.* **Q: What other senses do we have? Which parts of the body do we use?** Sight. We see with our eyes; Sound. We hear with our ears; Smell. We smell with our nose; Touch. We feel/touch with our hands.

1 ▶ Focus on the photos. Ss look at them in pairs and write as many things as they can in the table. Get feedback from the whole class, writing the words on the board.

Answers: Pic 1: red chili peppers Pic 2: oranges, grapefruits, limes, lemons, raspberries, grapes and apples Pic 3: chef, cooker, saucepan, frying pan Pic 4: waiter, customer, table, glasses

▶ Now give the Ss a few minutes to think in pairs of some more words for each category. Write the four categories on the board and have Ss tell you their ideas to complete each one.

2a ▶ Focus on the words in the box and check to see if Ss understand them. Give a clue for an expression and have Ss guess which one it is e.g. *How can we describe eating in a restaurant? What can you do if you feel fat? What are you if you cook on TV? What are you doing when you make food at home? What's another expression for when you stop eating something particular?*

▶ Have Ss complete the sentences with the words and phrases and check them with the whole class. Pay special attention to the pronunciation of *recipe* /ˈresɪpiː/.

Answers: give up (5) 1 vegetarian (3) 2 diet (2) 3 cook for yourself (6) 4 eat out (1) 5 celebrity chefs (4)

2b ▶ Tell Ss they are going to listen to some answers, six of which correspond to the questions given in Ex. 2a (including the example). Ss have to write the number of the correct answer next to the appropriate question. Play recording 3.1 twice.

3 ▶ Ss ask and answer all seven questions in pairs. Get feedback from the whole class about their answers.

EXTEND THE LEAD-IN

Ss work in pairs to write a recipe of a dish they know how to cook. Allow them to use dictionaries or help them with any difficult vocabulary. Have Ss read their recipes to the rest of the class without saying what the dish is. The rest of the class can guess the dish.

3.1 Jamie's kitchen

Over the last decade, celebrity chefs and TV cooking programmes have become increasingly popular in Britain. Jamie Oliver became an overnight success when he appeared on a documentary about the restaurant where he was working in London. The next morning he was called by five different TV production companies, who wanted him to work for them. He chose one and made the incredibly popular series *The Naked Chef*. He's since made several other TV programmes, written four books and performed his cooking shows in theatres in Britain, Australia and New Zealand.

In this lesson Ss read about Jamie's latest venture; a restaurant called '15', which trains unemployed young people to be chefs. They also listen to the plans of one of his trainee chefs and through this context analyse the grammar of *going to*.

OPTIONAL WARMER

Ask Ss questions about cooking programmes.

Q: Do you watch cooking programmes? Why or why not?

Q: What time are cooking programmes normally on the TV?

Q: Who do you think usually watches them?

Q: Are there any celebrity chefs who are very famous in your country?

Reading

▶ Focus the Ss on the first photo and tell them that the man is Jamie Oliver, a famous British celebrity chef. Ask:

Q: How old do you think he is? Jamie was born in 1975.

Q: Do you think he looks like a typical celebrity chef?

▶ Focus Ss on the second photo and tell them that this is his restaurant in London.

1▶ Ss read the text and choose a title with a partner (A success story for Jamie). Tell them not to worry about any words they don't understand yet.

2▶ Ss read the text again slowly and answer the questions in pairs.

Answers: 1 Because the recipes are simple, easy and tasty. 2 when he was eight 3 unemployed 16–24-year-olds 4 She failed her college exams but then became very successful in Jamie's restaurant. 5 She is very close to Jamie. He's like a big brother or a best friend to her. 6 in a top restaurant in New York

3a▶ Ss work in pairs to match the phrases. Get feedback from various Ss. Drill the pronunciation of *recipe* /resɪpiː/ which is often problematic.

Answers: open a restaurant top-class chef tasty recipe no previous experience work abroad

b▶ Ss work in pairs to make sentences about Jamie and KerryAnn using the phrases in Ex. 3a. Tell them to try to do this without looking back at the text. Get feedback from various Ss.

▶ Tell Ss to look back at the text one more time. Ask if there are any other phrases they don't understand. Encourage Ss to answer each other's questions.

4▶ Ss discuss the questions with a partner. Get feedback from the whole class.

OPTIONAL GRAMMAR LEAD-IN

Tell the Ss one of your plans for next summer e.g., *Next summer I'm going to go to the beach.* Write on the board the stem: *Next weekend I'm going to ...* Tell the Ss to complete the sentence with a true plan of their own, and then chain around the classroom with each student saying his or her sentence and asking the next student about theirs.

Grammar

5▶ Tell the Ss that they are going to listen to a trainee chef talking about her plans. Read through the two questions with the whole group and tell Ss to listen to the recording. Play recording 3.2. Ss answer the questions in pairs. Get feedback from the whole class.

Answers: 1 She's going to work in a small restaurant in the south of France. 2 She's going to get a job in the States.

6a▶ Focus Ss on the Active grammar box and tell them to listen again and complete the gaps. Point out that the sentences are not in order. Play recording 3.2 again. Allow Ss time to compare answers with a partner before you get feedback.

Active grammar

\+ I'm going to work for him over the summer.
– I'm not going to stay there longer than a few months.
? What are you going to do next?

▶ Point out that we use this tense to refer to future plans and intentions.

b▶ Tell the Ss to rewrite the sentences with *you, she* and *they* with a partner. When they have finished, tell them to check with the Reference on page 33.

7▶ Read through the example sentence with the whole group. Tell Ss to work with a partner to correct the other sentences. Get feedback from various Ss.

Answers: 1 They're going to visit their son in Australia in the summer. 2 What is he going to do this afternoon? 3 Are you going to see Sarah at the weekend? 4 We're going to play tennis on Sunday morning. 5 They're not going to work abroad this summer. 6 When are you going to come and visit me? 7 Marie-Ann isn't going to catch the train.

8a▶ Ss work in pairs to write the complete sentences.

b▶ Play recording 3.3 and have Ss check their answers.

Answers: 1 I'm going to start going to the gym. 2 Rachel isn't going to get a new job. 3 Are we going to visit your parents tomorrow? 4 They aren't going to come to dinner next week. 5 What are you going to do this weekend? 6 He's going to call you later. 7 Where are Peter and Tania going to stay? 8 Who's going to tell him the news?

▶ Model the pronunciation of *going to* /gəʊɪŋ tə/ or play the first sentence again and have Ss repeat it. Tell the Ss to practise saying the rest of the sentences with a partner. Go around checking they are saying them correctly.

Person to person

9▶ Tell Ss three plans of yours for this week. Ss discuss with a partner and guess which one is false. Encourage them to ask follow up questions in order to get extra information upon which to base their decision e.g., *'I'm going to go to the cinema.' 'What are you going to see?'*

▶ Tell them the three plans and the Ss discuss with a partner which is false. Get feedback from the whole class and reveal the correct answer.

▶ Tell the Ss to write three sentences about their plans for this week, one of which is false. Then they tell their sentences to a partner who must guess which is false. Again encourage them to ask follow-up questions.

OPTIONAL VARIATION

Follow the same procedure as above, but instead of the Ss doing this with only one partner, tell them to stand up and mingle telling their sentences to as many people as possible.

Speaking

10a▶ Tell Ss to think about their plans for the next couple of years. Focus their attention on the box and read through the suggested areas with the whole class. Ss make notes in relation to these areas as in the example. Help with any vocabulary or phrases they might need.

▶ Focus their attention on the How to ... box and read through the different sections with the whole class. Give the Ss an example of your own that they can use as a model e.g., *Next year I'm going to travel to England because my friend is going to get married.*

b▶ Ss in groups of three or four, ask each other about their future plans. Encourage Ss to use the How to ... box and to ask follow up questions about what they hear.

▶ Get feedback from different groups, encouraging them to say what they have in common and what is different about their plans.

OPTIONAL EXTENSION

Rearrange the class so that Ss are sitting in a different group than before. Ss tell their new partners about the plans of the people they were sitting with previously.

3.2 Big Night

Big Night is the name of an American film released in 1996 and directed by Campbell Scott and Stanley Tucci. It's a story about two Italian brothers trying to run a good Italian restaurant in 1950s America but struggling to find enough customers. They gamble all their money on one big night, inviting a famous jazz musician to have dinner there. Unfortunately he doesn't arrrive and the brothers lose a lot of money. In the end, they realise they won't be successful without changing some good things about their food/culture.

In this lesson Ss listen to a conversation about this film and through this context, discuss defining relative clauses.

OPTIONAL WARMER

Write *Films and Food* on the board. In pairs, Ss brainstorm films that are related in some way to food (in the plot or the title). Get feedback from the whole class and write the titles on the board. If the Ss haven't thought of many, add some from the list below.

Possible answers: *Breakfast at Tiffany's, Chocolat, Delicatessen, Fried Green Tomatoes, Supersize Me, Vanilla Sky*

▶ Tell Ss to talk to a partner and say which of the films they have seen and what they are about.

Listening

1a▶ Focus the Ss attention on the photo and tell them to discuss the questions with a partner. Get feedback from the class, asking Ss to give reasons for their answers.

b▶ Play recording 3.4 and Ss check their answers.

Answers: 1 They are Italian. 2 They are brothers. 3 It's about a restaurant that is not very successful and how the brothers organise a big night with a famous jazz musician to try to attract more customers.

2▶ Read through the stem sentences with the Ss and tell them to listen to the recording again and complete the notes. Play recording 3.4 again and then allow Ss to compare answers with a partner before getting feedback from the class.

Answers: 2 It's set in the 1950s in New York. 3 It's about two Italian brothers, Primo and Secondo, and Pascal, who owns the restaurant next door. 4 The problem is that the brothers want to serve the very best Italian food, but the customers only want spaghetti and meatballs. 5 They plan to organise a big night and advertise that Louie Prima, a famous jazz musician, is going to eat there.

3▶ Ss think of a film they know and make notes similar to those presented in Ex. 2. Help them with any difficult vocabulary. Ss then tell a partner about the film.

Pronunciation

4a ▸ Focus the Ss on the extract from the dictionary, and tell them to pronounce the word with a partner. Ask:
Q: Which letter is silent? (The second 'o'). Ss repeat the word after you.

b ▸ Ss look at the words in the box with a partner and identify the silent letter.

c ▸ Play recording 3.5 and Ss check their answers. Chain around the class, with different Ss pronouncing the words.

> Answers: spaghetti, comfortable, Wednesday, vegetable, knife, island, lamb, calm, hour, yoghurt

5a ▸ Play recording 3.6. Ss listen and read the sentences. Ss then practise saying the sentences in pairs. Go around the class checking pronunciation. Explain that *hour* takes the article 'an' not 'a' because of its silent letter.

b ▸ Ask the Ss to brainstorm some more words with silent letters, in pairs. Then ask them to either write the words on the board or spell them out so that you can write them on the board. Tell the rest of the class to copy the words and circle the silent letters. Get feedback from the class and practise pronouncing the words.

> Possible answers: knock, know, climb, science, autumn, psychology, exhibition, business, write

Grammar

> **OPTIONAL GRAMMAR LEAD-IN**
> Dictate the following stem sentences to the Ss:
> *Big Night is about two brothers who ...*
> *They own a restaurant which ...*
> *Next door there is a restaurant where ...*
> Tell the Ss to work in pairs to complete the sentences in some way. Get feedback to find out how many ways of completing the sentences Ss have found. Ask the class: **Q: What is the grammatical name of this type of sentence?** Defining relative clauses

6 ▸ Read through the examples with the whole class and then focus the Ss on the Active grammar box and tell them to complete the gaps using the examples as a guide. Get feedback and write the answers on the board.

> **Active grammar**
> Use *who* for people.
> Use *which* for things.
> Use *where* to say what happens in a place.

▸ Explain to the Ss that these clauses give extra information that is necessary for us to understand the noun. Write on the board *I saw the boy* and ask the Ss:
Q: Do we know which boy? (No.) Finish the sentence on the board so that it reads *I saw a boy who lives next door.* Ask: **Q: Do we know which boy?** (Yes.)
Point out the position of the relative pronouns and the absence of commas and tell the Ss that there is a complete explanation on page 33.

7a ▸ Ss complete the sentences with a partner. Check the answers with the whole class.

> Answers: 1 where 2 who 3 which 4 where 5 who 6 which 7 who 8 where

b ▸ Ss mark the sentences in which *that* can be used in pairs. Check the answers with the whole class.

> Answers: Sentences 2, 3, 5, 6 and 7.

8a ▸ Read through the example sentence with the class and tell Ss to make similar sentences with the prompts below. Let them check their sentences with a partner and then check them with the whole class.

> Answers: 1 Spinach is the only vegetable which/that I never eat. 2 The place where I feel happiest is my bedroom. 3 The village where I was born is beautiful. 4 My sister is the only person who/that I tell my secrets to. 5 The music which/that I listen to the most is jazz. 6 The thing which/that I like most about myself is my hair.

b ▸ Ss change the sentences to make them true for them and then tell a partner. Get feedback from various Ss.

▸ Read through the Lifelong learning box with the Ss. Explain how important it is to be able to communicate when you only have a limited vocabulary. Point out the use of *thing*, *stuff* and *person* and ask the Ss:
Q: Which would you use with the following words? doctor (person), sweet (thing), coffee (stuff), teacher (person), orange juice (stuff), vegetables (things)

9 ▸ Put the Ss in pairs. Student A looks at page 125 and student B looks at page 127. Tell them not to look at each other's book. Each student takes it in turn to describe one of their items using a defining relative clause.

Writing

10 ▸ Tell the Ss to look at the Writing bank on page 145, read through the information and do the exercises.

> 1 ▸ Answers: 1 He has been on holiday. 2 to invite her to a dinner party 3 six 4 let him know if she can come

> 2 ▸ Answers: Starting: I F F Ending: F I I F

▸ Ss complete the text on page 29. Read through the letter with the whole class to check the answers.

> Answers: 1 writing 2 reason 3 everything's

11 ▸ Ss put the activities in order with a partner.

> Answers: 1 d 2 a 3 b 4 c

12 ▸ Ss write the letter. Tell them they can either tell the truth or invent their news.

3.3 It's the place ...

Research carried out recently at Bournemouth University has shown that it is not so much the quality of the food as the place where you eat it, that contributes to the enjoyment of a meal. When exactly the same dish of 'chicken à la king' with 'Uncle Ben's rice' was served in ten different places, it scored lowest in an army training camp and a boarding school and highest in a four-star restaurant.

In this lesson Ss read an article about this research and listen to a woman making arrangements to go to a restaurant. Through this context the Ss analyse the use of the Present Continuous for future arrangements.

OPTIONAL WARMER

Tell Ss that you want them to imagine the best meal ever. Write the following cues on the board and give an example yourself of a perfect meal using the cues.

Where? (city/town) When? (season) Who with? Type of restaurant? Music? Food? Drink? Other things?

Allow Ss five minutes to make some notes and then put them into small groups to talk about their perfect meal. Get feedback from the whole class.

Reading

1▶ Ss answer the questions in pairs. For question 1, get feedback from the class, writing the words on the board under headings *favourite* and *least favourite*. For question 2, get feedback, write the answers on the board under three headings and ask the Ss about each picture:
Q: Do you like oysters? ... cake? ... asparagus?

2▶ Ss work in pairs to decide whether the adjectives are negative or positive and if they can use *absolutely* or *very* (*absolutely* is used with extreme adjectives, and *very* is used with the moderate adjectives).

Answers: + delicious (absolutely) + tasty (very)
+ mouth-watering (absolutely)
– tasteless (absolutely) – disgusting (absolutely)
– horrible (absolutely)

▶ Tell Ss to look back at the list of foods you wrote on the board after Ex. 1 and tell a partner what they think of the foods using the adjectives e.g., *I think beef is absolutely disgusting.*

3▶ Tell the Ss they are going to read a text about some research done on the importance of where you eat. Ask:
Q: Where do you think are nice places to eat?
Q: Where do you think are horrible places to eat?

▶ Ss read the text quickly. Tell them not to worry about any vocabulary they don't understand at the moment. Get feedback about the results from the whole class.

Answer: In many cases, the location is much more important than the food.

4▶ Read through the sentences with the whole class, checking that everybody understands. Ss then read the text more carefully and work with a partner to say if the statements are true or false. Check the answers with the whole class.

Answers: 1 T 2 F 3 T 4 F 5 T 6 F

5▶ Ss work in pairs to decide on the meaning of the vocabulary underlined in the text. Check the answers with the whole group.

Answers: 1 a) 2 b) 3 b) 4 a) 5 a) 6 a)

▶ Ask the Ss if there are any other words or phrases that they don't understand from the text. Encourage Ss to guess the meanings from the context.

6▶ Ss discuss the questions in small groups of three or four. Get feedback from the whole class.

Vocabulary

7▶ Ss match the illustrations and the sentences in pairs. Get feedback from various Ss.

Answers: 1 D 2 3 C 4 A 5 B

8▶ Focus Ss on the words in the box and check they understand all of them. Now read the example for the whole class. Tell Ss to work in pairs to make similar sentences. Get feedback from various Ss.

Suggested answers: Fresh coffee smells delicious. Being in love feels fantastic. A Ferrari looks very sophisticated. Madonna sounds awful. Your shoes look great. Old milk smells disgusting. Chillies taste hot. Cigarettes smell horrible.

OPTIONAL VARIATION

Ss write one or more sentences individually for some of the things and then work with a partner to say the sentences but using *this/these* rather than the name of the thing/person e.g., *These smell disgusting and they taste horrible* (cigarettes). The other student must listen and guess the thing.

Grammar

OPTIONAL GRAMMAR LEAD-IN

Tell the Ss what you are doing after class (invent it if you want). Say: *After class I'm having a meeting with the head teacher. What are you doing after class?* Chain around the class, eliciting answers. Don't worry if Ss use a mixture of Present Continuous and *going to.*

9a▶ Ss listen to the conversation and say what arrangement the woman has for that evening. Play recording 3.7 and allow Ss to check with a partner before getting feedback.

Answer: She's having dinner with Marcin, a friend of her brother's. It's a blind date.

▶ Write *blind date* on the board and ask they Ss if they know what it is. Elicit/teach the answer.

b▶ Focus Ss on the Active grammar box. Play recording 3.7 again and Ss complete the gaps. Get feedback and write the complete sentences on the board.

Active grammar

What are you doing tonight? I'm going out for dinner with Marcin. He's not coming with us.

▶ Point out that the Present Continuous is used to talk about future arrangements. Remind them that in lesson 1.3 they used the Present Continuous to refer to things happening now or around now. Explain that this tense has both functions.

▶ Write two example sentences on the board:
1 *Tonight I'm meeting Sue in the Mexican restaurant.*
2 *Next year I'm going to learn to drive.*

Ask Ss: **Q: Which sentence refers to a general plan or intention?** (2) **Q: What tense do we use?** (*going to* + infinitive) **Q: Which sentence tells us where and when the action is going to happen?** (1) **Q: Which tense do we use?** (Present Continuous: *be* + verb + *-ing*).

10a▶ Ss write sentences using the prompts. Get feedback from various Ss.

Answers: 1 I'm not doing anything tonight. 2 Karen's going to a restaurant next week. 3 He's not going out this weekend. 4 We're watching TV at home tonight. 5 Are they spending this summer by the beach? 6 I'm playing football tomorrow night.

b▶ Tell the Ss to change sentence 1 so that it is true for them. For the rest of the sentences Ss must find somebody in the class who is doing that thing. Model the first question: Are you doing anything tonight?

▶ Tell them to stand up and mingle, asking questions for numbers 2–6 until they find somebody who says *yes*. Then they write the person's name next to the sentence. Finally, get feedback from the whole class.

Speaking

11▶ Focus Ss on the How to ... box. Tell them to work with a partner to suggest different expressions for the underlined words. Get feedback from the whole group.

Suggested answers: Are you free on Friday night? I'm playing tennis with Jo. What about the Indian restaurant? That sounds good! I don't really like Italian food. Let's meet at the restaurant at 7p.m. I'd prefer 8p.m.

12▶ Tell Ss to write five true or imaginary arrangements for the weekend. Then they mingle and try to make arrangements with three different classmates.

Communication: Design a restaurant

In this lesson Ss listen to a man talking about his plans for a new restaurant and then design their own restaurant in groups.

1▶ Tell Ss they are going to talk about one of their favourite restaurants. Read through the different points they should cover, giving examples in relation to one of your favourite restaurants e.g., kind and quality of food – *In my favourite restaurant they serve top quality fish and salads.*

▶ Give the Ss a little time to think about their own favourite restaurants, making a few notes. Help with any difficult vocabulary and then put them in small groups so they can share their ideas.

2a▶ Play recording 3.8 and Ss answer the question (He's going to open a restaurant).

b▶ Focus Ss on the floor plan of the restaurant and on the menu. Explain the meaning of any of the new words on the menu.

▶ Tell the Ss to listen again and mark the words from the box on the plan and complete the menu. Play recording 3.8 again and then allow Ss to compare answers with a partner before you get feedback. If you feel it is necessary, play the recording again.

Answers: 1 It is one third kitchen and two thirds restaurant. The toilets are in the small room which is on one side of the restaurant and the main entrance is opposite. 2 tomato and orange soup, grilled salmon and new potatoes, chocolate mousse

3a▶ The Ss work in small groups to design their own restaurant. Ask one member of each group to take notes. Encourage them to pay attention to detail e.g., drawing a plan. Go around the class helping with any difficult vocabulary.

b▶ Each group presents their ideas and at the end, the whole class votes for the restaurant they think is most likely to succeed.

▶ Point out that Ss can consult the grammar Reference on page 33.

OPTIONAL EXTENSION

Tell the Ss to write two sentences, one of which is a general plan and one which is an arrangement for the near future. Chain around the class with Ss saying their sentences. Check that they are using the Present Continuous and *going to* correctly.

Review and Practice

1 ▶

Answers: 1 No, I'm going to have something later. 2 No, I'm going to take him/her after dinner. 3 No, I'm going to buy it at the weekend. 4 No, I'm going to paint it on Tuesday. 5 No, I'm going to clean it in the morning.

2 ▶

Answers: 1 When are you going to give up? 2 Are you going to buy her a present? 3 Where are you going to put it? 4 Are you going to wash the car?

3 ▶

Answers: 1 The waiter who/that brought us our food was very friendly. 2 This is the restaurant where John asked me to marry him. 3 The train which/that goes to the airport runs every twenty minutes. 4 The men who/that robbed the post office escaped in a black BMW. 5 This is the corner of the road where the accident happened.

4 ▶

Answers: Hi Tim! What are you doing this evening? I'm probably having a quiet evening at home alone. I'm inviting a few friends over for dinner. I'm going to see a film with my brother.

5 ▶

Answers: 1 She's going to the dentist's on Monday morning/at 11.00a.m. 2 She's having lunch with Jenny at 2.00pm. 3 She's going to Italian class in the evening/at 6.30p.m. 4 On Tuesday she's making a presentation in the morning/at 10a.m. 5 She's having a meeting with the Marketing Director in the afternoon/at 3.00p.m. 6 She's phoning the US office at 6.00p.m. 7 She's going to the cinema with Nathan in the evening/at 8.00pm.

6 ▶

Answers: 1 cooker 2 chef 3 vegetarian 4 work abroad 5 low marks 6 tasty 7 smells 8 recipe

Notes for using the Common European Framework (CEF)

CEF References

3.1 Can do: tell a friend about your future plans

CEF A2 descriptor: can discuss what to do in the evening, at the weekend (CEF page 77)

3.2 Can do: write an informal letter to a friend

CEF A2 descriptor: can write a series of simple phrases and sentences linked with simple connectors like 'and', 'but' and 'because' (CEF page 61)

3.3 Can do: make arrangements with a friend

CEF A2 descriptor: can discuss what to do, where to go and make arrangements to meet (CEF page 77)

CEF quick brief

The Common European Framework describes itself as 'a common basis for the elaboration of language syllabuses, curriculum guidelines, examinations, textbooks, etc'. It is not intended to be a definitive description of what to teach but it is designed to offer a 'framework' which the user can build on.

Portfolio task

Download the Total English Portfolio free from www.longman.com/totalenglish.

Objective: help students to complete the 'language learning and intercultural experiences' section of their Passport.

This task can be done in Ss' L1.

1 ▶ Remind Ss that their Passport enables them to demonstrate their relevant experiences and qualifications.

2 ▶ Explain that language learning and intercultural experiences are important in this. The Total English Portfolio has a section for students to give information about these.

3 ▶ Give some examples of your own relevant experiences (exchange trips, holidays, courses, friends with that first language, etc).

4 ▶ Ask students to write a list of their own relevant experiences and show a partner.

5 ▶ Ask students to complete this section of their Passport.

6 ▶ Remind students that they can update this at any time.

4 Survival

Overview

Lead-in	**Vocabulary:** survival
4.1	**Grammar:** comparatives
	Vocabulary: describing people
	Can do: compare people
4.2	**Grammar:** superlatives
	Vocabulary: survival skills
	Can do: write a thank-you note
4.3	**Grammar:** indirect questions
	Can do: ask polite questions
Com. Focus	Survival choices
Reference	
Practice	

Summary

Lesson 1: Ss read about Peter Habeler, Reinhold Messner and Tanya Streeter. Habeler and Messner were the first people to climb Mount Everest without oxygen and Streeter has held the record for the deepest 'free dive' – a dive without oxygen or equipment.

Lesson 2: Ss read a web page about a survival school that offers courses to people who want to learn survival skills. Then they listen to an instructor from that school give further information.

Lesson 3: Ss look at how to survive in England, encompassing the quirks and traditions like afternoon tea and saying 'sorry' every five minutes.

Communication Focus: Ss negotiate with each other to choose five objects to help them survive in a particular environment.

Film bank: Surviving in the Sahara (4'12")

An extract from a British TV survival programme

This extract is from a programme called *Ray Mears' World of Survival*. Ray Mears is a popular TV personality and is also an expert on the topic of how to survive in inhospitable places. In this extract he is in the Sahara and explains what to do if your vehicle breaks down.

Possible places to use this short film are:

- after Lesson 1 to extend the topic of extremes
- after Lesson 2 to extend the topic of survival skills
- at the end of the unit to round up the topic of survival

For ways to use this short film in class, see Students' Book page 136 and Teacher's Book page 190.

Lead-in

▶ Introduce Ss to the topic of survival.
Q: What does *survival* mean? Survival is when someone or something continues to live or exist after being in a dangerous situation.
Q: What is the verb? What is the person who survives? *Survive* and *survivor*.
Q: Which famous survivors can you think of? Robinson Crusoe, Gulliver, and many others from literature.
Q: What songs or TV shows do you associate with *survival*? *I Will Survive* by Gloria Gaynor, *I'm a Survivor* by Destiny's Child. There have been shows on British TV called *Survivor* where people had to survive on an island and every week one person was voted off.

1 ▶ Focus on the photos. Ask Ss to discuss their immediate reactions to the photos.

▶ Ss look at the photos in pairs and discuss what they can see. They also write words/phrases that they associate with each photo. Write some words/collocations on the board to help prompt ideas (see Answers box).

▶ Ss share their words with another pair and make a note of new language. Elicit what can be seen in the photos from the class and write the words/phrases on the board. Feed in more if you think your class will find them useful.

Possible answers: Pic 1: to go rock climbing, afraid of heights, to hold on, dangerous
Pic 2: to sail a boat, a rough/empty/deep sea, a sail, be sea-sick, sharks
Pic 3: to trek through the jungle, vegetation, snakes, creepy-crawlies, dangerous animals, humid
Pic 4: rush-hour, a tube train, packed, commuters, hot, over-crowded, delays

2a ▶ Books closed. Check that Ss understand the words from the box by asking questions: **Q: What's the noun of *strong*? Q: What verb goes with goal to mean *reach*?** Ask other questions as necessary.

▶ Open books. Ss match the words and phrases in the box to the definitions. Check in pairs. Don't give Ss the answers yet.

b ▶ Play recording 4.1 and Ss can check their answers.

Answers: 1 control your fear 2 achieve your goal 3 a challenge 4 rely on 5 physical/mental strength

3 ▶ Ask Ss to discuss the questions in pairs. Get feedback from the whole class.

EXTEND THE LEAD-IN

Ss order the activities in each picture according to these criteria:
1 scary 2 exciting 3 likely to do
Ss show their list to each other and explain why. e.g. *Rock climbing is very, very scary for me because I'm afraid of heights. Next is trekking through ...*

4.1 Going to extremes

In modern-day society many people seem to enjoy setting themselves dangerous and challenging goals, which according to psychologists is a result of the lack of risk in everyday life. As our daily routines can often be a little boring, thousands are turning to extreme sports from bungee-jumping to sky diving in order to get that 'adrenalin rush'. Some refer to these people as 'adrenalin junkies'.

In this lesson Ss read about two mountaineers and a diver who successfully achieved their goals despite pushing themselves to the limits. Through this context Ss consider adjectives for describing personality and the grammar of comparatives.

OPTIONAL WARMER

Write *Going to extremes* on the board. Ask Ss:
Q: What do you think this means? What type of people go to extremes?
Get feedback from the class and then ask them to brainstorm activities/hobbies/sports in which they think people push themselves to the limit. If they don't know the name of the sport they can just describe it.

Get feedback and write the activities on the board. If they don't mention some of the more recent sports listed below, add them to the list. **Possible answers:** *rock climbing, white-water rafting, trekking, racing-car driving, street-luge, bungee-jumping, skysurfing*

Ask Ss: **Q: Have you ever done any of these activities? Would you like to do one of them?**

Reading

1▶ Ss look at the photos and article headings in pairs and discuss the question. Get feedback from various Ss.

▶ Ss read the text quickly to check their answers. Tell them not to worry about anything they don't understand at this stage. Get feedback about what the people achieved.

2▶ Read through the statements with the whole class and check they understand. Ss read the text again and, in pairs, decide if the sentences are true (T), false (F) or (?) if the answer is not in the text. Get feedback from various Ss.

Answers: 1 T 2 F 3 T 4 ? 5 ? 6 ? 7 T 8 F 9 T

▶ Ask the Ss if there are any words or phrases in the text that they don't understand. Encourage Ss to answer each other's questions.

3▶ Ss discuss the question with a partner. Get feedback from the whole class.

Vocabulary

4a▶ Read the example with the whole class and tell Ss to work in pairs to replace the phrases with an adjective from the box and the verb *to be*.

b▶ Play recording 4.2 and Ss check their answers. Ask various Ss to read the sentences aloud to check pronunciation.

Answers: 1 is generous 2 is confident 3 is intelligent 4 is reliable 5 is ambitious 6 is determined 7 is talented

5a▶ Read the example with the class and give another example of your own e.g., *My friend Sally is very talented. She plays the violin very well.* Ss work in pairs to talk about people they know, using the adjectives from the box. Get feedback from various Ss.

b▶ Ss use the adjectives to describe Habeler, Messner and Tanya Streeter. Tell them to use all the adjectives, either in the affirmative or the negative, giving reasons where possible. Get feedback from the whole class.

OPTIONAL EXTENSION

Ss create a questionnaire to discover what kind of person their partner is. Write an example of the type of question Ss could ask on the board e.g., *Do you continue trying hard when things are difficult?* (determined).

Ss work in pairs to write questions for these adjectives. Go around the class helping with structure and vocabulary problems. Finally Ss change partners and ask and answer each other's questions. Ss decide what type of person their partner is.

Grammar

OPTIONAL GRAMMAR LEAD-IN

Books closed. Write *cat, horse* and *big* on the board. Ask the Ss to make a sentence to compare them. Elicit or model 'A horse is bigger than a cat'. Do the same with *pencil, table* and *small.*

Now write *car, bike* and *expensive* on the board. Ask the Ss to make a sentence to compare them. Elicit or model 'A car is more expensive than a bike'. Do the same with *mountaineering, swimming* and *dangerous.*

Elicit rules for making comparatives.

6▶ Ss look at the sentences in pairs and discuss how to make the comparative form. Get feedback from various Ss.

▶ Ss complete the Active grammar box, in pairs. Get feedback from various Ss. Write the answers on the board.

Active grammar

1 more boring (than) 2 happy 3 more interesting (than) 4 bad 5 better (than) 6 tall

▶ Focus Ss on *fit–fitter* and elicit/teach the reason why the 't' is doubled in the comparative form (when an adjective ends in vowel + consonant, we double the consonant).

▶ Ask Ss: **Q: What do you think the comparative form of *nice* is?** Elicit/teach *nicer* and point out that when an adjective already ends in *-e*, we only add 'r'.

▶ Check that the Ss understand the box by asking them to write the comparative forms of the following adjectives with a partner: *small* (*smaller*), *important* (*more important*), *easy* (*easier*), *big* (*bigger*), *strange* (*stranger*).

▶ Focus the Ss on the irregular adjectives and tell them to look at Reference page 43 to find other adjectives which have irregular comparative forms in English. Elicit the answers from the whole class (*little – less, far – farther/further*).

▶ Write the following sentences on the board.
1 *Peter is as tall as Paul.* 2 *Peter isn't as tall as Paul*
▶ Ask the Ss:
Q: In which sentence are Peter and Paul the same? (1)
Q: In which sentence are they different? (2)

7▶ Ss work with a partner to write the comparative forms of the adjectives in Ex. 4a.

Answers: more determined than, more intelligent than, more confident than, braver than, more ambitious than, more generous than, more talented than

8a▶ Ss work in pairs to make sentences about the illustrations using the adjectives in the box.

b▶ Play recording 4.3 and Ss check their answers.

Answers: Kurt is a bit taller than Pablo. Pablo isn't as tall as Kurt.
The grey car is a bit more expensive than the blue car. The blue car isn't as expensive as the grey car.
Teri is much funnier than Jan. Jan isn't as funny as Teri.

c▶ Play the recording again and ask Ss what they notice about the pronunciation of *than* (/ðæn/) and *as* (/æz/). Elicit/teach the fact that as these words are not stressed, the vowel sound is pronounced /ə/.

▶ Tell Ss to work with a partner and repeat the sentences with. Get feedback from a various Ss.

Person to person

9▶ Read through the example with the whole class and check they understand. Then Ss work in pairs to find five differences between them. When they have finished, each pair joins with another pair and they tell each other about their differences.

OPTIONAL EXTENSION

Write the names of various items that can be compared on the board e.g., *London, Tokyo, New York*; *Madonna, Michael Jackson, Britney Spears*; *fruit, cake, ice-cream*; *Monday, Friday, Sunday*; *January, June, August*.
Ss work in pairs to compare the items within each group in various ways. Get feedback from the whole class.

Lesson 4.2 Survival school

In recent years there has been a growing interest in how to survive in the wild. Game shows, documentaries and now survival schools cater to this new trend. These schools offer short courses in how to survive without any modern comforts in the wild.

In this lesson Ss read about a survival school and listen to a school instructor describe the courses that are on offer. Through this context Ss learn superlatives and how to write thank-you notes.

OPTIONAL WARMER

Ask Ss how well they could survive in the wilderness.
Q: Could you find food/kill animals to eat/build a place to sleep/make a fire?

Vocabulary

1a▶ Focus on the words/phrases in the box. Establish that the underlined words/phrases are the important ones to remember. Give Ss 2 or 3 minutes to match the words/phrases in the box to the underlined ones in the sentences. Avoid giving too much help. Ss should be able to work out parts of speech and meaning from the context. Check Ss answers as a class.

Answers: 1 nature 2 abilities 3 place to sleep outside 4 something difficult to do 5 try very hard 6 deal with

b▶ Listen to Ss as they discuss the questions and note down any obvious errors. Elicit answers to each question from the whole class and clarify any of the errors you heard, encouraging Ss to self-correct first.

▶ Ask Ss if they would like to learn any survival skills. Which one? Why?

Listening

2a▶ Focus Ss on the advert for a minute then ask them to cover it. Elicit ideas on what a survival school is and what you learn there. Write ideas on the board but don't confirm or reject anything.

b▶ Ask Ss to check the ideas on the board as they listen. Play recording 4.4. After listening, confirm with Ss which of the ideas on the board were mentioned.

3▶ Focus on the notes beneath the advert. Establish that Ss have to complete the notes with information from the listening. Play recording 4.4 again. Ss check their answers in pairs then check the answers as a whole class.

Answers: 1 He was in the army. 2 to learn and have fun 3 a weekend 4 throughout the year 5 £139 per person 6 between November and February 7 £149 per person 8 eighteen years old 9 at least four weeks before the course begins 10 groups of four or more

4▶ Ss discuss the question in pairs. Monitor their conversations, checking that they are giving reasons and noting down any important errors. Get feedback from Ss and go over errors, encouraging self-correction first.

Grammar

5▶ Focus on the thank-you notes. Establish that they were written by people who had been on a Hillside survival course. Ss read the notes and decide if each person feels positive or negative about the course. Elicit responses from Ss (each person feels very positive).

OPTIONAL GRAMMAR LEAD-IN

Tell Ss that you are going to test them on the notes. Ss read the notes again then close their books. Read the notes carefully but stop before each superlative to see if Ss can remember the next word.
Teacher: *A big thank-you for helping to make it the ...*
Ss: ... *most exciting ...*
Ask Ss: **Q: Look at the underlined words. What is the name for this construction?** (superlative)
Q: There are two ways to make superlatives. What are they? (1 adjective + *-est*, 2 *most* + adjective.)

6▶ Direct Ss to complete the Active grammar box. Write the grammar box on the board in preparation then elicit the correct answers from the whole class.

Active grammar

Short adjectives (one syllable) = (the) adjective + *-est*
Long adjectives (two+ syllables) = (the) *most* + adjective
Irregular adjectives: *good = best; bad = worst*

▶ Ss should be comfortable with this grammar, after doing comparatives in lesson 4.2. If not, move straight to the exercises to iron out any problems. If they are comfortable, introduce the finer points of superlatives.

▶ The word *the* almost always precedes superlatives (e.g., *the best, the most beautiful*); two-syllable adjectives ending in *-y* use *-est*. The *-y* changes to *-i*. (e.g., *the funniest*); when a one-syllable adjective ends in *-e*, simply add *-st* (e.g. *the nicest, the largest*); when a one syllable adjective ends in a vowel and a consonant, double the consonant (e.g., *fittest; biggest*)

▶ Direct Ss to Reference page 43 to review these points, particularly the irregulars, and the use of *in* and *on* after superlatives.

7▶ Ss find and correct the mistakes in pairs, then check with a partner. Get feedback from various Ss.

Answers: 1 Simon is the most experienced person in our office. 2 Which is the largest city in Africa. 3 Today is the hottest day of the year. 4 My sister is the most intelligent person in our family. 5 This is the most valuable of all the paintings. 6 Tim is the fittest player in our team.

8a▶ Direct Ss to Ex. 4a in lesson 4.1. Ss make the superlatives in pairs. Elicit answers from the whole class.

Answers: the most determined, the most intelligent, the most confident, the bravest, the most ambitious, the most generous, the most talented, the most reliable

OPTIONAL EXTENSION

Ss make sentences about friends and family using superlatives and these endings: ... *that I know.* ... *in my family.* ... *of all my friends.* ... *that I've ever met.* E.g., *My mother is the cleverest person in my family.*

b▶ Ss write complete sentences from the prompts. Elicit the answers from Ss and write them on the board. Often more than one tense is possible but tell Ss to use the Present Simple to keep this easy.

Answers: 1 This is the most exciting holiday I've ever had. 2 Everest is the highest mountain in the world. 3 What is the best department store in New York? 4 This is the wettest day of the year so far. 5 This is the most boring film I've ever seen. 6 Football is the most popular sport in Brazil. 7 This is the most difficult exam I've ever taken.

Pronunciation

9a▶ Stress patterns in superlative sentences are often emphasised to heighten the meaning. Focus attention on the sentences Ss wrote for Ex. 8b. Read out the first sentence. Ask Ss where the stressed words are (*exciting, holiday, had*).

b▶ Play recording 4.5. Ss mark the stressed words in the sentences. Check that Ss have got this correct. Ss identify what kinds of words are most likely to be stressed (nouns, verbs, adjectives). Note that stress changes depending on the meaning and the situation.

▶ Ss repeat the sentences to each other in pairs.

Answers: See the underlined words in Ex. 8b.

Person to person

10▶ Focus Ss on the questions and model 1 or 2 of the answers. Ss listen for examples of superlatives.

▶ Ss work in pairs to answer the questions. If some Ss finish early, they can swap partners and remember their previous partner's answers.

Writing

11a▶ Focus Ss back on the thank-you notes in Ex. 5. Ss underline any useful phrases that could be used in other thank-you notes.

Answers: A big thank-you for ... I would love to do it again. Thanks a million for ... I had a fantastic time.

b▶ Ask Ss to think of real reasons for thank-you notes e.g., *Someone cooks dinner for you/gives you a present.* Ss choose one of the situations and write a thank-you note using the phrases above and superlatives.

4.3 Surviving in English

It is increasingly important to know about the cultural background of people from other countries, especially when learning to speak the language of that country.

In this lesson Ss reconsider some of the stereotypes that exist about England and through this context look at the use of indirect questions to express politeness.

OPTIONAL WARMER

Write a number of countries on the board e.g., *Spain, USA, Japan, Sweden, France, Egypt, India* (don't include England yet). Ss work in pairs to write three things that they associate with each country.

Now write *fact* or *stereotype* on the board and check the Ss understand. Get Ss to read out the words they put for each country and discuss, as a group, if they are facts or stereotypes.

Reading

1a▶ Books closed. Give Ss two minutes to write a list of words they associate with England. Get feedback from the whole class, writing the words on the board. Ask the Ss to discuss, in pairs, if these things are fact or stereotype.

b▶ Ss read the text quickly and circle the topics that are mentioned. Tell them not to worry about any words they don't understand at this stage. Get feedback from the whole group.

Answers: drinking tea, the weather, English food and being polite.

▶ If Ss didn't mention the other topics (football, driving habits and libraries) in Ex. 1a, give them a few minutes to discuss what they know about these things in England with a partner. Get feedback from the whole class.

2▶ Read through the statements with the whole class, checking everybody understands all of them. Ss then read the text again and answer T (true) or F (false) with a partner. Get feedback from various Ss.

Answers: 1 F 2 T 3 T 4 F 5 T 6 F

▶ Ask the Ss if they have any vocabulary questions from the text and encourage other Ss in the class to clarify any doubts before explaining them yourself.

3▶ Ss discuss any facts that are particularly surprising. Get feedback from the whole class and add any information you would like to e.g., *It's not normally foggy in London. Not all English people are reserved.*

Lifelong learning

▶ Read through the questions with the whole class and Ss discuss their answers in pairs. Get feedback from the whole class, feeding in other ideas e.g., using a dictionary/a phrase book or asking for clarification, repetition or paraphrasing what you want to say. Encourage Ss to watch English language films and TV shows, as these contain lots of useful natural language.

Listening

4▶ Ss look at the places in the box with a partner and predict sentences they might hear in each place e.g., *Can I have the bill?* (in a restaurant). Get feedback.

▶ Play recording 4.6. Ss match each dialogue to a place.

Answers: 1 on a bus 2 in a clothes shop 3 in a bank 4 in a taxi 5 in a restaurant

5a▶ Read through the questions with the class and then play recording 4.6 again. Ss take notes as they listen and then compare in pairs. If necessary, play the recording again. Get feedback from the class.

Answers: 1 Carson Street. How much is it?/Can you tell me how long it takes? 2 a size 12, the assistant has a look 3 how much they charge to change euros into pounds, to change 200 euros 4 Queens Road, near Victoria station. She offers to tell the taxi driver where to go when they get nearer. 5 the bill, by credit card (Mastercard)

b▶ Ss work in pairs to practise the conversations, using the tapescript as a guide. After they have read through it once, Ss can be given freer practise by repeating the conversations but with only one of them looking at the tapescript and the other student improvising.

6▶ Ask Ss to brainstorm other situations that they might find themselves in if they visited an English speaking country, e.g., *in a hotel, at the airport, in a museum, in a pub*, etc.

▶ Get feedback from the whole class and write the situations on the board. Ask Ss to work in pairs to write a conversation for one of the situations. Go around the class correcting errors and ask some, more confident Ss to perform the dialogue for the rest of the class.

Grammar

OPTIONAL GRAMMAR LEAD-IN

Write the following stems on the board:
Do you know ... Can you tell me ...
Tell the Ss to imagine they are in London and they are lost. They want to go to Trafalgar Square. In pairs Ss discuss how they would complete the stem sentences. Get feedback and elicit/teach the correct form (*Do you know/Could you tell me where Trafalgar Square is*?)
Do the same with the following situation. You phone the theatre and you want to know what time the show starts. Elicit the correct answer (*Do you know/could you tell me what time the show starts*?)

7▶ Focus Ss on the Active grammar box and point out the distinction between direct and indirect questions. Explain that we often use indirect questions to be more polite. Read through the examples with the class and Ss complete the rules and answer the questions in pairs.

▶ Copy the rules from the box onto the board and elicit words to complete the gaps.

Active grammar

a) Questions with the verb *to be:*
Direct: question word/phrase + verb *to be* + subject
Indirect: indirect phrase + question word + subject + verb *to be*

b) Questions with main verbs:
Direct: question word + auxiliary verb + subject + verb
Indirect: indirect phrase + question word + subject + verb

1 Auxiliary verbs disappear.
2 We make Yes/No questions by using *if* or *whether*.
Point out that Ss can consult Reference page 43 for further examples.

8a▶ Ss work in pairs to make the questions indirect.

b▶ Play recording 4.7 and Ss check their answers.

Answers: 1 Can you tell me how much that is? 2 Do you know where I can get an application form? 3 Can you tell me if you have any 1st class stamps? 4 Do you know how far it is to the library? 5 Can you tell me if there's a post office near here? 6 Do you know what the time is? 7 Can you tell me where I get off the bus?

▶ Play the first sentence of recording 4.7 again and get the Ss to repeat with the correct intonation. Then they practise the rest of the sentences in pairs.

OPTIONAL EXTENSION

Tell Ss to write a question that they might ask in the place where they are studying. Some of these questions could be the same as those in Ex. 8a or some could be slightly different e.g., *Could you tell me the way to the bank?* Ss stand up and mingle, asking and answering their questions.

Speaking

9a▶ Elicit/explain the meaning of 'market research company' (a company that specialises in finding out information from the general public about a new product, for example). Then in pairs Ss choose a topic they would like to research.

b▶ Ss write about five questions for their survey. At this stage the questions Ss write should be direct. Go around the class helping with vocabulary and correcting errors.

c▶ Read through the How to ... box with the whole class. Tell the Ss to mingle in order to conduct the survey. Remind Ss that they should now use indirect questions and make a note of the answers they are given.

10▶ Give Ss five minutes to compile their results in pairs. Then ask them to report back to the class.

Communication: Survival choices

In this lesson Ss consider which objects or items are the most and least essential for surviving in a forest, up a mountain or in a desert.

1▶ Focus Ss on the items in the box and tell them to work with a partner to name the things they can see in the photo. Get feedback from various Ss, eliciting/explaining the meaning of problematic words with the whole class e.g., *We use a torch at night to see.*

Answers: a torch, a box of matches, a first-aid kit, chocolate, water, a penknife, rope, a mirror, a tent, blankets, pen and paper, scissors, an umbrella, a radio, a plastic bowl and some candles

2▶ Read through the questions with the whole class and then play recording 4.8. Ss listen and note down their answers. Allow them to compare with a partner and then get feedback from several Ss.

Answers: 1 a – (the trees and leaves and things).
2 blankets, penknife, matches, tent and chocolate

3▶ Tell Ss to look at the tapescript on page 156 and play recording 4.7 again. As they listen, tell them to underline ways of expressing opinion and making suggestions and comparisons. Get feedback, writing the expressions on the board.

Answers: Espressing opinions: I think we should take ...; In my opinion ...
Making suggestions: How about ...; Why don't we have ...
Making comparisons: Do you think they are more important than ... ?

4▶ Ss work in groups of three or four. Tell them to choose a place from Ex. 2 and discuss which five things they are going to take with them. Stress that they must try to come to an agreement.

▶ Get a member of each group to explain what they chose, giving reasons for their decisions.

OPTIONAL VARIATION

Assign a place to each group so that at least two groups have the same place. Follow the same procedure as above but when they have finished, two members of each group sit with a different group. The Ss must then try to convince each other that their list is the best.

Review and practice

1 ▶

Answers: 1 quieter 2 more exciting 3 worse 4 happier 5 further/farther

2 ▶

Answers: 1 The gold watch is more expensive than the silver watch. The silver watch is not as expensive as the gold watch. 2 The Brighton train leaves later than the London train. The London train doesn't leave as late as the Brighton train. 3 Health is more important to me than money. Money is not as important to me as health. 4 Brown bread tastes better than white bread. White bread doesn't taste as good as brown bread.

3 ▶

Answers: 1 the most expensive 2 the hottest 3 the tallest 4 the fastest 5 the friendliest

4 ▶

Answers: 1 one of the hottest (days) of 2 one of the best (swimmers) in 3 one of the most intelligent (boys) in 4 one of the oldest (houses) in 5 one of the worst (shocks) of 6 one of the bravest (soldiers) in

5 ▶

Answers: 1 Do you know why he isn't home yet? 2 Do you know if I can pay by credit card? 3 Can you tell me where I can find a garage? 4 Can you tell me whose car this is, please? 5 Do you know what time the next train for Manchester leaves?

6 ▶

Answers: (*Do you know*/*Can you tell me* can be used interchangeably) 1 ... where I can find a cheap hotel? 2 ... if there is an Internet café near here? 3 ... how much a taxi to the airport is? 4 ... where I can buy a map of Britain? 5 ... if I need a visa to go to Ireland?

7 ▶

Answers: 1 torch 2 reliable 3 achieve my goal 4 scissors 5 skills

Notes for using the Common European Framework (CEF)

CEF References

4.1 Can do: compare people

CEF A2 descriptor: can describe people, places and possessions in simple terms (CEF page 59)

4.2 Can do: write a thank-you note

CEF A2 descriptor: can write very simple personal letters expressing thanks and apology (CEF page 83)

4.3 Can do: ask polite questions

CEF A2 descriptor: can exchange limited information on familiar and routine operational matters (CEF page 81)

CEF quick brief

The Common European Framework believes that language learning can be measured not by how much grammar or vocabulary a learner knows, but by what a learner can achieve with the language that they know. Grammar and vocabulary are only important in terms of what they empower a learner to do. This is an 'action-oriented' approach to language.

Portfolio task

Download the Total English Portfolio free from www.longman.com/totalenglish.

Objective: help students to complete the qualifications section of their Passport.

This task can be done in Ss' L1.

1 ▶ Remind Ss of the purpose of the Portfolio and the Passport.

2 ▶ Explain that their formal qualifications are also important and that this is the other section of the Passport to complete.

3 ▶ Ask Ss to list their formal qualifications and compare with a partner.

4 ▶ Ask Ss to complete this section of their Passport.

5 Stages

Overview

Lead-in	**Vocabulary:** age and life stages
5.1	**Grammar:** *should, can, have to*
	Can do: exchange opinions with a friend
5.2	**Grammar:** Present Perfect with *for/since*
	Vocabulary: friendship
	Can do: write a personal profile
5.3	**Grammar:** *used to*
	Vocabulary: habits
	Can do: describe yourself when you were younger
Com. Focus	This is your life
Reference	
Practice	

Summary

Lesson 1: Ss read about three young adults of different nationalities talking about their life experiences, hopes and obligations. Then they discuss rules and obligations in their own countries.

Lesson 2: Ss read a website for 'Friends United', which is a company that helps old school friends to get in touch with each other. Then they tell a story about friendship.

Lesson 3: Ss do a quiz about ageing and listen to a radio programme about factors that affect life expectancy. Then they talk about their past habits.

Communication Focus: Ss listen to a programme called *This is your life*, which presents the life of actor, Pierce Brosnan. Then they interview a partner in order to make a similar presentation.

Film bank: On Golden Pond (2'50")

An extract from the classic Hollywood film

On Golden Pond stars Katherine Hepburn, Henry Fonda and his daughter, Jane Fonda. The film centres around the relationship between characters from three different generations. In this extract Jane has just met her parents again for the first time in ages and she's brought the teenage son of her new boyfriend.

Possible places to use this short film are:

- ▶ before the Lead-in to introduce the topic of ages and stages
- ▶ after Lesson 1 to extend the topic of adolescence and adulthood
- ▶ at the end of the unit to round up the topic and language

For ways to use this short film in class, see Students' Book page 137 and Teacher's Book page 191.

Lead-in

▶ Write *stage* on the blackboard and ask the Ss if they know what it means. Elicit/tell the Ss that it's a level or period of time in a process.

▶ Write the following ages on the board: 1, 15, 30, 50, 65 and 80. Ask the Ss to brainstorm one or two things normally associated with each stage of a person's life. Give the following example: *When you are one you can't speak and you sleep a lot.* Get feedback from the whole class.

1 ▶ Write *early/late/mid-twenties* on the board. Ask Ss which one they would use for a person who is 21. And for a person who is 25 or 28. Tell them to look at the photos and discuss with a partner what the people are doing and how old they are. Ss share their ideas with the rest of the class.

2a ▶ Check that Ss understand the words in the box.
Q: When you are six months old, what are you? (a baby)
Q: When you are two years old, what are you? (a toddler)
and so on.

▶ Tell the Ss to write an age range for each word individually.

b ▶ Have Ss compare with a partner to see if they agree or disagree with each other and then discuss each concept with the whole class.

3 ▶ Ss work in pairs to discuss the age at which people in their country normally do the activities in the box. If your class is of mixed nationality, it might be a good idea to group Ss according to their country of origin. Go around the class helping the Ss with any expressions they don't understand. Have Ss share their ideas with the whole class.

4 ▶ Read the example out loud to the Ss and tell them they have to talk about themselves or somebody they know well in a similar way. Give Ss a couple of minutes to think and make brief notes about what they are going to say. Have them work with a partner to tell their stories. Get some feedback by asking individual Ss to tell you about what their partner had told them.

EXTEND THE LEAD-IN

Tell the Ss to look back at the words or phrases in Ex. 3. Ask them to think about the age at which people did these things 100 years ago. Do they think that it was better in the past or do they prefer the way things are now?

5.1 Turning eighteen

In many countries a person's eighteenth birthday is of great importance, as it marks the age at which a teenager is generally recognised to be a legal adult. In Britain, for example, you can't vote, get married without your parents' permssion or drink alcohol in a pub until you are eighteen. In the USA it's the same, except that the legal age for drinking alcohol is twenty-one.

In this lesson Ss read about three young people, from different cultural backgrounds, commenting on life at eighteen. Through this context they analyse the grammar of *should(n't)*, *can(can't)* and *(don't) have to*.

OPTIONAL WARMER

Write a number of dates on the board e.g., *August 2003, December 2001, 1992, 1989*. Ask Ss to think about these dates and to tell their partner what they remember or know about their life at that point. Get feedback from a number of Ss.

Reading

1▶ Ss discuss the question in pairs. Encourage them to give reasons for their answers. Get feedback.

2a▶ Divide the class into three groups. Group A reads the text on page 46, group B reads the text on page 125 and group C reads the text on page 130. Ss work together in groups, completing the table for the person in their text. Get feedback from various Ss from each group.

Answers: Wong Fei: education, free-time, career, money and family
Isabel: education, free-time, career, money and family
Gregor: the army, education, free-time and money

b▶ Rearrange the class into new groups of three, one student from group A, one from B and one from C. Ss take it in turns to tell the others about the text they have read. Encourage Ss to use their own words.

3▶ Read through the questions with the whole class and then Ss work in the same groups as in Ex. 2b, discussing their answers. Get feedback from various Ss.

Grammar

OPTIONAL GRAMMAR LEAD-IN

Write the following sentences on the board:
You should speak in English in class.
You can smoke in class.
You have to be a good swimmer to study English.
Ss work in pairs to say if the sentences are true or false, correcting the verb form of the false sentences to make them true. Elicit feedback from the whole class.

4▶ Focus Ss on the Active grammar box and read through the example sentences. Ask the Ss if they can remember who said each one; Wong Fei, Isabel or Gregor.

▶ Ss complete the rules in pairs. Write the rules on the board and complete them by eliciting answers from Ss.

Active grammar

Use *can* to say something is possible.
Use *have to* to say something is necessary.
Use *should* to say something is a good idea. (opinion)
Use *can't* to say something is not possible.
Use *don't have to* to say something is not necessary.
Use *shouldn't* to say something is not a good idea. (opinion)

▶ Tell Ss to look back at the example sentences and ask:

Q: How is *have* different from *should* and *can*? Ss discuss the question in pairs. Elicit/teach the answers (*have* takes the full infinitive and the auxiliary verb, *should* and *can* take the infinitive without *to* and no auxiliary verb)

▶ Point out that Ss can consult Reference page 53.

5▶ Ss work in pairs to choose the best alternative. Check the answers with the whole class.

Answers: 1 can't 2 don't have to 3 have to 4 shouldn't 5 should 6 can

6▶ Read the example sentence with the whole class and then Ss work in pairs to complete the rest of the sentences. Check the answers with the whole class.

Answers: 1 can 2 don't have to 3 should 4 doesn't have to 5 shouldn't 6 have to

Pronunciation

7▶ Read through the sentences with the whole class and then play recording 5.1. Give the Ss time to answer questions 1–4 in pairs before you get feedback from various Ss.

Answers: a) The *t* is pronounced before a word which starts with a vowel.
b) The *t* isn't pronounced before a word which starts with a consonant.

▶ Tell the Ss to practise saying the sentences with a partner. Ask a few Ss to say the sentences for the whole class.

8▶ If you have Ss from various different countries, try to group them so that those from the same country are together. If your Ss are all from the same country, have them work in pairs. If they are all from different countries, Ss can work individually.

▶ Read through the example with the whole class and tell Ss to write similar sentences with the rest of the prompts. Go around the class, correcting errors.

▶ Rearrange the class so that Ss are working with a different partner (from a different country if possible). Tell them to explain their ideas and to see if their partner agrees or disagrees. Get feedback from the whole class.

OPTIONAL EXTENSION

Arrange the class so that Ss are working in groups of three. Student A looks back at the text on page 46, student B looks back at the text on page 125, and student C at the one on page 130. Organise this so that Ss are reading a text that they didn't read before.

Each student writes sentences with *(don't) have to*, *should(n't)* and *can(n't)* about their text. When they have finished, Ss tell their partners their sentences and discuss if they like this way of life or not.

Listening and speaking

9▶ Read through the statements with the whole class and play recording 5.2. Allow Ss to compare with a partner and get feedback from the whole class.

Answers: Dialogue 1: Eighteen is too young to get married.
Dialogue 2: Young people should do military service.

10▶ Give Ss a minute to read through the How to ... box and then play recording 5.2 again. Ss tick the phrases they hear. Allow them to compare with a partner and then get feedback from the whole class.

Answers: Dialogue 1: I think ... I mean ...
What do you think? ... I'm not so sure ...
Dialogue 2: In my opinion ... ... because ...
Don't you think so? ... you're probably right ...

11▶ Ss choose one of the statements with a partner and exchange opinions, using the How to ... box as a guide. Go around the class monitoring the conversations. Ask one or two of the more confident pairs to act out their conversation for the rest of the class.

OPTIONAL EXTENSION

Write the following statements on the board:
All school children should wear uniform.
Young people shouldn't be allowed to drive until they are twenty-one.
Children should always look after their parents when they are old.

Divide the class into two groups, A and B. Tell group A that they have to think of arguments to support all three of the statements and group B that they have to think of arguments against those statements.

Ss work together for five to ten minutes. Reorganise the class so that one student from group A is with a student from group B. Using the How to ... box as a guide, they discuss the statements from the position they have been given.

Alternatively, have a whole class debate about the issues. After the arguments for and against have been presented, you could allow Ss to vote, expressing their own personal point of view

5.2 Old friends

The Internet has transformed means of communication over the last decade and staying in touch with people is now easier than ever. One kind of website that has become increasingly popular is one which allows you to get in contact with old school friends, workmates, people from university, colleagues from the army and old neighbours. You can either search the web by place, putting in the name of your school, university etc. or by name. In November 2004, there were 11 million people registered to these sites.

In this lesson Ss read the profile of a woman who is registered to this kind of website and through this context consider the use of the Present Perfect Simple with *for* and *since* and vocabulary related to friendship.

OPTIONAL WARMER

Tell the Ss to write the name of a friend from primary school or secondary school who they no longer see. They then work in pairs to talk about their memories of that person. After a few minutes, ask the Ss:

Q: Would you like to meet this person again? Have you any idea what this person is doing now?

Grammar

OPTIONAL GRAMMAR LEAD-IN

Refresh Ss' memory of the Present Perfect as compared with the Past Simple (lesson 2.3) by asking the following questions and eliciting answers from the Ss: **Q: Have you ever been to Paris?**
Q: What did you do last night?

Write the two questions on the board and ask Ss what tense they are. Elicit rules for when we use each tense. If they don't remember, tell them to look back at Reference page 23.

Ask Ss to write one more question in the Present Perfect and one in the Past Simple. Ss mingle, asking and answering each other's questions.

1▶ Focus Ss on the extract from the website and tell them to read through the text quickly, without worrying about things they don't understand at this stage.
Ask them what the purpose of the website is (to give information about what Tina Armstrong is doing now and allow her old friends to get in touch with her).

2▶ Focus Ss on the part of the text that is underlined and tell them to answer the questions with a partner. Check the answers with the whole class.

Answers: 1 two years ago 2 Yes, she does.

3▶ Focus Ss on the Active grammar box and tell them to work with a partner to complete the sentences with the correct past participle. Write the sentences on the board and elicit the answers to complete the gaps.

Active grammar

+ My dad has been in hospital for a week.
– We haven't seen her since university.
? Have you lived in Paris for long?

Focus Ss on the rules and tell them to work with a partner to complete them, using the example sentences as a guide. Write the rules on the board and elicit the correct word to complete them.

1 Use *since* to refer to the start of the action.
2 Use *for* to refer to the time period of the action.

▶ Contrast the two uses of the Present Perfect that Ss have studied so far, writing the following example sentences on the board:
I have been in hospital twice (an action in the general past – we don't know when it happened).
I have been in hospital for three days/since Tuesday (an action that started in the past and continues now).

▶ Point out that the rules are given on Reference page 53.

▶ If you feel Ss are not clear about *for* and *since* do some extra practice. Dictate the following prompts and tell them to Ss them down in pairs with *for* or *since*; last week (*since*); ten years (*for*); two hours (*for*); four o'clock (*since*); I was a child (*since*); a long time (*for*); primary school (*since*).

4a▶ Ss work in pairs to complete the dialogue.

b▶ Play recording 5.3 and Ss check their answers.

Answers: 1 since 2 for 3 since 4 for

5▶ Read through the example sentences with the whole class, then Ss work in pairs to write the replies. Check the sentences with the whole class.

Answers: 1 No, I haven't seen her since last Christmas. 2 No, I haven't had a summer holiday for years. 3 No, I haven't played since last summer. 4 No, I haven't worked at the weekend for months.

OPTIONAL EXTENSION

If you feel Ss need extra practise, tell them to write down the name of five things that they haven't done for a long time. Ask them to talk to a partner about these things. Give an example yourself e.g., see my sister – *I haven' t seen my sister for two years because she's living in Australia and I can' t afford to go.*

Person to person

6▶ Ss choose three words from the box. In pairs they tell each other how long they have had or known this thing or person. Encourage them to ask questions as they listen e.g., *I have had my shoes for two weeks. Where did you buy them?* Get feedback from various Ss.

Vocabulary

7▶ Ss work with a partner to match items from each column. Check the answers with the whole class.

Answers: 1 b) 2 e) 3 d) 4 f) 5 a) 6 c)

8▶ Ss complete the story in pairs. Tell them to make any necessary changes to verb forms. Check the answers with the whole class, reading through the text and eliciting a phrase for each gap.

Answers: 1 an old school friend 2 got on well 3 lost touch 4 got in touch 5 was going out with 6 colleague 7 go out

9▶ Tell Ss to work in pairs, putting the pictures in order. Get feedback from various Ss to see if everybody agrees. It's fine if some Ss have a different order as long as they can justify it's logic.

Suggested answer: D, C, A, E, B

10▶ Now ask Ss to tell the story with their partner, using the vocabulary from Ex. 7 and inventing extra details like the names of the characters, the place and year it took place, etc. Ask a few Ss to tell their story for the rest of the class.

Writing

11▶ Ss read Tina's profile in Ex. 1 again and tick the topics she mentions (work, relationships and home).

▶ Ask Ss if there is any vocabulary in the profile they don't understand, and encourage other Ss to explain, if they can. If not, explain yourself.

12▶ Tell Ss they are going to write their own profile. Explain that they can include any of the topics from Ex. 11 and anything else they consider important.

▶ First, Ss make notes and then write out their complete profile.

OPTIONAL VARIATION

Ss write their profiles in the same way but don't include their names. When they have finished, take them in and redistribute them so that a different student has each profile. Ss then read the profile they have aloud and other members of the class try to guess who it is.

5.3 The truth about ageing

Although life expectancy around the world has generally risen, there is still a great difference between countries. The highest life expectancy can be found in countries such as Japan, Australia or Andorra, where many people live to be over 80 and the lowest in African countries such as Ethiopia, Botswana or Mozambique (35–45).

In this lesson Ss listen to a radio programme about ageing and through this context analyse the grammar of *used to* for past habits and situations.

OPTIONAL WARMER

Write the following lists of countries and numbers on the board: Australia, Turkey, United Kingdom, Poland, Argentina and 77.8, 71.2, 75.3, 73.4, 79.9.

Tell the Ss that the numbers represent the life expectancy in these countries. In pairs, they match a country and a number, giving their reasons for the order they choose. Get feedback from the whole class (Australia – 79.9, United Kingdom – 77.8, Argentina – 75.3, Poland – 73.4, Turkey – 72.2).

Speaking and listening

1a▸ Focus Ss on the quiz and tell them to answer the questions in pairs. Get feedback and discuss points that Ss do not agree over, but don't give them the correct answers yet.

b▸ Play recording 5.4 and Ss check their answers. Ask the Ss if anything has surprised them and discuss why.

Answers: 1 The Japanese 2 twenty-six years 3 20% 4a) non-smokers b) married people c) pet owners

2▸ Read the statements with the whole class and tell Ss to comment in pairs on which statement they agree with the most. Get feedback from the whole class.

3a▸ Tell Ss to listen to part of a radio programme that says which one of the statements in Ex. 2 is probably true. Play recording 5.5 and ask them which one (statement 2).

b▸ Read through the statements with the whole class. Then play recording 5.5 again and Ss mark these statements true or false. Allow them to compare with a partner before checking the answers with the whole class.

Answers: 1 F 2 T 3 T 4 T 5 F 6 T

4▸ Ss discuss the question in pairs. Get feedback.

Grammar

5▸ Focus the Ss on the phrases in the box. Ask them how much each factor contributes to reaching an old age.

Q: Do you think physical exercise is very important if you want to live a long time?
Q: Is mental exercise as important as physical exercise?
Q: How important is thinking positively?

▸ Now Ss read the quotes in pairs and match a phrase to each one. Check the answers with the whole class.

Answers: Text 1: thinking positively Text 2: physical exercise Text 3: mental exercise

OPTIONAL GRAMMAR LEAD-IN

Tell the Ss look at the quotes for one minute and try to remember what the people say. Tell them to close their books and ask the following questions:

Q: The first man believes in thinking positively, but what did he use to do? Elicit: *sport.*
Q: The woman dances now, but did she use to do physical exercise? Elicit: *No, she didn' t.*
Q: What did the second man use to do when he was younger? Elicit: *smoke.*

6▸ Focus the Ss on the Active grammar box and tell them to complete the sentences with a partner, referring back to the quotes when necessary. Write the sentences on the board and elicit words to complete the gaps.

Active grammar

\+ I used to play tennis.
– She didn't use to play tennis.
? Did you use to play tennis?

▸ Read through the rule at the top of the box with the Ss and ask: **Q: Does *I used to play tennis* refer to a habit or a situation?** (habit)

▸ Write an example of a situation on the board e.g., *I used to live in a big house*. Ask Ss to turn to Reference page 53 and ask: **Q: Does the form of *used to* change with he or she?** (No)

7▸ Ss complete the sentences in pairs. Check the answers with the whole class.

Answers: 1 I used to have long hair but now it's short. 2 I didn't use to like olives but I do now. 3 Did you use to play any sports at school? 4 We used to be friends but we're not now. 5 Did they use to live together? 6 Paul used to work for me but now he's my boss. 7 Zuza didn't use to be interested in fashion but now she loves it.

8a▸ Focus Ss on the picture and read the example sentence with the whole class. Tell the Ss to work in pairs, writing sentences using a phrase from each column.

b▸ Play recording 5.6 and Ss check their answers.

Answers: Thomas used to have a lot of hair but now he doesn't have much. Thomas used to be quite slim but now he's overweight. Thomas didn't use to have a girlfriend but now he's married. Thomas used to have a bicycle but now he he's got/has a car. Thomas didn't use to have much money but now he gets a good salary.

Pronunciation

9a▶ Play recording 5.6 again and tell Ss to focus on the pronunciation of *used to* /juːst tə/ and *didn't use to* /dɪdnt juːst tə/. Point out the weak form of *to* in these sentences. Elicit the correct pronunciation from the Ss and practise the sounds as a class.

b▶ Ss repeat the sentences in pairs, paying special attention to pronunciation. Ask a number of Ss to read the sentences aloud for the whole class.

Person to person

10▶ Focus the Ss on the categories in the box and read the example below. Give some more examples about yourself from the other categories e.g., *I used to play hockey when I was younger but now I prefer swimming*; *I used to love meat and I used to hate vegetables, but now it's really different. I'm a vegetarian.*

▶ Ss talk in pairs about their past and present with regard to the categories. Get feedback from various Ss.

OPTIONAL VARIATION

Divide the class into six groups and give one category to each group. Each group has to think of two questions for their category e.g., Pets: *Did you use to have a dog? Did you used to have a cat?*

When they have written their questions, Ss mingle and interview the other Ss in the class. Then they go back to their original group, compare results and present the final results to the rest of the class e.g., *four Ss used to have a cat, three Ss used to have a dog and seven Ss didn't used to have a pet.*

Vocabulary

11a▶ Ss work in pairs to match the verb and noun phrases. Check the answers with the whole class.

Answers: eat junk food eat healthily be mentally active be a heavy smoker drink a lot of water do physical exercise think positively go to bed very late

b▶ Ss discuss the questions with a partner. Get feedback from the whole class.

OPTIONAL EXTENSION

Write on the board: *Advice for people who want to live to be 100*. Ss work in small groups of three or four to make lists of things that you should and shouldn't do if you want to live to be very old. They can use the habits already given but encourage them to think of other things too. Finally, the Ss present their advice to the rest of the class.

Communication: This is your life

This lesson is based on an idea taken from a popular TV programme called *This is your life* that was first shown in the USA in the 1950s and then in Great Britain (1955–2003). On this programme celebrities were surprised by a presentation of their past life in the form of a narrative and reminisces by relatives and friends.

In this lesson Ss listen to an extract from the programme in which the past life of Pierce Brosnan is presented.

1▶ Ss talk in pairs about the actors. Get feedback from the whole class.

2a▶ Play recording 5.7 and Ss listen to find out which actor they are talking about (Pierce Brosnan). Ask Ss what other information they heard about him.

b▶ Focus the Ss on the words and phrases in the box and the example sentence. Tell them to listen to find out the significance of the other things. Play recording 5.8. Allow Ss time to compare with a partner before getting feedback.

Answers: He lived with his grandparents until he was six years old. He had a job washing dishes when he was sixteen. He used to have long hair and a beard. He has been an actor since he was twenty-one. He found success in 1980 with the TV series *Remington Steele*. The film *Goldeneye* took $350 million at the box office.

3a▶ Focus Ss on the fact file and elicit the question forms they will need to use to complete it. Ss work in pairs to ask the questions and complete the form.

b▶ Ss work with a different partner to prepare questions for the topics provided in the box. Go around the class correcting any errors.

c▶ Ss work with their original partner to ask their questions, making notes about the answers they are given.

4a▶ Ss prepare a presentation using the information they have. If you have time, play recording 5.8 again so that Ss can use it as a model.

b▶ Ss make the presentation for the whole class (if you have large numbers of Ss, you can divide the class into several groups).

Review and practice

1 ▸

Answers: 1 In the UK you have to wear seat belts in the back of a car. 2 I can do my homework while I watch TV. 3 You should go to Germany to improve your German. 4 You have to show your student card to get a reduction. 5 You don't have to drive me to the airport. I'll get a taxi. 6 You shouldn't drink coffee just before you go to bed. 7 I can't finish this report today.

2 ▸

Answers: 1 I can't lift this box. It's really heavy. 2 Does he have to work this weekend? 3 Correct. 4 They don't have to wear school uniform. 5 Should you take a coat with you? 6 Correct. 7 Are you sure you have to take all your certificates to the interview?

3 ▸

Answers: 1 for 2 for 3 since 4 since 5 for

4 ▸

Answers: 1 I have played the guitar since I was a child. 2 My parents have lived in Bristol since April. 3 I have had a dog for two years. 4 I have known Jack since October. 5 They haven't had a holiday for ten years. 6 She has driven a car since 2001. 7 I have studied English for three years. 8 He hasn't seen Angie for five years.

5 ▸

Answers: 1 Correct. 2 Did you use to play football at school? 3 She didn't use to get good marks at school. 4 Where did you use to live before you came here? 5 Correct. 6 I used to like my job more than I do now. 7 Correct. 8 My parents didn't use to have a television.

6 ▸

Answers: 1 -aged 2 heavy 3 got 4 in 5 lost 6 against 7 place 8 active

Notes for using the Common European Framework (CEF)

CEF References

5.1 Can do: exchange opinions with a friend

CEF A2 descriptor: can agree and disagree with others (CEF page 77)

5.2 Can do: write a personal profile

CEF A2 descriptor: can write a series of simple phrases and sentences about their family, living conditions, educational background, present or most recent job (CEF page 62)

5.3 Can do: describe yourself when you were younger

CEF A2 descriptor: can give a short, rehearsed, basic presentation on a familiar subject (CEF page 60)

CEF quick brief

Chapters four and five of The Common European Framework set out 'reference levels' as a way to describe someone's ability in language. There are six basic reference levels: A1, A2, B1, B2, C1, C2 (though these can be subdivided if required). These reference levels are designed to describe ability in any language, not just English.

Portfolio task

Download the Total English Portfolio free from www.longman.com/totalenglish.

Objective: to introduce students to the Biography section of the Portfolio.

This task can be done in Ss' L1.

The second section of the Portfolio is the 'Biography'. The Biography is for the students to keep a more detailed and personal record of their language learning history, objectives and progress.

1 ▸ Explain the purpose of the Biography section of the Portfolio.

2 ▸ Ask Ss to think about their language learning objectives. Give some examples of your own objectives in a different language.

3 ▸ Ask Ss to think about their own language learning objectives and makes a list. Ss compare objectives with their partner.

4 ▸ Ask Ss to complete this section of their Biography.

6 Places

Overview

Lead-in	**Vocabulary:** places
6.1	**Grammar:** *will*
	Can do: make general predictions about the future
6.2	**Grammar:** *too, too much/many, enough*
	Vocabulary: machines at home
	Can do: give explanations for choices
6.3	**Grammar:** uses of *like*
Can do:	Describe a favourite place
Com. Focus:	Where shall we go?
Reference	
Practice	

Summary

Lesson 1: Ss listen to some tour guide information about New Zealand and read a text about the effects of the filming of *The Lord of the Rings*, on tourism, there. Then they talk about the positive and negative effects of tourism.

Lesson 2: Ss read about a TV programme called *Frontier house* in which a Californian family live for six months as if it were the Wild West of 100 years ago. Then they listen to two people talking about that experience.

Lesson 3: Ss read a leaflet called 'Garden of Freedom', which talks about a prison garden inspired by Nelson Mandela and set up to help prisoners in Zambia.

Communication Focus: Ss listen to two people talking about where to go on holiday and then choose themselves between various cities, discussing options in small groups.

Film bank: Around the world (5'05")

Four people talk about where they are from and how they feel about that place.

This series of interviews shows four people from different English-speaking countries talking about their home and what they like about it. The interviewees are from Ireland, the US, Trinidad and Australia. Shots of each country offer a flavour of what they are like.

Possible places to use this short film are:

- after Lesson 3 to extend the topic of doctors and health
- at the end of the unit to round up the topic and language

For ways to use this short film in class, see Students' Book page 138 and Teacher's Book page 191.

Lead-in

▶ Write *places* on the board and the example *beach*. Give Ss a couple of minutes to brainstorm in pairs names of places e.g., *village*, *town*, *city*, *mountain*, *countryside*, *desert*, *forest*, etc. Ss may also suggest more concrete places such as *school*, *shop*, *restaurant* etc. Get feedback from the Ss, writing the place names on the board.

▶ In pairs, Ss talk about their favourite places in their home town/country/abroad, saying why they like these places. Ask various Ss to share their ideas with the rest of the class.

1a▶ Focus Ss' attention on the photos and tell them to work in pairs to guess which continent each photo was taken in. Elicit answers from different Ss and see if all the class agree.

Answers: Pic 1: Africa Pic 2: Asia
Pic 3: North America. Pic 4: Europe

b▶ Elicit the continents that are not shown in the photos (South America, Antarctica, the Arctic and Australasia) and write them on the board. Tell Ss to work in pairs to say which continent each country in the box belongs to. Go around the class, asking Ss to pronounce the name of the countries in turn and where you can find them.

c▶ Ss talk in pairs about the countries they have/haven't visited and those they would/wouldn't like to visit and why. Get some Ss to share their opinions with the class.

2a▶ Refer the Ss to the example and elicit the common endings used for nationalities (*-ian*, *-ish* and *-ese*). Remind Ss that there also some exceptions e.g., Greece – Greek. Ss write the nationality for each country in pairs.

b▶ Ss then mark the stress and practise pronouncing the words. Play recording 6.1 so that Ss can check the pronunciation and then go around the class having different Ss pronounce each nationality.

▶ Tell the Ss to close their books and divide the class into two teams. One person from team A says a country and one person from team B has to say the corresponding nationality and vice versa. Ss are not necessarily limited by those countries given in the book. The teams score a point for each correctly pronounced word.

3▶ Have the Ss discuss the meaning of the underlined expressions in the questions with a partner for a few minutes. Check the meanings with the whole class and have the Ss answer the questions in pairs. Get feedback.

EXTEND THE LEAD-IN

Play 'Guess my country'. Think of a country and tell the Ss they have twenty questions to which you can answer only *yes* or *no* in order to guess which country it is. Ss ask questions e.g., *Is it in Europe? Is it big? Are there mountains/beaches? Is the capital city ...?* Give each student a country written on a piece of paper or have them choose one themselves. Ss play the game in groups or as a whole class.

6.1 New Zealand

New Zealand consists of a group of islands that lie in the South Pacific, almost 2,000 km from Australia. It has two official languages, English and Maori. The Maori, who settled on the islands in about 1,000 AD, make up about 9% of the total population. Many of their ancient traditions are still kept alive, although New Zealand has a mainly European feel to it.

In this lesson Ss listen to some tour guide information about New Zealand and consider the future of the tourist industry. Through this context Ss analyse the use of *will* for predictions.

OPTIONAL WARMER

Write the following words on the board: *Kilimanjaro*; *Loch Ness*; *Copacabana*; *Majorca*; *the Mediterranean*; *the Atlantic*; *the Thames*; *the Amazon*; *the Sahara*. Ask Ss: **Q: What are these things and where can you find them?** Get feedback from the whole class. Teach the words Ss don't know.

Kilimanjaro is a mountain in Tanzania; Loch Ness is a lake in Scotland (*loch* means lake); Copacabana is a beach in Brazil; Majorca is an island off Spain; the Mediterranean is the sea found between Southern Europe, the Levant and Northern Africa; the Atlantic is an ocean found between America and Europe/Africa; the Thames is a river in London; the Amazon is a river in South America and the Sahara is a desert in Africa.

Listening

1a ▸ Ss work with a partner to label the map.

b ▸ Play recording 6.2 and Ss listen and check their answers. Pay special attention to the pronunciation of *island* /ˈaɪlənd/.

Answers: 1 Beach 2 mountain 3 Sea 4 Ocean 5 river 6 Lake 7 Island

▸ All the words are used except *forest* and *desert*.

2a ▸ Ss read the sentences in pairs and guess what information is correct. Get feedback from the whole class.

b ▸ Play recording 6.3 and Ss check their answers. Ask a number of Ss to read the correct sentences aloud.

Answers: 1 4 million 2 40 million 3 Wellington 4 English and Maori 5 kiwi bird 6 North Island 7 South Island

3 ▸ Ss talk about the question in pairs. Get feedback from the whole class.

Reading

4 ▸ Focus Ss on the photos and ask what they are (a poster from *The Lord of the Rings* and a 'village' in New Zealand). Ask Ss what they think the relation is between these photos and New Zealand (It was filmed there).

▸ Read through the possible titles for the text with the whole class. Ss read it and choose one with a partner (The new New Zealand). Tell them not to worry about any vocabulary they don't understand at this stage.

5 ▸ Ask different Ss to read the statements aloud and check everybody understands. Ss then read the text again and mark the statements true (T) or false (F) with a partner. Check the answers with the whole class.

Answers: 1 F 2 F 3 T 4 F 5 T 6 F

6 ▸ Focus Ss on the example, locate *they* in the text and read the complete sentence. Now Ss do the same in pairs for the other words or phrases. Check the answers with the whole class.

Answers: 1 *The Lord of the Rings* film 2 the LOTR effect 3 tourists 4 the number of tourists 5 the negative effects of tourism (changes to the natural beauty and wildlife)

▸ Ask Ss if there are any words or phrases in the text that they still do not understand. Encourage other Ss to explain the meaning if they can. If not, explain yourself.

7 ▸ Ss discuss the questions in small groups. Encourage Ss to ask follow-up questions as they do this. Get feedback from the whole class.

Grammar

OPTIONAL GRAMMAR LEAD-IN

Ask the Ss the following questions about the future of tourism. Elicit/model short answers with *will* and *won't* and Ss' reasons.

Q: In the future, do you think: people will travel to other planets for their holidays?/people will stop sunbathing?/the sea will become too dirty to swim in?/people will have more holidays/people will invent a new quicker form of transport?

8 ▸ Focus Ss on the Active grammar box and tell them to complete the sentences in pairs. Copy the sentences on the board and elicit the answers to fill the gaps.

Active grammar

\+ The number of tourists will double in the near future.
– It won't (will not) stop there.
? Will tourism change the natural beauty of the landscape?

▸ Refer Ss to Reference page 63. Allow Ss a few minutes to look at the information. Then ask:

Q: Does the verb form change with he, she or it? (No).
Q: What can we use if we would like something to happen? (I hope ...)
Q: What do we use if we think something is not going to happen? (I don't think ...)
Q: Apart from making predictions, when else do we use *will*? (For promises and spontaneous decisions)

OPTIONAL EXTENSION

Dictate the following sentences. Ss write them down, compare with a partner and decide if they are predictions, promises or spontaneous decisions. Get feedback, writing the sentences on the board.

1 *I'm cold. I think I'll shut the window.* (spontaneous decision)
2 *I don't think he'll be famous.* (prediction)
3 *I'll help you tomorrow.* (promise)
4 *I think she'll come to the party.* (prediction)
5 *I'll repair your bike for you.* (promise)
6 *If you're going shopping I'll stay at home.* (spontaneous decision)

9▶ Check the Ss understand all the verbs in the box and then they work in pairs to complete the sentences. Check the answers with the whole class.

Answers: 1 will be 2 won't go 3 won't see 4 will get 5 will pass 6 will rain 7 won't hurt 8 will like

Pronunciation

10a▶ Play recording 6.4 and Ss write the sentences. Each sentence is repeated but pause at the end of each sentence if necessary. Ss compare in pairs. Check with the class and write the sentences on the board.

Answers: See transcript on page 155.

b▶ Tell the Ss to say the sentences in pairs, focusing particularly on the difference between the pronunciation of *want* and *won't*. Elicit the difference.

c▶ Tell the Ss to change the sentences so that they are true for them. Ss then compare with a partner. Get feedback from the whole class.

Person to person

11▶ If you have Ss from different countries or regions try to group them so that those from the same country/ region are together. Tell Ss to work in pairs to draw the map and discuss the questions, making notes about their answers.

▶ Rearrange the class so that Ss are working with a different partner. Tell them to show each other their maps and explain about the places they chose and the future of tourism in that area. Get feedback from the whole class.

OPTIONAL VARIATION

Ss work in pairs to plan a new tourist complex for the city/town where they are studying. They must draw a map and make notes about the different facilities it will have. Each pair presents their complex to the class and Ss vote for the one they think is the best.

6.2 Frontier house

This lesson is based on an American TV series known as *Frontier house*, first broadcast in April 2002. Three families were taken to a remote area of Montana and left to set up their own homes, rear animals, catch fish and make food without the assistance of modern technology, just as the first settlers had done. More information can be found at: www.pbs.org/wnet/frontierhouse.

In this lesson, Ss listen to two people talking about *Frontier house* and through this context, they consider the grammar of *too, too much/many,* and *enough*.

OPTIONAL WARMER

Write the date *1850* on the board. Ask Ss to work with a partner to imagine what life would have been like at that time. What things would they like and what things would they miss. Ask:
Q: Do you think life is better now or then? Why?
Get feedback from the whole class.

Listening

1a▶ Ss read through the text and look at the photos. Tell them to discuss with a partner what they think *Frontier house* is about. Get feedback from the whole class by asking the following questions:
Q: What is *Frontier house*? (a TV programme)
Q: What's it about? (nineteenth century life)
Q: How long did the family try this lifestyle? (six months).
Q: How many children were there? (four)
Q: Where was the family from? (California)

b▶ Ss make predictions in pairs and make notes in the box. Get feedback from various Ss.

2a▶ Play recording 6.5 and ask Ss to listen to see if their predictions were right or wrong. Allow them time to discuss with a partner what they heard and then ask:
Q: Did they have a hard time? (Yes, particularly the mother and father. The children did at first but later they seemed to enjoy it more.)

b▶ Give the Ss a moment to read through the sentences, then play recording 6.5 again. Ss circle the correct alternative. Allow them to compare with a partner and check answers with the whole class.

Answers: 1 1880 2 sixteen 3 thinner 4 missed 5 didn't like 6 shopping 7 less

3▶ Ask Ss to predict what happened when the family arrived home with a partner. Get some feedback and then play recording 6.6. Ss listen and then compare with a partner to discuss what they heard. Get feedback from the whole class.

4▶ Ss discuss the questions with a partner. Get feedback from the whole class.

Grammar

OPTIONAL GRAMMAR LEAD-IN

Write the following words on the board. Ss work in pairs to put them in order to make sentences. Elicit the answers, writing the sentences on the board.

1 *hard too life was* (Life was too hard.)
2 *was work much there too* (There was too much work.)
3 *too many there cars were* (There were too many cars.)
4 *water the enough wasn' t hot* (The water wasn't hot enough.)
5 *weren' t shops there enough* (There weren't enough shops.)

5a▶ Ss discuss the question with a partner. Elicit the answer (They have the same meaning).

b▶ Ss match the examples and the rules. Check the answers with the whole class.

Active grammar

1 B – I'm too tired to do any more work today.
2 C – I had too much time and nothing to do.
3 E – There were too many things to do.
4 A – They weren't warm enough.
5 D – They often didn't have enough food.

▶ Tell the Ss to look at Reference page 63. Give them a moment to read through the notes and then ask:
Q: What's the difference between *too* and *very*? (*Too* is used with a problem and *very* when something is difficult but not impossible.)

▶ Write the following sentences on the board and ask the Ss to discuss the difference in pairs. Elicit/teach the difference.
This coffee is very sweet. (No opinion is expressed)
This coffee is too sweet. (A negative opinion is expressed)

6▶ Ss work with a partner to correct the mistakes. Check the answers with the whole class.

Answers: 1 The weather here is too cold for me. 2 I'm not going on holiday this year because it'll cost too much money. 3 She's not old enough to get married. 4 He didn't get the job because he didn't have enough experience. 5 The children are making too much noise. 6 I didn't have enough time to finish the exam. 7 The town isn't near enough to walk from here.

7▶ Read the example and tell Ss to complete the sentences in pairs. Check the answers with the whole class.

Answers: 1 I'm hungry. I didn't have enough breakfast this morning. 2 I'm very tired. I went to bed too late last night. 3 I'm not fit enough to run a marathon. 4 I'm very busy today. I've got too many things to do. 5 I didn't have enough time to do my homework yesterday. 6 I often spend too much money on clothes. 7 Most English people speak too quickly for me to understand. 8 This tea is too hot to drink.

Person to person

8▶ Ss discuss with a partner whether the sentences in Ex. 7 are true for them. Get feedback from various Ss.

OPTIONAL EXTENSION

Write the following things on the board: *free time*; *good clubs in your city*; *good food in England*; *sports facilities in your city*; *job opportunities in your city*; *good films*; *reality shows on TV*. Ss discuss them using *too, enough, too much* and *too many.*
Give Ss the example: *I think there aren' t enough sports facilities in my town. They are also too expensive. I think they should be free.*

Vocabulary

9▶ Ss work in pairs to match the words and the pictures. Check the answers with the whole class, making sure Ss know how to pronounce the words correctly.

Answers: A mobile phone B answerphone C vacuum cleaner D hairdryer E dishwasher F washing machine G fridge H freezer I DVD player J radio K CD-walkman

10a▶ Highlight the example for the Ss. In pairs, Ss write five definitions of the machines. Go around the class, correcting errors and helping with vocabulary.

b▶ With a different partner, Ss test each other on the five machines they chose with their books closed.

Speaking

11▶ Play recording 6.7 and Ss listen to see what task is being performed (choosing five machines to take with them to the Wild West) and what they agree on (radio and washing machine).

12▶ Read through the How to ... box with the class. Ss do the same task in groups of 3 or 4. They must try to come to an agreement. When they have finished, different groups explain their choices.

OPTIONAL VARIATION

Each student writes down the machines in order of importance in modern-day society. Then Ss compare in pairs and discuss the differences they have.

6.3 Mandela's garden

Nelson Mandela was born in 1918 in South Africa. He studied to be a lawyer and joined the African National Congress in 1942 in order to fight against the laws of apartheid and for the freedom of the black people of South Africa. During years of struggle he was arrested many times and spent decades in prison. He was finally released in 1990. A firm believer in democracy and equality, he was given the Nobel peace prize in 1993.

In this lesson Ss read about the garden Mandela looked after during his years in prison and through this context, look at the different uses of *like*.

OPTIONAL WARMER

Ask the Ss to think about people who are in prison for a very long time. Tell them to brainstorm with a partner the things that prisoners do to keep themselves occupied. Get feedback from the whole class (e.g., some prisoners have studied degrees, written books, learned to paint.)

Reading

1 ▶ Ss write down the information they know about Nelson Mandela and then compare with a partner. Get feedback from the whole class.

2a ▶ Focus the Ss on the charity leaflet and check they know what it is. Give examples of international charities e.g., *Red Cross/Cresent*; *Oxfam*, etc. Tell them to work in pairs to match the illustrations with the words in the box. Check the answers with the whole class.

Answers: Pic 1: plant seeds Pic 2: water plants Pic 3: get rid of weeds Pic 4: harvest the fruit/ vegetables

b ▶ Ss discuss the question in pairs. Get feedback from the whole class.

3 ▶ Ss answer the question with a partner and then read quickly through the text. Tell them not to worry about any vocabulary that they don't understand at this point. Ask various Ss to tell you what the text is about in their own words.

4 ▶ Ask different Ss to read each question aloud. Then tell Ss to read the text again and answer the questions in pairs. Check the answers with the class.

Answers: 1 The charity *Seeds for Africa* 2 It helped him to increase his self-esteem. 3 To increase prisoners' self-esteem. 4 It was a way of escaping what surrounded him. 5 in oil drums on the roof 6 the staff 7 Because he could control it and look after it. 8 his life

▶ Ask the Ss if there are any words they don't understand in the text and encourage other Ss to explain before giving an explanation yourself.

5 ▶ Ss answer the question in pairs. Get feedback from the whole class.

Grammar

OPTIONAL GRAMMAR LEAD-IN

Ask Ss to write a question with the word *like* in it. Tell them it can be in any tense and encourage them to be as imaginative as possible. As they are writing the question, go around the class correcting errors.

Tell Ss to stand up and mingle, asking and answering each other's questions. Allow five to ten minutes and then tell them to sit down and get each student to read their questions aloud and comment on the answers they were given.

Write examples of the questions on the board, explaining the way in which *like* is being used. Tell Ss that *like* has many meanings in English.

6a ▶ Focus the Ss on the Active grammar box and tell them to match the questions and answers in pairs. Check the answers with the whole class.

Active grammar

1 B 2 A 3 D 4 C

b ▶ Ss match the definitions in pairs. Tell them to look back at the example questions and answers for clues. Check the answers with the whole class.

Answers: 1 d) 2 b) 3 c) 4 a)

▶ Refer Ss to Reference page 63 and read through the examples with the whole class. As this is rather complicated it may be useful for the Ss to translate these into their mother tongue.

7a ▶ Read the example with the Ss and then tell them to work in pairs to write the rest of the questions. Check with the whole class. Point out that the difference between questions 1 and 3 is that the first is a general description and the second is appearance only.

Answers: 1 What is your best friend like? 2 Would you like to go out tonight? 3 What does your best friend look like?

b ▶ Ss ask and answer the questions in pairs, including the example question. Get feedback from the whole class, paying special attention to the answers given to questions 1 and 3 (The most common response to question 1 would refer to personality, although it could include a physical description too. Question 3 is clearly only physical).

8 ▶ Read the example and tell Ss to work in pairs to find and correct the mistakes. Check the answers with the whole class.

Answers: 1 Would you like to visit South Africa? 2 What is the weather like today? 3 What do you like doing at weekends? 4 Which famous person would you like to meet? 5 What sports do you like playing? 6 Do you look like your mum or your dad? 7 Where would you like to go on your next holiday?

Pronunciation

9a▶ Explain to the Ss that when we ask a question we usually only stress the most important words. Focus them back on Ex. 8 and tell them to listen to the sentences and underline two words which are stressed the most. Play recording 6.8. Get feedback from various Ss.

> Answers: 1 Would you like to visit South Africa? 2 What is the weather like today? 3 What do you like doing at weekends? 4 Which famous person would you like to meet? 5 What sports do you like playing? 6 Do you look like your mum or your dad? 7 Where would you like to go on your next holiday?

Person to person

10▶ Ss ask and answer the questions in Ex. 8 in pairs. Go around the class monitoring their conversations. Encourage Ss to ask follow-up questions.

> **OPTIONAL EXTENSION**
>
> If you feel Ss need extra practise, ask them to work in pairs to adapt the questions in Ex. 8 e.g., *What was the weather like yesterday*? Go around the class to check they are doing this correctly. When they have finished, Ss ask and answer the new questions in pairs with a different partner.

Writing

▶ Read through the Lifelong learning box with the whole class and explain the importance of brainstorming. Very often Ss have problems with writing because they lack ideas.

11a▶ Ask Ss to think of their favourite natural place. Tell them to close their eyes for a minute and imagine it. Now they brainstorm ideas, writing things down on a piece of paper. Tell Ss to ask you for any vocabulary items that they don't know.

b▶ Ss share their ideas with a partner. Again encourage Ss to ask follow-up questions as this will push the speaker to develop more detailed ideas.

12▶ Refer Ss to the Writing bank on page 147 and give them time to do the exercises. Check with the whole class.

> **1▶** Answers: 1 Many trees are very old. 2 You can keep cool under the trees. 3 Autumn 4 different

> **2▶** Answers: 1 the trees 2 the wood 3 the wood 4 the weather 5 the wood 6 the wood

▶ Ss write about their favourite places. If you wish, Ss can exchange their writing and let other Ss read it.

Communication: Where shall we go?

In this lesson Ss listen to two people discussing where to go on holiday. They then role-play a similar discussion in small groups.

1▶ Ss match the cities and the photos and discuss what they know about each one. Get feedback from the whole class.

> Answers: St Petersburg (top right), Barcelona (left), Rio de Janeiro (upper middle), Cairo (lower middle), Edinburgh (bottom right)

2a▶ Focus Ss on the chart and give them a few minutes to look at the information. Ask a few questions to check that Ss understand the chart e.g.,

Q: What's the daytime temperature in Edinburgh in March? (4 °C)

Q: How much does a meal cost in Rio de Janeiro? (15 euros)

▶ Play recording 6.9 and Ss listen to see which city the two people choose (Barcelona). Get feedback from the whole class.

b▶ Ask a number of Ss to read through the statements for the whole class. Then play recording 6.9 again and Ss tick the reasons for the decision. Check the answers.

> Answers: 1 ✗ 2 ✗ 3 ✓ 4 ✓ 5 ✓

3▶ Tell the Ss that they have to work individually to choose a city. They have to make notes about why they chose that city and why they didn't choose the others. Check the cities Ss have chosen so that you can group them in an appropriate way for the next exercise.

▶ Put Ss (with different choices) in small groups of three or four and tell them to discuss their holiday plans. Each one must try to convince the others of their choice. Get feedback to find out if Ss have reached an agreement or not.

Review and practice

1 ▸

Answers: 1 I'll go 2 I usually like 3 I won't forget 4 I'll go 5 do you 6 it'll be 7 arrives 8 I'll have

2 ▸

Answers: 1 'll have 2 won't forget 3 'll phone 4 won't walk 5 'll stay 6 'll pay 7 'll help 8 'll come

3 ▸

Answers: 1 The food was too hot to eat. 2 There isn't enough sugar in my tea. 3 It's too far to walk home from here. 4 She's not old enough to get married. 5 There were too many people in the pool. 6 Don't eat too much chocolate. 7 There aren't enough shop assistants in this department store. 8 She always eats her dinner too quickly.

4 ▸

Answers: 1 This suitcase is too heavy for me to carry. 2 The hotel was too noisy for us to sleep in. 3 The food is too spicy for me to eat. 4 The homework was too difficult for us to do. 5 The top shelf is too high for me to reach.

5 ▸

Answers: 1 Where would you like to go for your next holiday? 2 What's your street like? 3 What does your cat look like? 4 What would you like to do this evening? 5 What do your new shoes look like?

6 ▸

Answers: 1 hairdryer 2 desert 3 freezer 4 Ocean 5 dishwasher 6 answerphone 7 mountain

Notes for using the Common European Framework (CEF)

CEF References

6.1 Can do: make general predictions about the future

CEF B1 descriptor: can correct mix-ups with tenses or expressions that lead to misunderstandings provided the interlocutor indicates there is a problem (CEF page 65)

6.2 Can do: give explanations for choices

CEF B1 descriptor: can briefly give reasons and explanations for opinions, plans and actions (CEF page 59)

6.3 Can do: describe a favourite place

CEF A2 descriptor: can recall and rehearse an appropriate set of phrases from his/her repertoire (CEF page 64)

CEF quick brief

The reference levels in the Common European Framework (A1–C2) are mostly written in the form of 'Can do' statements. These statements give examples of what a learner can do at the different reference levels. Teachers, syllabus designers, writers, etc. can write and add their own statements according to the needs of their users.

Portfolio task

Download the Total English Portfolio free from www.longman.com/totalenglish.

Objective: to help learners complete the 'language learning history' section of their Portfolio Biography.

This task can be done in Ss' L1.

By completing details of their language learning history, learners are encouraged to reflect on successful and unsuccessful language learning experiences and hence to further develop their language learning skills.

1 ▸ Explain the benefits for any language learner of thinking about their history and what has been successful for them.

2 ▸ Ask Ss to write details of their English language learning history (twelve years at school, etc.) and compare with a partner.

3 ▸ Encourage Ss to reflect critically on what has been successful and what hasn't been successful for them.

4 ▸ Ask learners to transfer this information to the language learning history section of their Biography.

7 Body

Overview

Lead-in	**Vocabulary:** body
7.1	**Grammar:** First Conditional
	Vocabulary: appearance
	Can do: describe a person's physical appearance
7.2	**Grammar:** gerunds and infinitives
	Vocabulary: personality
	Can do: describe someone's personality
7.3	**Grammar:** purpose/reason/result
	Vocabulary: illness and injury
	Can do: talk about illness and give advice
Com. Focus	Stress? What stress?
Reference	
Practice	

Summary

Lesson 1: Ss discuss celebrity magazines and TV programmes and read about Renée Zellweger, who plays the part of Bridget in the film *Bridget Jones's Diary*.

Lesson 2: Ss consider different types of hands and the way in which they can be related to different types of personalities and listen to two friends discussing the same topic. Then they analyse each other's hands.

Lesson 3: Ss listen to *Doctor, doctor* jokes and then tell jokes to each other. Then they look at symptoms of illness and read texts about homoeopathy and acupuncture.

Communication Focus: Ss do a quiz to find out how stressed they are and then discuss different ways of relaxing.

Film bank: Carry on Doctor (2'48")
An extract from a classic British comedy film

During the 1950s, 60s and 70s about thirty *Carry On* films were made in the UK. They are all very light-hearted and slapstick. This extract from one of the most famous films, *Carry on Doctor*, shows the unfortunate series of events suffered by Mr Francis Bigger when he falls off a stage.

Possible places to use this short film are:

▶ after the Lead-in to practise the language of descriptions

▶ before Lesson 2 to introduce the Past Simple tense in an interesting and different way

▶ at the end of the unit to round up the topic and language

For ways to use this short film in class, see Students' Book page 139 and Teacher's Book page 192.

Lead-in

▶ Write *body* on the board and check that the Ss understand. Tell them to brainstorm parts of the body in pairs.

▶ Write 'point to your hand' on the board and tell the Ss to do this. Now explain that you are going to play a game. Have the Ss stand or sit in a circle. One student begins by saying 'point to (+ a part of the body)' to the next student. If the student follows the instruction correctly, they have a turn and must tell the next student what to do. If they don't follow the instruction correctly, they are eliminated, and the next student continues. The game finishes when Ss can think of no more words to say.

▶ While the Ss are doing this, write the words on the board. At the end of the game, give instructions to the whole class to point to the parts of the body that have seemed more problematic.

1a▶ Ss work in pairs to categorise the words. Tell them to practise saying the words as they do this and go around the class checking pronunciation.

b▶ Play recording 7.1 so that the Ss can check their answers. Now check that Ss know the exact meaning of any new words by telling them to point to these body parts or have different Ss give these instructions.

Answers: Head: hair, face, ear, nose, lips, eyes, mouth Torso: waist, back, stomach Arm/Hand: elbow, wrist, finger, thumb Leg/Foot: knee, toe, ankle

▶ Have the Ss look at the photos and tell them to discuss the following questions in pairs.
Q: What can you see? (a person doing yoga, a runner, an elderly man and a dancer) **Q: Which part of the body do these people use the most?** (various body parts)

2a▶ Tell the Ss to read the sentences in pairs, discussing the meaning of the words that are underlined.

▶ Get feedback from the class and elicit/explain the meanings. Ss read the sentences again and mark them T (true) or F (false) according to their personal opinion.

b▶ Ss compare their opinions in groups of three or four. Encourage them to explain why they think what they do. Get some general feedback from the whole class.

EXTEND THE LEAD-IN

Ask Ss to look at the words that are underlined in Ex. 2a again. Ss work in small groups to write some similar statements using some of those words e.g., *If you eat chocolate you put on weight; Travelling on public transport makes people stressed.*
Go around the class helping Ss and correcting errors.

Ss then swap their sentences with another group. They read and discuss each other's sentences, saying if they agree or disagree.

7.1 Changing bodies

The film *Bridget Jones's Diary*, released in 2001, was a huge success. It tells the story of a rather desperate girl in her thirties, who is obsessed with losing weight and finding the right man to spend the rest of her life with. It starred Renée Zellweger, Hugh Grant and Colin Firth and was based on a book by Helen Fielding. A sequel to the film *Bridget Jones: The Edge of Reason* was released in 2004.

In this lesson Ss read about Renée Zellweger and learn vocabulary related to appearance. Through this context they consider the grammar of the First Conditional.

OPTIONAL WARMER

Write *celebrity* on the board and ask the Ss what this means (a famous person who appears frequently in magazines or on TV). Ask the Ss to give you the names of some celebrities and why they are famous. Now ask: **Q: Would you like to be a celebrity?** Allow Ss to discuss this with a partner and get feedback.

Reading and speaking

1 ▶ Focus the Ss on the questions and tell them to discuss their answers in pairs. Get feedback from the class, but don't confirm or reject their suggestions yet.

2 ▶ Ss read quickly through the text to find the answers to the questions in Ex. 1. Tell them not to worry about any vocabulary they don't understand at this stage.

Answers: 2 Renée Zellweger 3 She's an American actress. 4 Because she put on weight for the film *Bridget Jones* and lost it again afterwards.

3 ▶ Read the statements with the whole class and then tell Ss to read the text again to mark each statement true (T), false (F) or (?) if the answer is not given in the text. Allow Ss to compare with a partner before getting feedback.

Answers: 1 T 2 ? 3 T 4 F 5 ? 6 F 7 T

▶ Ask Ss if they have any vocabulary problems with the text and encourage other Ss to explain any words before doing so yourself.

4 ▶ Ss read the opinions individually and decide if they agree or disagree. Tell Ss to share their ideas in pairs or small groups. Discuss the issues with the whole class.

Vocabulary

5a ▶ Focus Ss on the chart and read the headings (weight/build; height; attractive or not) with the whole class. Tell the Ss to work in pairs to put the words from the box in the correct category.

▶ Ask different Ss to read out their answers so that you can check for correct pronunciation.

Answers: Weight/build: slim, skinny, fat, thin, overweight, muscular. Height: tall, medium height, short. Attractive or not: beautiful, (un)attractive, handsome, ugly, good-looking.

b ▶ Ss discuss the differences in pairs. Get feedback from the whole class.

Answers: Slim is always positive and is considered to be an ideal build. Skinny often means too thin and can therefore be negative. Fat is a less polite way of saying overweight. However, overweight can also be used to describe being heavier than the average weight for someone of your height and gender, e.g., you can be 1 kg overweight. Handsome is traditionally used for men and beautiful for women.

6a ▶ Focus Ss on the pictures and play recording 7.2. Ss have to identify which people are being described. Allow Ss to compare with a partner before getting feedback.

Answers: B and E

b ▶ Focus Ss on the How to ... box. Tell them to listen again and complete the gaps. Check the answers with the whole class. Make sure they understand that the first set of modifiers in each section is the most extreme.

Answers: He's very/really good-looking.
He's quite/fairly muscular.
She's really/very skinny.
He's a bit/slightly overweight.
She's much/a lot more attractive than most.
She's a bit/slightly taller than average.

▶ Check that Ss know how to use the adjectives and the modifiers by asking them to describe Renée Zellweger in the two photos on page 66. Give them a few minutes to do this in pairs and then get feedback from the whole class (Ss will not necessarily agree about all of the adjectives).

c ▶ Ss play 'Guess who ...?' in pairs. Remind them not to say if it's a woman or a man as this would make it too easy.

OPTIONAL EXTENSION

Play twenty questions with internationally famous celebrities. Choose a celebrity e.g., David Beckham and Ss ask you twenty questions in order to guess the celebrity to which you answer 'yes/no/don't know'. Tell Ss to ask first about appearance and then other things e.g. nationality, job, marital status.

Ss now play the game in small groups. Go around the class monitoring their question formation.

Grammar

OPTIONAL GRAMMAR LEAD-IN

Write the following stem sentences on the board. Ss complete them in pairs: *If I'm very tired tonight I'll ...' 'If it rains next weekend, I'll ...' 'If I get a cold, I'll ...'* Get feedback from various Ss. Explain that this grammatical structure is called the First Conditional.

7 ▶ Tell the Ss they are going to listen to a radio advert. Read the questions with the class. Play recording 7.3. Ss compare in pairs before you get feedback.

Answers: 1 'Face Saver' face cream 2 men

8 ▶ Tell Ss to read through the Active grammar box and choose the correct alternatives. Ss compare in pairs. Elicit the answers, writing the rules on the board.

Active grammar

The First Conditional talks about a possible situation in the future.
The *if clause* comes either first or second.

▶ Refer Ss to Reference page 73 and give them time to read through the notes. To check comprehension, ask:
Q: Can we use *will* in the *if clause*? (No)
Q: When do we need to use a comma? (if the *if clause* comes first).
Q: What other types of verbs can we use instead of *will*? (modals such as *could, may* and *might*).

9a ▶ Ss complete the sentences in pairs.

b ▶ Play recording 7.4. Ss listen and check their answers. Then play the recording again for Ss to repeat with the same intonation.

Answers: 1 If you eat a lot of junk food, you'll put on weight. 2 You won't sleep well tonight if you drink all that coffee. 3 If he doesn't call you, what will you do? 4 He won't have any money left if he buys any more DVDs. 5 If you don't start training now, you won't be able to run the marathon. 6 Will you call me if your bus is late?

Person to person

10a ▶ Ss work individually to complete the sentences. As they do this, go around the class correcting any errors.

b ▶ Ss compare what they have written with a partner.

OPTIONAL VARIATION

Tell the Ss that they have to try to find somebody who has written the same as they have in Ex. 10a. Elicit the questions they would need to ask e.g., *What will you do if you have time tomorrow*? Ss stand up and mingle, asking the questions until they find somebody who will do the same as they will. Get feedback about how much the class has in common.

7.2 Hands up

People have suggested many ways of analysing people's personality, from astrology to graphology (the study of handwriting) and palmistry. Palmistry was part of the university curriculum in the European middle-ages, and the subject of one of the earliest known books. Aristotle studied it; so did Alexander the Great. These days people often take it less seriously.

In this lesson Ss consider the relationship between the shape of a person's hand and their personality. Through this context they analyse the grammar of gerunds and infinitives with *to*.

OPTIONAL WARMER

Write *personality* on the board and ask Ss to brainstorm related adjectives in pairs. Give them a couple of minutes and then get feedback, writing the words on the board. Now ask: **Q: Which of these adjectives would you use to describe yourself?**

Ss discuss their answers in pairs, giving reasons for what they say. Get feedback from a number of Ss.

Vocabulary

1 ▶ Focus Ss on the photos and tell them to discuss the question in pairs. Get feedback from the whole class.

2a ▶ Read out the adjectives with the class and tell Ss they are going to find definitions for them. Ss match the adjectives and the underlined phrases with a partner. Get feedback from various Ss.

Answers: 1 sensitive 2 open organised 4 hard-working 5 unreliable 6 chatty 7 reserved 8 ambitious

b ▶ Put Ss in pairs and tell student A to cover the definitions with a piece of paper. Student B tests student A by reading out four definitions. Then they change roles.

Pronunciation

3a ▶ Write the word *beautiful* on the board and elicit from the Ss where the stress falls (*beautiful*). Now play recording 7.5 and Ss underline the stress in the words in the box in Ex. 2a. Ss compare in pairs and practise saying each word. Get feedback from the whole class.

Answers: ambitious, hard-working, reserved, open, organised, unreliable, chatty, sensitive

b ▶ Play recording 7.6, stopping at the end of each question to give Ss time to write it down. Ss compare answers in pairs. Check with the whole class.

Answers: See transcript on page 156.

c ▶ Ss ask and answer the questions in pairs. Get feedback from various Ss.

Listening

4a▶ Tell Ss they are going to listen to two people talking about how you can predict personality by looking at somebody's hands. Focus them on the questions and play recording 7.7. Get feedback from the whole class.

Answer: a

b▶ Play recording 7.7 again and Ss tick the sentences in Ex. 2a which are true for Daniel. Check with the class.

Answers: The true sentences are 2, 3, 6 and 8.

5▶ Ss discuss the question in pairs. Get feedback.

OPTIONAL EXTENSION

Ask Ss what other methods they know for analysing personality e.g., astrology or graphology. Ask:
Q: Are these methods better than studying hands?
Q: What does your horoscope sign say about your personality. Do you think it is true?

Grammar

OPTIONAL GRAMMAR LEAD-IN

Write the following questions on the board.
1 *What did Helen want to do?* 2 *What seem to be fairly straight?* 3 *What does Daniel really enjoy doing?* 4 *What does somebody whose thumb doesn't bend back avoid doing?*

Ss discuss the answers in pairs from what they can remember. If necessary play recording 7.7 again. Check the answers with the whole group and write the full answers on the board: 1 *Helen wants to look at the shape of Daniel's fingers.* 2 *Daniel's fingers seem to be fairly straight.* 3 *He really enjoys talking about his feelings.* 4 *He/she avoids talking about his/her feelings or problems.*

Ss underline the verbs in each sentence. Elicit the two structures: verb + infinitive and verb + gerund.

6▶ Ss read the examples and choose the correct alternatives to complete the rules with a partner. Tell Ss that they don't need to fill in the gap at this stage, as this will be done later. Check answers with the whole class.

Active grammar

Some verbs are followed by the gerund e.g., *enjoy, avoid.*
Some verbs are followed by the infinitive with *to* e.g., *want, seem.*

▶ Refer Ss to Reference page 73 and give them a moment to read through the notes. Ask one of the Ss to read out the list of verbs followed by the gerund and check that all the Ss understand these verbs. Do the same with the verbs followed by the infinitive with *to*. Explain to the Ss that there are no rules for this, they simply have to remember which verbs are in which list.

7a▶ Ss work in pairs to choose the correct alternative. Tell them to do this without referring to page 73, basing their answers on what they remember and what sounds right (very often Ss know these structures subconsciously from having heard or used them before). Check the answers with the whole class.

Answers: 1 to read 2 not to be 3 learning 4 writing 5 to be 6 to go 7 not to be 8 seeing

b▶ Ss write the verbs in bold in the correct gaps in the Active grammar box. To give the Ss extra practice, put them in pairs and tell student A to close their book. Student B tests student A on five verbs, then they change roles.

Person to person

8a▶ Divide the class into pairs and Ss complete the sentences about their partner. They cannot speak at this stage. Go around the room monitoring their work.

b▶ Ss speak to their partner to find out if they were right. If Ss were wrong they have to change the sentence. Give an example yourself with one student e.g.,

'I think you want to move to England next year.' 'No, I don't.' 'What do you want to do?' 'I want to finish university.' Get feedback from several Ss.

OPTIONAL EXTENSION

Ss work in pairs to write questions with two verbs from the lists in the Active grammar box. They must be personal questions that other Ss could answer. They can be in any tense. Ss then take one question each, stand up and mingle with the others asking and answering questions. Get feedback from each student about the question and the answers.

Reading and speaking

9a▶ Ss read the text with a partner and decide what type of hands they have got. Encourage them to help each other with any difficult vocabulary. Ask the Ss if they think the description of their personality is accurate.

b▶ Pair Ss so that they are working with someone new. Encourage them to act as if they were professional palm readers, analysing their partner's hand using the information in Ex. 2a and Ex. 9a.

c▶ Ss comment on how accurate they think the character analysis was.

OPTIONAL VARIATION

Ss analyse their partner's hand and write a short piece describing his/her character. Collect in the pieces of writing and redistribute them. Then each student reads out the piece they have been given. The rest of the class guess who is being described.

7.3 Doctor, doctor

In recent years, alternative forms of medicine such as homoeopathy and acupuncture have become increasingly popular in the Western world. Homoeopathy is based on treating like with like. If my symptoms are similar to those of having been bitten by a tarantula then I'd be treated with tarantula venom. Acupuncture is a branch of Chinese Medicine, and is over 3,000 years old. It can treat conditions for which conventional medicine has no treatment.

In this lesson, Ss work on vocabulary related to illnesses and read about homeopathy and acupuncture. Through this context they consider the grammar of purpose, reason and result.

OPTIONAL WARMER

Write *illness and injury* on the board. Elicit/teach the difference (illness is poor health and injury is the result of an accident or aggression). In pairs, Ss brainstorm different types of illnesses and injuries. Get feedback, writing the words on the board.

If you feel the class are comfortable together, have Ss talk to their partner about the words, saying if this has ever happened to them, when and how.

Listening

1▶ Focus Ss on the joke and elicit/teach *swallow*. Explain that this is a *Doctor, doctor* joke, and these are very popular in England and normally consist of short, simple and often silly plays on language.

▶ Ss answer the questions with a partner. Get feedback.

2▶ Play recording 7.8 and Ss note down the problem the patients describe in each joke. Allow them to compare with a partner before getting feedback.

Answers: 1 She's lost her memory. 2 She gets a pain in her eye when she drinks coffee. 3 When she presses her finger on her stomach it hurts.

3▶ Focus the Ss on the How to ... box. Read through the different ways of reacting to jokes with the whole class. Play recording 7.8 again, but stop after each joke. Elicit a reaction from the Ss.

▶ Tell Ss to think of a joke or jokes in pairs. Give them time to work out how to tell it/them, making notes if necessary. Have each student tell their jokes to a different partner. The listener must react, using expressions from the How to ... box.

Vocabulary

4a▶ Focus the Ss on the chart and read the headings with the whole class. In pairs, Ss put the vocabulary items into the correct category. Tell Ss that some items could go into more than one category.

▶ Ask different Ss to read out the answers, paying particular attention to the pronunciation of *ache*.

Answers: Illness: flu, a cold, food poisoning
Injury: a broken arm/leg
Symptom: a headache, a sore throat, earache, a pain in my chest, stomachache, feel sick, a high temperature, toothache, backache

b▶ Ss answer the question in pairs (The answer is *have*, although we could also use *get* with all the others except for *a broken arm/leg*).

c▶ Play recording 7.9. Ss listen to check their answers.

Lifelong learning

▶ Focus st on the Lifelong learning box. Read through the suggestion with the whole class and discuss the usefulness of this advice with the whole class. Point out that they can listen to the recording when driving, cooking, cleaning etc. and it's a good way of studying while doing something else at the same time.

5▶ Read the example sentence with the whole class and then Ss work in pairs to match the symptoms and suggestions. Go around the class helping with any difficult vocabulary.

Answers: 1 a high temperature 2 backache 3 feel sick 4 a sore throat 5 a headache 6 earache

6a▶ Play recording 7.10 and Ss listen. Then they act out the dialogue with a partner. Tell them to try to use good pronunciation and intonation.

b▶ Ss write similar dialogues with other health problems and advice. They should use the vocabulary form Ex. 4a and the phrases from Ex. 6a, but encourage them to be imaginative too. Go around the class monitoring their work.

c▶ Ss practise the dialogues with their partner. Go around the class correcting any pronunciation problems. Ask any of the more confident Ss to act out their situation for the rest of the class.

Reading and speaking

7▶ Focus Ss on the photos and tell them to answer the questions in pairs. Get feedback from the whole class.

8▶ Divide the class into two groups, A and B. Group A reads the text on page 125 and group B reads the text on page 130. Encourage Ss within the same group to help each other with any difficult vocabulary and tell them to complete their part of the table on page 71.

9a▶ Put a student from group A with a student from group B. Ss then work in pairs in order to tell each other about each type of medicine. When student A talks, student B completes the table and vice versa.

▶ Get feedback from the whole class about both types of alternative medicine.

b▶ Ss discuss the question in pairs. Get feedback from the whole class.

Grammar

10▶ Ss read through the letter individually and guess the problem (backache). Check that Ss understand all the new vocabulary.

OPTIONAL GRAMMAR LEAD-IN

Ss to close their books. Ask the following questions to see how much Ss remember from the letter. Elicit answers, but model the correct form if necessary.
Q: Why is backache a common problem? Because people don't stand or sit in the right way.
Q: Why should you get the right chair? To support your back.
Q: Why should you sleep on a hard mattress? In order to keep your back straight during the night.
Q: Why should you take regular breaks? So that you change your sitting position.

11a▶ Focus the Ss on the Active grammar box. In pairs they read the examples and complete the rules. Write the rules on the board and elicit words to complete the gaps.

Active grammar

Giving a reason: *because* + subject + verb
Explaining a result: *so* + subject + verb
Expressing purpose: *to* + infinitive; *in order (not) to* + infinitive; *so that* + subject + verb

▶ Tell the Ss to look at Reference page 73. Give them a moment to read through the notes and ask: **Q: How do we express purpose in formal situations?** (in order to)

b▶ Ss work in pairs to correct the sentences. Check the answers with the whole class.

Answers: 1 I eat a lot of garlic because I don't want to get flu. 2 I'm careful when I lift boxes so that I don't hurt my back. 3 I drink water in order not to feel sick on car journeys. 4 I did a lot of yoga today so I feel very relaxed now. 5 I want to buy a special chair to help me sit properly. 6 I usually drink milk in order to get rid of a stomachache.

OPTIONAL EXTENSION

In pairs, Ss choose one of the problems or results above e.g., not to get the flu, not to hurt your back. Then they write about other possible actions that have the same result, reason or purpose e.g., *I drink a lot of orange juice so that I don't get the flu.* Go around the class, monitoring their work.

Writing

12a▶ Ss write a letter (like those found in magazines) asking for advice about a health problem. Tell them they must describe the problem and address it to Doctor Darren.

b▶ Ss work with a partner and read each other's letters. Then they write a reply, giving advice.

c▶ Ss read their partner's reply and decide if it is good advice. Get feedback from the class.

Communication: Stress? What stress?

In this lesson Ss do a quiz to find out how stressed they are and discuss ways of relaxing.

▶ Write *stress* on the board and elicit/teach the meaning (a negative emotional condition caused by external pressures). Ask the Ss:
Q: What's the adjective of *stress*? Elicit/teach the two possibilities. *Stressed* (only for people) and *stressful* (things that cause stress).

Focus Ss on the photo and ask:
Q: How does the person feel? What stressful things can you see?
Ask them to brainstorm causes of stress in pairs. Get feedback from the whole class.

1▶ Ss discuss the questions in pairs or small groups. Get feedback from the whole class.

2▶ Focus Ss on the quiz and read through the introduction with the whole class. Tell Ss to do the quiz, writing a number to represent their reactions in each situation.

3a▶ Ss add up their points and look at the results on page 129. Ask the Ss which category they fall into.

b▶ In groups, Ss discuss whether they agree with the results, giving their reasons why and why not.

4▶ Ss answer the questions in pairs.

5▶ Tell the Ss to stand up and mingle with other Ss asking how they relax. Give them time to talk to most other Ss and then get feedback on the most popular way of relaxing.

Review and practice

1 ▶

Answers: 1 We'll be late if we don't leave now. 2 If it rains, we won't play tennis this afternoon. 3 Will you buy me a newspaper if you go shopping later? 4 If I don't see Holly today, I'll phone her. 5 If you put your hand on the cooker, you'll burn yourself. 6 I won't meet you at the cinema if I don't finish my work. 7 If you lend me five pounds, I'll pay you back tomorrow. 8 If you get home before me, will you make the dinner?

2 ▶

Answers: 1 If they offer me the job, I'll take it. 2 I'll have a party if I pass my exam. 3 If you don't use sun cream, you'll get burnt. 4 I'll be late for work if I don't get up now. 5 If we don't invite her, she'll be upset. 6 If I see Jon, I won't tell him about the party. 7 You won't have any money left if you buy those jeans. 8 If we don't leave now, we'll be late.

3 ▶

Answers: 1 going 2 not to tell 3 to wash 4 doing 5 to go 6 living 7 to see 8 talking

4 ▶

Answers: 1 going 2 to lose 3 to help 4 arriving 5 to do 6 talking

5 ▶

Answers: 1 because 2 in order to 3 so that 4 so 5 in order not to 6 to

6 ▶

Answers: 1 skinny 2 sore throat 3 reliable 4 muscular 5 reserved 6 high temperature 7 ambitious

Notes for using the Common European Framework (CEF)

CEF References

7.1 Can do: describe a person's physical appearance

CEF A2 descriptor: can tell a story or describe something in a simple list of points. Can describe everyday aspects of his/her environment e.g. people, places, a job or study experience. (CEF page 59)

7.2 Can do: describe someone's personality

CEF A2 descriptor: can write short, simple imaginary biographies and simple poems about people. (CEF page 62)

7.3 Can do: talk about illness and give advice

CEF A2 descriptor: has a sufficient vocabulary for coping with simple survival needs (CEF page 112)

CEF quick brief

Though the reference levels in the Common European Framework suggest that Ss progress 'vertically', from A1 to A2, etc., the Framework itself says that 'learning a language is a matter of horizontal as well as vertical progression'. This means that some learners might like to move from A2 level in a business context to A2 level in a tourist context. The CEF identifies four basic 'domains' that help to understand this horizontal language development: the public domain, the personal domain, the educational domain and the occupational domain.

Portfolio task

Download the Total English Portfolio free from www.longman.com/totalenglish.

Objective: to help learners complete the 'significant linguistic and intercultural experiences' section of their Portfolio Biography.

This task can be done in Ss' L1.

Students can further improve their language learning skills by reflecting on significant experiences that have helped them to learn another language or about another culture.

1 ▶ Refer Ss back to the section of their Passport where they listed their language learning and intercultural experiences.

2 ▶ Ask Ss to choose the most important experiences that have helped them learn a language or learn about a culture. It can help to give your examples of your own.

3 ▶ Ask Ss to compare with each other and explain why they were important.

8 Speed

Overview

Lead-in	**Vocabulary:** speed
8.1	**Grammar:** Present Simple Passive
	Vocabulary: verbs about change
	Can do: describe simple changes
8.2	**Grammar:** questions
	Vocabulary: phrasal verbs about relationships
	Can do: find out personal information
8.3	**Grammar:** Past Simple and Continuous
	Can do: ask and answer questions about past actions
Com. Focus	Race to the finish
Reference	
Practice	

Summary

Lesson 1: Ss read a text about speed in modern-day society, focusing on the areas of fast food, communication and information technology and travel. Then they discuss recent changes in their country/area.

Lesson 2: Ss talk about relationships using various phrasal verbs. Then they read about speed-dating, in which twenty men and twenty women meet and talk to each person for three minutes in order to decide who they would like to date.

Lesson 3: Ss read an extract from Mark Haddon's novel *The Curious Incident of the Dog in the Night-time,* which tells the story of a 15-year-old autistic boy who decides to investigate the mysterious death of his neighbour's dog.

Communication Focus: Ss play a board game in which they have to answer questions related to this unit.

Film bank: Speed-dating (2'19")

An extract from a current affairs TV programme about speed-dating.

In this short film about speed-dating we meet two people as they are getting ready to attend their first speed-dating event. We see the questions they ask each other and find out if they put a tick by each other's name.

Possible places to use this short film are:

▶ before Lesson 2 to introduce the topic of speed-dating

▶ after Lesson 2 to extend the topic of speed-dating

▶ at the end of the unit to round up the topic and language

For ways to use this short film in class, see Students' Book page 140 and Teacher's Book page 192.

Lead-in

▶ Ask Ss to brainstorm in pairs a list of things that are fast e.g., runner/athlete, trains, cars, various types of animals, food, Concorde etc. Then ask them to choose one or two things from their list and write definitions of the words. Have one student from each pair read out their definitions and the rest of the class guess the word.

▶ Write the words on the board. Then ask Ss to tell you any other words they have on their list and write them on the board too.

▶ Now write *speed* on the board and tell Ss that the next unit is about this topic.

1a▶ Ss look at the photos and say what they can see and comment on the connection in pairs.

Answers: Pic 1: a cheetah Pic 2: fast food Pic 3: a traffic sign showing maximum speed Pic 4: speeding cars at night

b▶ Ss complete the sentences using the words or phrases in the box. Let them check with a partner and then check with the whole group.

Answers: 1 can run at 2 a top speed of 3 speed limit 4 fastest-selling

2a▶ Ss discuss in pairs or small groups which two sentences they think are false. Encourage them to give their reasons. Get feedback, put do not tell them the answers yet.

b▶ Play recording 8.1 and Ss check their answers (1 and 3 are false. Cheetahs can run at 112 kilometres an hour and the speed limit on motorways in Spain is 120 kilometres an hour).

3a▶ Give the Ss a few minutes to work in pairs to discuss the meaning of the words and phrases that are underlined. Ask for volunteers to explain the expressions one by one or give examples of how they would use them.

b▶ Ss ask and answer the questions in pairs and then decide which of them has a 'faster' life. Ask various students to explain how fast their partner's life is.

EXTEND THE LEAD-IN

Draw a chart with two columns on the board with the headings: 'advantages' and 'disadvantages'. Put Ss in groups and have one member of each group copy the chart. Give Ss about ten minutes to think about modern-day society and the advantages and disadvantages of speed in our lives. e.g., 'advantages': *travel quickly, communicate by the Internet, don't have to cook, can do lots of things in a very short time* etc; 'disadvantages': *stress, no time for family and friends, fast food is unhealthy, accidents on the road* etc. Then get feedback from each group, allowing other Ss to agree or disagree.

8.1 Fast world

In an increasingly fast world, many organisations are springing up to defend the right to take your time. These organisations claim that the speed of daily life threatens our health, family and relationships, weakens communities and leads to higher levels of unemployment.

In this lesson Ss read a text about how fast modern-day life is and tips about how to slow it down. Through this text they analyse the grammar of the Present Simple Passive.

OPTIONAL WARMER

Ask the Ss about their habits with regard to fast food, use of mobile phones and emails and travel.

Q: How often do you eat fast food? How many emails do you usually send a day? How many text messages do you usually write a day? When do you switch off your mobile phone? How often do you use your car?

Reading

1▶ Focus Ss on the photos and explain what the Slow Movement is. Tell them to answer the questions in pairs. Get feedback from various Ss.

2▶ Ss read through the text quickly and choose a title (b). Tell them not to worry about any vocabulary they don't understand at this stage.

3▶ Ss work in pairs to correct the sentences, referring back to the text where necessary. Check the answers with the whole class.

Suggested answers: 1 The text doesn't recommend having lunch in front of your computer. 2 British people send more than fifty million text messages every day. 3 The text says you should leave your phone at home or switch it off sometimes. 4 The average speed of cars in London's rush hour is thirteen kilometres per hour. 5 Most people speed up when the traffic lights turn amber. 6 The text says walking is probably quicker then driving. 7 The text suggests relaxing in a garden or park for twenty minutes each day.

▶ Ask the Ss if there are any words in the text that they haven't understood and encourage other Ss to explain those words before doing so yourself. Avoid explaining the underlined words yet, as this is included in Ex. 8.

4▶ Ss look at the 'Slow tips' again and answer the questions with a partner. Ss share their ideas for other tips with the rest of the class.

Grammar

OPTIONAL GRAMMAR LEAD-IN

Write the following sentences on the board but with the words in the wrong order. Ss work in pairs to order the words and write the sentences.

1 *million day 65 eaten USA fast-food every in are meals the* (65 million fast-food meals are eaten in the USA every day).
2 *text fifty over million UK the each messages in day sent are* (Over fifty million text messages are sent each day in the UK).
3 *around world over million cars used 400 the currently are* (Over 400 million cars are currently used around the world).

Elicit/teach the name of this grammatical structure (Present Simple Passive).

5a▶ Ss read through the Active grammar box and choose the correct alternatives. Elicit the answers and write the structures on the board.

Active grammar

Active: Form: subject + verb + object.
Passive: Form: am/is/are + past participle.

b▶ Ss find two more examples in the text. (If you have done the optional grammar lead-in, this exercise is not necessary).

▶ Refer Ss to Reference page 83 and give them a few minutes to read through the notes. Ask the Ss:
Q: What preposition do we use to say who did the action in passive structures? by
Q: What happens to the object of active sentences when we change them to passives? It becomes the subject.
Q: When do we use *is*? when the subject is singular
Q: When do use *are*? when the subject is plural.

▶ If the Ss still have some doubts about this structure, work through a few more examples on the board.

e.g., *A man in that shop repairs my bike.*
My bike is repaired (by a man) in that shop.
People in Canada speak two languages.
Two languages are spoken (by people) in Canada.

6▶ Ss complete the sentences in pairs. Check the answers with the whole class.

Answers: 1 Pizzas are delivered in twenty minutes or you get your money back. 2 Service is included in the bill. 3 Many people are caught by speed cameras. 4 London Underground is used by thousands of people every day. 5 Millions of people are employed in the fast-food industry.
6 Customers are charged 35 yen per minute to eat in the Totenko restaurant in Tokyo.

7a▶ Play recording 8.2 and Ss listen and write the sentences. Each sentence is repeated twice. Pause the recording at the end of the second repetition to give the Ss time to write and compare with a partner.

Answers: See tapescript on page 157.

b ▶ Elicit a full answer from the class for question 1 e.g., *Most international phones calls are made in English.* Then, in pairs, Ss write full answers for the rest of the questions and check to see if they were right on page 130.

Vocabulary

8 ▶ Tell Ss that they are going to study verbs used to describe change. Focus them on the underlined verbs in the text in Ex. 2 and tell them to answer the questions in pairs. Check with the whole class.

Answers: 1 *Rise* and *go up* have similar meanings.
2 *Improve* means to get better.

9 ▶ Distinguish the concept of change in quantity and change in quality with the whole class. Ss work in pairs to classify the verbs. Get feedback from the whole class.

Answers: Changes in quantity (A): rise/fall, go up/go down.
Changes in quality (B): improve/deteriorate, get better/get worse.

10a ▶ Ss work in pairs to choose what they think is the correct alternative, giving reasons for their choice.

b ▶ Play recording 8.3 and Ss listen to check their answers.

Answers: 1 going up 2 got worse 3 risen 4 fallen 5 deteriorating 6 gone down

Speaking

11a ▶ Focus the Ss on the words in the box and tell them to make notes about the changes that have taken place in their area/country. Go around the class as they do this monitoring their work.

b ▶ Focus Ss on the How to ... box. Read through the different sections with the whole class.

▶ Put Ss in pairs and have them tell each other about the changes they have noted down, using language from the How to ... box. If you have Ss from different countries/areas, make sure the pairs are mixed.

OPTIONAL EXTENSION

Ss work in pairs to think of other things that have changed in the world during recent years and make sentences using the How to ... box. They then share their ideas with the rest of the class.

8.2 Speed-dating

Speed-dating is a new craze that has hit Britain and the US. It entails a group of singles gathering at a café or bar that has been rented out for the evening. The café is filled with 'tables for two', and participants are given a set time (three–ten minutes) to talk to a member of the opposite sex on suggested topics to help break the ice. At the end of the set time, there is usually a DJ that rings a bell or plays music to let you know it's time to move on to the next date. Participants write on a form if they would like to see this person again.

In this lesson Ss read a letter from a speed-dating company to one of their clients and through this context they analyse the grammar of question formation.

OPTIONAL WARMER

Write *romantic relationships* on the board. Tell Ss that this is the topic of the lesson. In pairs, Ss brainstorm words related to this topic. Get feedback from the whole class and write the words on the board.

Vocabulary

1 ▶ Write *phrasal verb* on the board and elicit/teach the meaning (verb + one or two particles e.g., adverb or preposition which changes the meaning of the verb). Give the Ss an example of a phrasal verb e.g., *get up*.

▶ Focus Ss on the box and the example, *ask someone out*. Read through the definition with the whole class. Tell the Ss to read the questions in pairs and write the other phrasal verbs next to the correct definitions. Check with the whole class.

Answers: A go out with B split up with C grow apart D ask someone out E get over F put up with

2 ▶ Ask Ss which of the verbs in the box are irregular and elicit/teach the Past and Past Participle of those verbs (*go–went–gone; split–split–split; grow–grew–grown; get–got–got; put–put–put*).

▶ Ss complete the sentences in pairs with the correct form of the phrasal verb. Check the answers with the whole class.

Answers: 1 Pete asked me out yesterday. He wants to take me to a restaurant. 2 Jade's been single since she split up with her boyfriend last year. 3 Oliver never does the washing-up and Maria just puts up with it. 4 When my sister got divorced, she found it difficult to get over her ex-husband. 5 Linda and Guy are a couple. They started going out/to go out with each other last month. 6 We used to be good friends but we've grown apart over the last year.

3 ▶ Ss discuss the questions in Ex. 1 in pairs. Get feedback from the whole class.

Reading

4a▶ Focus Ss on the photo and tell them to answer the question with a partner. Get feedback from the class.

b▶ Ss read the letter quickly. Tell them not to worry about any vocabulary they don't understand at this stage. Ask the class to tell you what speed-dating is.

5▶ Ss read the letter again and answer the questions with a partner. Check the answers with the whole class.

> Answers: 1 forty 2 three minutes 3 give it to the organisers 4 those of the people whose name you ticked and who also ticked you 5 boring ones like 'What do you do?' 6 interesting ones like 'How would your best friend describe you?'

▶ Ask the Ss if there is any vocabulary in the letter that they still don't understand and encourage other Ss to explain before doing so yourself.

6▶ Ss discuss the questions with a partner. Get feedback from the whole class.

> **OPTIONAL EXTENSION**
>
> In pairs, Ss discuss what advice they might give someone who wants to find a partner. Get feedback from the class and discuss the advantages and disadvantages of each idea (e.g., put an advert in the newspaper, a traditional dating agency, join a club, do an English course, go clubbing).

Listening

7a▶ Tell Ss they are going to listen to two conversations about speed-dating. Focus their attention on the questions and play recording 8.4.

> Answer: The pair in dialogue 2 follow the advice.

b▶ Play recording 8.4 again and Ss write the names of the different speakers. Allow them to compare with a partner before checking with the whole class.

> Answers: 1 Melanie 2 Steve 3 Steve 4 Melanie, 5 Kieron 6 Rachel 7 Kieron

Grammar

> **OPTIONAL GRAMMAR LEAD-IN**
>
> Play recording 8.4 again. Ss try to remember the questions. Then write the following answers from recording 8.4 on the board and Ss write the questions in pairs. Check the questions with the whole class, pointing out any errors in question formation. (Sometimes another question is possible.)
>
> *I'm Steve; Oh, I'm a teacher; Yes, I do. It's very interesting; No, this is my first time; Well, I think my best friend would say that I'm friendly and open; Oh, Canada definitely; Well actually, it was a teach-yourself Italian CD.*
>
> See tapescript on page 157 for questions.

8▶ Focus Ss on the Active grammar box and tell them to read through the notes and choose the best alternatives. If you have done the optional warmer, it is not necessary for them to find examples in the tapescript.

> **Active grammar**
>
> 1 When the main verb is *to be*, put the verb before the subject.
>
> 2 With the Present Simple and Past Simple, put *do/does/did* before the subject.
>
> 3 With other tenses, put the auxiliary verb or modal verb before the subject.

▶ Tell Ss to look at Reference page 83 and give them a few minutes to read through the notes. Ask:
Q: How many common question words are there? (8)
Ask Ss to give you some examples with these questions words. Say: *How* – elicit a question e.g., *How are you?*
Q: What other words can we put with the question word *what?* (time, kind)
Q: What other words can we put with the question word *how?* (many, much).
Q: What happens when the question word is the subject of the sentence? (The verb comes after the question word and we don't use the auxiliary). If you feel Ss are not very comfortable with this, write another example on the board, contrasting the question word as subject and as object of the question. e.g., 1 *Who kissed the girl?* (*who* is the subject and *girl* is the object) and 2 *Who did the girl kiss?* (*who* is the object and *girl* is the subject). Ask the Ss to identify the subject and the object in each sentence.

9▶ Ss work in pairs to correct the mistake in each sentence, referring to the grammar reference if necessary. Check the answers with the whole class.

> Answers: 1 What kind of weather do you like best? 2 What is your favourite kind of holiday? 3 What are you going to do this weekend? 4 Can you cook a really good meal? 5 Are you good at making things? 6 Do you collect anything unusual? 7 What did you dream about last night? 8 How many countries have you visited in your life?

10▶ Ss work in pairs to write six more questions suitable for asking at a speed-dating event. Encourage them to be imaginative. Go around the class checking that they are using questions forms correctly.

Speaking

11a▶ Tell the Ss to stand up and imagine they are at a party. Ask them to find out some interesting information about one person, using the questions they wrote in Ex. 10. Tell them they have two minutes. After that time is up, say 'change partners' and Ss have two minutes with another person. Repeat several times.

b▶ Ss report back to the class about what they found out and were asked.

8.3 The curious incident

Mark Haddon's first novel *The curious incident of the dog in the night-time* (2003) tells the story of Christopher, a 15-year old autistic boy who turns private investigator when the neighbour's pet poodle is found dead. The book won the 2004 Whitbread prize (Britain's longest-running literary competition), and provides great insight into what it is like to live a life of autism in which there are no filters to order or eliminate the millions of pieces of information that one receives every day.

In this lesson Ss read an extract from the novel and through this context consider the grammar of Past Simple and Past Continuous.

OPTIONAL WARMER

Copy two face icons (happy and sad) from extract 2 on the board and elicit their meaning. In pairs, Ss discuss the things they associate with these feelings. Get feedback from the class and see if everybody agrees.

Reading

1 ▶ Ss discuss the questions in pairs. Get feedback from various Ss.

2a ▶ Focus the Ss on the photo and tell them that this is the front cover of a book. Read the title with the whole class and ask them to discuss with a partner what they think happens in the book. Get feedback from the class.

b ▶ Read through the questions with the whole class. Ss then read the first extract and answer the questions with a partner. Elicit the answers from the whole class.

Answers: 1 He knows lots of facts but he doesn't understand his feelings very well. (Elicit/teach the fact that he's autistic and ask the Ss to tell you what they know about this disability.) 2 Accept any viable answers but clarify that she is, in fact, his teacher. 3 He doesn't recognize/understand certain emotions.

3a ▶ Ask Ss to look at the illustration and discuss, in pairs, what they think is happening.

b ▶ Read through the questions with the whole class and instruct Ss to read through the second extract. Tell them not to worry about any words they don't understand at this stage. Ss answer the questions with a partner.

Answers: 1 Because they have uniforms and numbers and you know what they are meant to be doing. 2 Accept any viable answers but clarify the fact that she is a neighbour. 3 Because the policeman doesn't give him enough time to work out the correct answer. 4 Ss' own answers.

▶ Ask the Ss if there are any words they don't understand from the first two extracts and encourage other Ss to explain before doing so yourself.

4 ▶ Read the questions with the whole class. Ss turn to page 130, read the last extract and answer the questions in pairs.

Answers: 1 No, he didn't. 2 Because there is too much information going into his head, 3 Because he didn't like him touching him in that way.

5 ▶ Ss discuss the questions in pairs. Get feedback from the whole class.

Grammar

OPTIONAL GRAMMAR LEAD-IN

Ask Ss the following question about the story and tell them to write a complete answer with a partner. Elicit the answer and write it on the board: **Q: What was Christopher doing when the police arrived?** When the police arrived, Christopher was holding the dog.
Tell Ss to underline the verbs in the sentence and ask: **Q: What grammatical tenses are being used?** Elicit/teach Past Simple and Past Continuous.

6a ▶ Focus Ss on the Active grammar box and tell them to complete the gaps in pairs. Check with the whole class.

Active grammar

Use the Past Continuous to talk about an action in progress at a particular time in the past.
Use the Past Simple to talk about complete actions in the past.
Use the Past Continuous to talk about a longer action interrupted by another action.

b ▶ Ss find five more examples of the Past Continuous in the extracts and underline them. Ask various Ss to read them aloud for you. Comment on the interrogative form i.e., the fact that was/were goes before the subject.

Answers: And what, precisely, were you doing in the garden? (extract 2); I was holding the dog. (extract 2); And why were you holding the dog? (extract 2); He was asking too many questions ... (extract 3); and he was asking them too quickly ... (extract 3)

▶ Tell the Ss to look at Reference page 83 and give them a few minutes to read through the notes. Ask:
Q: Are Past Continuous actions complete at the time you are talking about? (No)
Q: Which tense do we normally use to set the scene to a story? (Past Continuous)

7 ▶ Ss complete the sentences in pairs. Check the answers with the whole class.

Answers: 1 was walking/met 2 took/wasn't looking 3 was reading/arrived 4 were you driving/happened 5 saw/was working 6 told/wasn't listening

8 ▶ Ss finish the sentences appropriately using their own ideas. Go around the class monitoring Ss' work and making any corrections. Then Ss read out their sentences for the class to hear.

9▶ Put Ss in pairs and tell them to think about their partner but not to speak yet. Ask them to write down what they think that person was doing at the stated times. Now tell them to talk to their partner to see if they were right.

Pronunciation

10a▶ Play recording 8.5 and Ss write the sentences they hear. Each sentence is repeated twice. Pause the recording after the second repetition to give Ss time to finish the sentence and compare with a partner. Check with the whole class.

> Answers: See tapescript on page 157.

b▶ Play recording 8.5 again and ask Ss to pay attention to the pronunciation of *was* and *were*. Elicit the fact that these words are not stressed in the sentences and are pronounced with weak forms: /wəz/ and /wə/.

▶ Ss practise saying the sentences with a partner. Go around the class listening to pronunciation.

Speaking

11a▶ Divide the class into groups of four, with two As and two Bs (If you have odd numbers, have three student Bs).

▶ Tell the As to look at page 126 and the Bs to look at page 128. Give them time to read the instructions. If possible separate the As and Bs while they prepare.

▶ Now send one of the As from each group out of the class while the 'police' interview the first suspect. Give them five minutes and then send the first suspect out of the class while the second suspect is interviewed.

b▶ Finally, everybody returns to the class and the police decide if the suspects were guilty or not. Ask each set of police to report back to the class with their verdict.

Writing

12▶ Ss read the story in the Writing bank on page 147 and do the exercises. Check with the whole class.

> **1▶** Answers: 1 bored 2 on his own 3 good 4 his cousin's house 5 made a lot of noise 6 followed 7 didn't stay

> **2▶** Answers: A 2 B 1 3 good C 3

13▶ Ss write a story starting with the words given. Allow time for Ss to brainstorm ideas before writing.

> **OPTIONAL VARIATION**
>
> Ss each write the first line on A4 paper. After two minutes they pass their paper on to the next student who reads that line, folds it over and writes a second line, and so on. When the papers have gone around the class, Ss open up their paper, and read the stories aloud.

Communication: Race to the finish

In this lesson Ss play a board game in which they answer questions related to this unit.

1▶ Read through the rules with the whole class and divide the students up into groups of three or four.

2▶ Ss write seven 'choice' questions on small pieces of paper for another group based on things they have studied in the book so far or general interest. Go around the class monitoring their work.

▶ Collect in the 'choice' questions and redistribute them among groups.

3▶ Give the Ss counters and dice and tell them to play the game. If any of the groups finish much earlier than the others, have them write similar questions about other topics in the book. These can be used to conduct a mini-quiz at the end of the lesson.

Review and practice

1 ▶

Answers: 1 are cleaned 2 are invited 3 is recycled 4 are cut down 5 is covered 6 are locked 7 is served 8 are opened

2 ▶

Answers: 1 don't pronounce 2 are taken 3 is not invited 4 are employed 5 don't use 6 are cancelled 7 is made 8 are played 9 is closed

3 ▶

Answers: 1 Have you ever seen a cheetah? 2 What time are your friends coming? 3 Why do you always drive to work? 4 How long has she lived in that flat? 5 When did you last see a good film? 6 Are you going to do your homework tonight? 7 Would you like to come to dinner tomorrow? 8 Where are you going on holiday next year?

4 ▶

Answers: 1 What do you like eating for breakfast? 2 Where do you usually go for your holidays? 3 What instrument did she play as a child? 4 What did you buy? 5 What can your mother do really well? 6 When are you going to start driving lessons? 7 How many times were they late for school last week?

5 ▶

Answers: 1 was raining 2 were driving 3 stopped 4 didn't hit 5 fell 6 wasn't 7 was walking 8 was following 9 started 10 looked 11 saw

6 ▶

Answers: 1 getting 2 down 3 up 4 hour 5 in 6 limit 7 apart

Notes for using the Common European Framework (CEF)

CEF References

8.1 Can do: describe simple changes

CEF A2 descriptor: can communicate what he/she wants to say in a simple and direct exchange of limited information on familiar and routine matters, but in other situations he/she generally has to compromise the message (CEF page 129)

8.2 Can do: find out personal information

CEF A2 descriptor: can ask for and provide personal information (CEF page 81)

8.3 Can do: ask and answer questions about past actions

CEF B1 descriptor: can briefly give reasons and explanations for opinions, plans and actions (CEF page 59)

CEF quick brief

The reference levels in the Common European Framework (A1–C2) allow a correlation with common international exams as well as exams within a country or institution. This means that employers can have a more accurate idea of what a student with a particular qualification can actually do. For more information see the introduction at the start of this Teacher's Book.

Portfolio task

Download the Total English Portfolio free from www.longman.com/totalenglish.

Objective: to help learners start using the Portfolio to assess their progress and priorities in English.

This task can be done in Ss' L1.

The Biography section of the Portfolio contains the Can do statements from each lesson in the book. Learners can use this section to review and keep track of their progress. It is helpful to remind students to complete the tick boxes in this section at regular intervals, perhaps at the end of every unit or at the end of every semester.

1 ▶ Ask learners to look at the Can do statements in the Biography section of their Portfolio. Show how the statements relate to the work they have completed in their course books.

2 ▶ Ask students to look through the statements at A2 level and complete the tick boxes.

3 ▶ Explain that as they progress through the course, they will be able to achieve more Can do goals at A2 and will also start to complete goals at B1 level.

9 Work

Overview

Lead-in	**Vocabulary:** work
9.1	**Vocabulary:** work
	Can do: respond to simple job interview questions
9.2	**Grammar:** *can, could, be able to*
	Vocabulary: make/do
	Can do: talk about your abilities
9.3	**Grammar:** Past Simple Passive
	Vocabulary: crime
	Can do: write a short article
Com. focus	Let's talk
Reference	
Practice	

Summary

Lesson 1: Ss listen to three people talking about job interviews and discuss the difference between pairs of vocabulary items related to work. Then they read a text giving advice about how to be successful at a job interview.

Lesson 2: Ss read a text about Carl Churchill, who runs an IT empire and is number one on *the Rich List 2020*, despite being only 19 years old. Then they ask and answer questions using *do* and *make*.

Lesson 3: Ss answer questions related to crime and then listen to a news story about a car thief who cleaned all the cars he stole before leaving them at the side of the road. Then they tell stories based on a series of pictures.

Communication Focus: Ss look at strategies for negotiating and then role-play a situation in which the owners of a company and the employees negotiate over pay and conditions.

Film bank: The interview (4'45")

A short film about a man getting unwelcome advice on his way to an interview.

In this film the main character is on his way to an interview for a job as a sales rep. He is not very well prepared and gets some advice en route to the interview on how he could prepare better.

Possible places to use this short film are:

▶ before Lesson 1 to introduce the topic of job interviews

▶ after Lesson 1 to extend the topic of job interviews

▶ at the end of the unit to round up the topic and language

For ways to use this short film in class, see Students' Book page 141 and Teacher's Book page 193.

Lead-in

▶ Write *work* on the board and tell the Ss that the next unit is about work. Have Ss work in pairs to brainstorm a list of jobs. Give them two minutes only. Elicit words from the Ss and write them on the board.

1a▶ Ss look at the photos and name the jobs.

> Answers: Pic 1: fire fighter Pic 2: plumber
> Pic 3: fashion designer Pic 4: lawyer
> sales rep. isn't shown.

b▶ Tell the Ss to practise pronouncing the words from the box with a partner. Play recording 9.1 and Ss check their pronunciation. Ask various Ss to pronounce the words for the whole class. Point out that the *b* in plumber is silent.

c▶ Read through the questions/instructions with the whole class and check they understand what they have to do. If the majority or a large percentage of the class does not work, write the following question on the board:
Q: What job would you like to do in the future?

▶ Tell the Ss that if the answer they are given to the first question (Do you have a job?) is *no*, they should ask the question from the board.

▶ Ss stand up and mingle, if possible, asking and answering the questions. Help any Ss who don't know how to say their own job in English.

2▶ Ss answer the questions in pairs or small groups. Get feedback from the whole class.

3a▶ Read through the phrases in the box with the class. Ss. In pairs, Ss put the phrases in a logical order. Tell them there is not necessarily one correct answer, and that they must justify the order that they choose.

▶ Get feedback from one of the groups and see if the rest of the class agree or disagree with the order. Have them give reasons for what they say.

> Suggested answers: prepare a CV, apply for a job, have an interview, be offered a job, take a job, get promoted, work long hours, resign, run your own company.

b▶ Ss answer the question in pairs. Get feedback from the whole class.

EXTEND THE LEAD-IN

Write five jobs on the board, e.g., *teacher, professional football player, cleaner, pilot* and *social worker*. Ss work in small groups to put these jobs and the jobs in Ex. 1a in order from highest paid to lowest paid. Get feedback and discuss any differences. In small groups again, Ss discuss if they think that each job has the right salary or should be paid more or less.

9.1 Make an impression

Nowadays, there are hundreds of books and websites that give advice on how to do well in a job interview. Advice is generally given about the pre-interview stage e.g., finding out about the company, the interview stage itself e.g., answering difficult questions, and the post-interview stage e.g., sending a thank-you letter. These books and sites also offer tips on writing CVs and covering letters.

In this lesson Ss consider vocabulary related to work and read some advice on being successful at a job interview.

OPTIONAL WARMER

Ask Ss about their experience with job interviews:
Q: Have you ever had a job interview? For what job(s)? Did you get the job? Did you feel very nervous? Have you ever interviewed somebody for a job?

Listening

1a▶ Focus Ss on the pictures. Tell them to discuss with a partner what is happening in each one. Elicit and accept various answers from Ss at this stage.

Answers: Pic A: The interviewer is throwing an ashtray at the interviewee. Pic B: The interviewee is parking in the Managing Director's personal parking space.
Pic C: An interviewee is spilling water (because he is very nervous).

b▶ Play recording 9.2. Ss listen to the stories and match them to the pictures.

Answers: Dialogue 1: Pic C Dialogue 2: Pic B
Dialogue 3: Pic A

2▶ Read through the sentences with the whole class and play recording 9.2 again. Ss write the correct person next to each sentence. Allow them to compare with a partner before checking the answers.

Answers: 1 Alison 2 Charlie 3 Kevin 4 Alison
5 Charlie 6 Kevin

3a▶ Divide the class into groups of three and give each student a letter A, B or C. Ss A read Story 1, Ss B Story 2, and Ss C Story 3 on page 157. Tell them to make brief notes about what they read.

b▶ With books closed, Ss explain their story to the rest of their group.

Vocabulary

4a▶ Ss discuss the words in pairs. Get feedback from the whole group.

Answers: 1 An employer is the boss; an employee is the worker. 2 An interviewer is the person who conducts the interview; an interviewee is the person who is applying for the job. 3 An application form is provided by the company and you complete it to apply for a job; a CV is a summary that you provide about your qualifications and experience. 4 Experience refers to the things you have done related to the job; qualifications refer to education and courses you have completed. 5 A salary is the money you earn from your job monthly or annually; a bonus is a special payment you are given for good work.
6 A receptionist works on a desk at the entrance to a business dealing with new arrivals; a secretary deals with general administration. 7 A company refers to a business in general; a factory refers to a building where things are produced. 8 A managing director is a person who manages and owns part of a company; a sales rep. is an employee who is responsible for selling the things the company makes.

b▶ Ss choose the correct alternative in pairs. Check answers with the whole class.

Answers: 1 employees 2 sales rep. 3 experience (point out to the Ss that experience is the correct answer because it is uncountable) 4 receptionist
5 bonus 6 interviewer 7 application form

Pronunciation

5a▶ Focus the Ss on Ex. 4a again and tell them to listen and mark the stress as in the example. Play recording 9.3. Allow them to compare with a partner before checking with the whole group.

Answers: 1 an interviewer/an interviewee 2 an application form/a CV 3 experience/qualifications
4 a salary/a bonus 5 a receptionist/a secretary
6 a company/a factory 7 a managing director/
a sales rep.

b▶ Ss practise pronouncing the words/phrases in pairs.

6▶ Ss discuss the questions in pairs. Go around the class monitoring the conversations and making a note of any errors. Get feedback about the questions, and then go through the errors with the whole class, encouraging them to self-correct before explaining yourself.

OPTIONAL EXTENSION

Ss talk in pairs about the job they do or would like to do, using some of the words from Ex. 4a e.g., what qualifications or experience you need to have or if you normally receive a bonus.

Reading

▶ Focus Ss on the picture. Ask them to discuss in pairs what is happening and if they think the interviewee will be successful. Elicit answers from the class.

7a▶ Ss close their books and discuss ideas about how to be successful in a job interview in pairs and make a list under the headings given.

b▶ Give the Ss about five minutes to do this and then ask each pair to join with another pair and share their ideas, adding to their lists where appropriate. If they don't agree with the others they shouldn't add the items.

8▶ Tell Ss to read through the text quickly and tick the things on their list.

▶ Find out from the whole class if they had anything on their lists that is not mentioned in the article.

9▶ Read through the questions with the whole class. Tell Ss to read the text again and answer the questions with a partner. Check with the whole class.

> **Answers:** 1 You need to find out about the company. 2 You should wear smart clothes. 3 You should go and have a coffee in a local café. 4 You should take two or three slow, deep breaths. 5 You should shake hands firmly, look the interviewer in the eye and say 'Pleased to meet you'. 6 not too short and not too long 7 You should give clear, direct answers. 8 You should look at the interviewer. 9 You should be positive and show enthusiasm. 10 If you think you haven't answered a question well, you should phone the interviewer and explain yourself.

10▶ Ss discuss the questions in pairs or small groups. Get feedback from the whole class.

Speaking

11▶ Put the Ss in pairs (A and B) and tell them to look at the job adverts on page 131. Explain that they are going to role-play an interview, with student A as the interviewee and student B as the interviewer. Student A can choose the job they want to apply for.

▶ Give them a few minutes to prepare their roles and make notes. Encourage them to follow the advice from the text.

▶ Ss act out their dialogues and then reverse their roles. Interviewers should give reasons at the end why the person got or didn't get the job. Ask for volunteers to act out an interview for the rest of the class.

> **OPTIONAL VARIATION**
>
> Ss act out the interview as above but each interviewer interviews all the student As in turn (Ss rotate around the class) and chooses the person who they think is the best for the job. Allow a maximum time (e.g., four minutes for each interview). Tell the interviewees that they can either tell the truth or invent their 'CV'. Finally, have each interviewer tell the rest of the class who they chose and why.

9.2 Teen tycoon

The Rich List 2020 has been drawn up in Britain to predict which twenty people under the age of twenty-one are likely to be the millionaires of the future. Eleven on the list are male and nine female. Four are involved in the music business, eight in sport (including a skateboarder), four in business and technology, three in acting, one in modelling and one in fashion design. They are tipped to make many millions during their careers, independent of any inherited wealth.

In this lesson Ss read about Carl Churchill, number one on this list, and through this context, consider the grammar of *can, could* and *be able to*.

> **OPTIONAL WARMER**
>
> Ask Ss to discuss in pairs in which jobs they think it is the easiest to make money quickly. Get feedback from the class. Ask them to give you examples of young, rich or successful people from their countries.
>
> Write *Teen Tycoon* on the board. Elicit/teach the meaning (*tycoon* is a businessman or woman with great power and wealth; *teen* is short for teenage).

Reading

1▶ Focus Ss on the photos and ask them to discuss the questions with a partner. Get feedback (they are all wealthy teenagers).

2a▶ Ss read through the first text quickly to see if they were right.

b▶ Tell Ss to turn to page 131 and read the rest of the text and discuss the question in pairs. Get feedback from the whole class.

3▶ Read through the sentences with the class. Ask Ss to decide with a partner where in the text they should go. Tell them to look carefully at the sentences which are immediately before and after each gap.

> **Answers:** A 3 B 4 C 2 D 1

4▶ Read through the statements and tell the Ss to read through the text again to decide if they are true (T) or false (F). Check the answers with the whole class.

> **Answers:** 1 F 2 F 3 T 4 T

5▶ Ss discuss the questions in pairs. Get feedback from the whole group.

Vocabulary

6▶ Ss work in pairs to put the words with *make* or *do*. Check the answers with the whole class. Tell Ss there are no real rules for when we use these, so it's best to learn the verb phrase itself.

> **Answers:** *make*: money, a decision, an effort, progress, an appointment, a mistake, a complaint
> *do*: nothing, business, homework, your best, someone a favour, research

7a▶ Refer Ss back to the text in Ex. 2 and on page 131. Tell them to underline five examples of these verb phrases in the text. Check the answers by asking the questions: **Q: How much money is Carl expected to make by 2020?** (£100 million). **Q: How many hours a day does he do business?** (10 hours). **Q: What type of decisions does he sometimes make?** (difficult ones). **Q: Is he happy with the progress the business has made?** (yes) **Q: Have they made any mistakes?** (yes)

b▶ Read through the example with the Ss, emphasising the fact that they may need to change the form of *do* or *make*. Ss then complete the questions in pairs. Check with the whole class.

> Answers: 1 made 2 did 3 made 4 doing 5 making

c▶ Ss ask and answer the questions in pairs. Go around the class monitoring their conversations, encouraging them to ask follow-up questions to each other and to self-correct when you notice an error.

> **OPTIONAL EXTENSION**
>
> Ask Ss to choose one of the expressions from the box in Ex. 6 and write a question in pairs (if they choose one that has already been used in Ex. 7 then they must change the context). Tell them that the question must be written so that other Ss can really answer it e.g., *When was the last time you made an appointment at the dentist's?* Ss stand up and mingle, asking and answering their questions. At the end, each pair reports back to the rest of the class.

Grammar

> **OPTIONAL GRAMMAR LEAD-IN**
>
> Write the following questions on the board:
> **Q: Could you go out until late when you were 14?**
> **Q: Can you speak any other languages apart from your own and English?**
> **Q: Do you think you will be able to travel around the world in the future?**
> Ss discuss the questions in pairs. Get feedback and ask Ss which sentences refer to the past, present and future.

8▶ Focus Ss on the Active grammar box. Tell them to read through the notes and choose the correct alternative. Elicit the correct answers and write them on the board.

> **Active grammar**
>
> Use *can* to talk about ability in the present.
> Use *could* to talk about ability in the past.
> Use *be able to* to talk about ability in the future.

▶ Tell Ss to look at Reference page 93. Give them a few minutes to read through the notes and ask:

Q: When do we use *can, could* and *be able to?* (to talk about ability and possibility).
Q: What verb form do we use after these expressions? (the infinitive; point out that this infinitive is without *to*).
Q: Do we use an auxiliary verb? (no; point out the change of subject-verb order in interrogatives and the use of *not* in negatives).

9a▶ Ss complete the sentences in pairs. Check the answers with the whole class.

> Answers: 1 can 2 couldn't 3 can't/Can 4 could 5 couldn't 6 Could 7 won't be able to 8 Will you be able to

b▶ Play recording 9.4, pausing after every sentence so that the Ss can repeat. Point out that *can* is pronounced in two different ways. Elicit/model the two different ways and explain that normally we pronounce the weak form /kən/ in the context of a sentence except with short answers (Yes, I can or No, I can't) where the strong form is used /kæn/.

10▶ Focus Ss on the table and the example sentence. Give Ss one more example, e.g., *She couldn't cook at all five years ago.*

▶ Ss make similar sentences in pairs. Go around the class, monitoring their work. Elicit sentences from the whole class.

Lifelong learning

▶ Read through the notes with the whole class and tell Ss to make a list for the three points given. Then, in pairs, Ss ask each other about those points e.g., *What couldn't you do a year ago?*

▶ Finally, the Ss plan how to improve and reach targets in pairs.

▶ Get feedback from the whole class about these plans and possible dates. Make a note of these things and ask later in the course how Ss are progressing. The question should appear to be one of personal interest. Be careful not to pressurise as Ss need to become autonomous in their learning and not feel that this is a teacher-imposed homework task.

Person to person

11a▶ In pairs, Ss talk about their abilities with relation to playing the guitar, cooking, swimming and painting.

b▶ Ss choose two more activities to talk about.

> **OPTIONAL VARIATION**
>
> Before doing Ex. 11b, brainstorm possible activities e.g., play other musical instruments, do other sports, ride a bike or moped, use a computer, speak a foreign language etc. Tell each student to write a question (present, past or future) with one activity e.g., *Could you use a computer when you were seven?*
>
> Ss mingle, asking and answering questions. At the end, each student reports back to the whole class about what they found out.

9.3 Crime doesn't pay.

Many strange crimes are committed every year all over the world. One such case is that of Peter Blain, a British man, who compulsively stole cars from showrooms, drove them around for several hours, then washed and cleaned them until they were spotless before leaving them at the side of the road. He was committed to six year's imprisonment in April, 2004.

In this lesson Ss listen to a news story about Peter Blain and analyse the grammar of the Past Simple Passive through this context.

OPTIONAL WARMER

Write *crime* on the board and ask Ss to brainstorm any words related to this topic. Get feedback from the whole class and write the words on the board. Ask Ss if they can make any other word (adjectives, nouns, verbs or adverbs) from the words already on the board e.g., if you have written *prison* elicit *prisoner*.

Vocabulary

1 ▶ In pairs, Ss answer the questions using one of the words from the box. Check the answers with the class.

Answers: 1 thief 2 police officer 3 jury 4 judge

2 ▶ Read through the questions with the class checking that they understand all of the questions. Ss then discuss their answers in pairs. Get feedback from the class.

Listening

▶ Focus the Ss on the pictures and ask them what they can see (a man and a car). Ask: **Q: Does the man look happy?** (No) **Q: Is the car new?** (Yes) **Is it clean?** (Yes)

3 ▶ Tell Ss they are going to hear a news story related to the pictures and the words in the box. Focus on those words and check student comprehension.

▶ Ask Ss to predict the story in pairs. Get ideas from the whole class.

4 ▶ Play recording 9.5 and Ss listen. Ask them if anybody in the class was right about the story and elicit information about what they have heard.

5 ▶ Read through the statements with the whole class. Ss listen to recording 9.5 again and mark them true (T) or false (F). Give them time to compare with a partner before checking the answers.

Answers: 1 T 2 F 3 T 4 F 5 F 6 T 7 F

6 ▶ Ss discuss the questions in pairs or small groups. Go around the class monitoring their conversations and encouraging self-correction of errors.

OPTIONAL EXTENSION

Ss work in pairs to think of a crime that they have heard about recently in the news. They make notes about what happened and explain the story to the rest of the class. Each pair has to decide what punishment they think is suitable for each crime. Get feedback and encourage Ss to discuss the different possibilities.

Grammar

OPTIONAL GRAMMAR LEAD-IN

Write the following stem sentences on the board:
65 million fast food meals ...
Over fifty million text messages ...
Over 400 million cars ...

Tell Ss that these are the beginning of sentences taken from a text about speed in lesson 8.1. In pairs, and without looking back at the text, ask them to finish the sentences in an appropriate way.

Get feedback and tell the Ss to check their version with the original on page 76. Write the full sentences on the board. Now ask:
Q: How do you think you say this in the past?
Allow Ss to talk about this with a partner and then get feedback. Elicit the correct form.

7 ▶ Focus the Ss on the Active grammar box. Tell them to read through the notes and choose the correct alternatives.

Active grammar

Use the active form to say what the subject did.
Use the passive to say what happened to the subject.

8 ▶ Tell Ss to look at the tapescript on page 157 and underline five examples of the Past Simple Passive.

Answers: All the cars were stolen ... He was arrested by police ... Every car was later found ... He was once called ... Blain was taken away by police ...

▶ Tell Ss that further notes are provided on Reference page 93. They should feel fairly comfortable with this grammar point having already studied the Present form.

9 ▶ Ss complete the sentences in pairs. Get feedback from the whole class.

Answers: 1 were sent 2 was invented 3 were met 4 were arrested 5 was cleaned 6 was painted

10 ▶ Ss complete the sentences in pairs. Check the answers by having two Ss read out each of the dialogues.

Answers: 1 We weren't given very long to do our test./ How long were you given? 2 Someone broke into my flat but my computer wasn't taken./What was taken? 3 This house wasn't built recently./When was it built?

11▶ Focus Ss on the picture and ask them to describe it with a partner and to say what they think is happening. Get feedback from the class.

▶ Tell Ss to read through the whole text in order to get the general idea of the story. At this stage they do not choose alternatives.

▶ Then ask if there is any vocabulary they don't understand. Encourage other Ss to explain before intervening yourself.

▶ Ss read through the text again choosing the correct alternatives. Check the answers with the whole class.

Answers: 1 was given 2 felt 3 was told 4 waited 5 ran 6 took 7 told 8 was arrested 9 was taken

Writing

12▶ Focus the Ss on the How to ... box and give them a few minutes to read through the information. Ask:
Q: What do we normally put in the introduction to an article?
Q: What sequencers can we use? Ask Ss if they can think of any more sequencers apart from the ones already given (e.g., *at first*, *later*, *in the end* etc.)
Q: How can we finish the article?

▶ Now tell the Ss to divide the story in Ex. 11 into three parts. Get feedback from the class. (The first complete sentence is the introduction, the last complete sentence is the conclusion, and the rest is the story.)

13a▶ Divide the class into two groups, A and B. Group A look at the pictures on page 126 and group B look at the pictures on page 128.

b▶ Within each group Ss work in pairs to describe what is happening in each picture and make a note of vocabulary they need to do this task. If you have dictionaries allow Ss to use them, if not, Ss request the vocabulary from you.

c▶ Put a student A with a student B. Each one tells their story while the other listens. Tell the Ss they are responsible for explaining new vocabulary to their partner either by giving a definition or pointing to the thing in the pictures (discourage translating into the mother tongue).

14▶ Ss write their article using the How to ... box as reference.

OPTIONAL VARIATION

Ss work in small groups to invent a 'disastrous crime' story. Tell them they must think of things that could possible go wrong for a criminal. Give Ss some time to prepare it and then have each group tell the rest of the class the story. Finally, Ss write up their story.

Communication: Let's talk

In this lesson Ss talk and read about how to negotiate before role-playing a situation of negotiation themselves.

1▶ Read through the examples given of negotiation situations and ask the Ss if they ever find themselves in these situations.

▶ Now tell Ss to brainstorm other situations in which they negotiate. Get feedback from the whole class.

▶ Focus Ss on the pictures and ask them to imagine what is happening and what the people might be saying. Get several Ss to share their ideas.

2▶ Ss discuss the question in pairs.

3▶ Focus Ss on the five-step negotiation plan. Tell them to read through it and underline anything they don't understand. Go through problems of comprehension with the whole class.

▶ Ss discuss in pairs whether they agree with all the points or not and if they have anything to add. Get feedback from the whole class.

4▶ Tell the Ss that they are going to listen to a father and his daughter negotiating. Ask the Ss what they think it might be about.

▶ Read through the questions with the whole class and play recording 9.6. Allow Ss to discuss the answers with a partner before checking with the whole class.

5▶ Divide the class into two groups, A and B. Ss A look at page 126 and Ss B look at page 128. Give Ss time to read through the information with a partner from the same group and discuss how they are going to approach the 'negotiation'.

6a▶ Two Ss A and two Ss B work together to act out the negotiation process. Give them a limited time (e.g., ten minutes) and tell them to stop.

b▶ Ss work out their scores to see who has 'won'.

Review and practice

1 ▶

Answers: 1 can tell 2 couldn't take 3 can you help 4 could stand 5 won't be able to play 6 couldn't sleep 7 won't be able to finish

2 ▶

Answers: 1 Can she read music? 2 Could you see the sea? 3 How much can he afford (to spend)? 4 When will he be able to walk again? 5 What can it do? 6 When will he be able to start? 7 How many languages could she speak?

3 ▶

Answers: 1 This letter was posted last Friday. 2 The animals were given some food. 3 They were invited to Raul and Sharon's wedding. 4 All the flights were cancelled because of the weather. 5 This chair was made in Italy in the sixteenth century. 6 We were warned to stay indoors until morning. 7 A lot of money and jewellery were stolen from their house.

4 ▶

Answers: 1 More than fifty people were arrested by the police. 2 The store was opened at exactly 9a.m. 3 I was paid a lot of money to do the job. 4 We weren't met at the airport. 5 Everybody was rescued from the ship. 6 All the classrooms were cleaned yesterday.

5 ▶

Answers: 1 interviewee 2 qualifications 3 correct 4 correct 5 receptionist

6 ▶

Answers: 1 apply 2 jury 3 employee 4 complaint 5 favour 6 company 7 appointment

Notes for using the Common European Framework (CEF)

CEF References

9.1 Can do: respond to simple job interview questions

CEF A2 descriptor: can answer simple questions and respond to simple statements in an interview (CEF page 82)

9.2 Can do: talk about your abilities

CEF A2 descriptor: can give a simple description or presentation of people, living or working conditions, daily routines, likes/dislikes, etc. as a short series of simple phrases and sentences linked into a list (CEF page 58)

9.3 Can do: write a short article

CEF B1 descriptor: can write short, simple essays on topics of interest (CEF page 62)

CEF quick brief

One of the key ideas within the Common European Framework is that learning a language is a lifelong task; it requires 'lifelong learning' skills. Like all skills, we can improve how we learn and one of the teacher's responsibilities is to show students how to do this. The Lifelong learning boxes in Total English offer help in this task and showing students how to use their Portfolio is another way that teachers can help.

Portfolio task

Download the Total English Portfolio free from www.longman.com/totalenglish.

Objective: to introduce learners to the 'Dossier' section of their Portfolio.

This task can be done in Ss' L1.

The Dossier section of the Portfolio allows Ss to record and store examples of good work in English to show other people. It can include anything from stories to recorded interviews to videos.

1 ▶ Explain the purpose of the Dossier section of the Portfolio to Ss.

2 ▶ Ask Ss to look back at their work over the last few months and choose one or two pieces of work which they feel proud of.

3 ▶ Ask Ss to compare the work in groups and explain why they feel proud.

4 ▶ Ask Ss to record details of the work relevant section of their Dossier and store the work separately in a Dossier folder. If necessary, learners might like to redo the work, correcting mistakes from the original version.

10 Wildlife

Overview

Lead-in	**Vocabulary:** animals
10.1	**Grammar:** phrasal verbs **Can do:** talk about people who influenced you
10.2	**Grammar:** countable/uncountable nouns **Can do:** write a short contribution for a bulletin board
10.3	**Grammar:** the definite article (*the*) **Vocabulary:** verb + prepositions (1) **Can do:** speculate about sounds and pictures
Com. Focus	Animal protection
Reference	
Practice	

Summary

Lesson 1: Ss read a text about children who were raised by animals and discuss the meaning of the phrasal verbs that are used. Then they listen to a woman talking about her childhood and the people who influenced her.

Lesson 2: Ss talk about the advantages and disadvantages of zoos and read an Internet bulletin board where people express their points of view with regard to this issue.

Lesson 3: Ss identify different animal noises and then read about a TV programme designed to be watched by pets. Then they listen to a radio programme about pet TV.

Communication Focus: Ss read about the World Wildlife Fund, the Monkey Sanctuary and the Royal Society for the Prevention of Cruelty to Animals and then discuss what they would do if they had £1,000 to spend on helping animals.

Film bank: Wolves (3'07")

A documentary about wolves and our fear of them

From fairy tales to horror films, we are expected to be afraid of wolves. But what are wolves really like and should we really be afraid of them? This film explores the topic through cartoons, film trailers and documentary footage.

Possible places to use this short film are:

▶ after Lesson 1 to extend the topic of the relationship between man and animals

▶ before Lesson 2 to introduce the topic of freedom and captivity for animals

▶ at the end of the unit to round up the topic and language

For ways to use this short film in class, see Students' Book page 142 and Teacher's Book page 193.

Lead-in

▶ Introduce Ss to the topic of wildlife.

Q: What is wildlife? Wildlife generally refers to animals that live in the wild as opposed to domesticated animals or pets.

Q: Do you have any pets? Did you have any pets when you were younger? Would you like to have a pet? What kind?

Q: What wild animals can you think of? Have you ever seen any of these animals? Do you ever watch documentaries about wild animals? What kind?

1a▶ Ss look at the photos and name the animals they can see with a partner. Get feedback from various Ss.

Answers: Pic 1: horses Pic 2: eagle Pic 3: spider Pic 4: killer whale

b▶ In pairs, Ss divide the animals into four groups. Tell Ss that some words can go into more than one group.

Suggested answers: wild animals: tiger, lion, elephant, hyena, bear, wolf, snake, zebra, eagle, whale; domestic animals: dog, cat, horse, cow; insects: spider; sea animals: snake, whale

c▶ Ss add two more examples to each list. Get feedback from the whole class and write the extra animals on the board.

2a▶ Ss work in pairs to complete the sentences. Tell them to think about the animals' behaviour and the meaning of the expressions in their own native language in order to make educated guesses. Get feedback from various Ss.

Answers: 1 mouse 2 horse 3 fish 4 rat 5 cat 6 birds

b▶ Ss try to find similar expressions in their own language. In multilingual classes, try to group students with the same mother tongue together.

▶ If you want to give Ss extra practice with these expressions, have them work in groups to make sentences using the expressions in a definite context, e.g., *If I go to England and get a job, I can make some money and practise English, and kill two birds with one stone.*

EXTEND THE LEAD-IN

Play 'Guess my animal'. Think of an animal and tell the Ss that they have to guess what it is by asking questions with *yes/no* answers. Give the Ss a minute to think of some questions in pairs before you begin e.g., *Is it big? Is it brown? Is it wild? Does it live in forests? Is it from Africa? Does it eat fruit?*
Now have the Ss play the game in small groups.

10.1 Raised by animals

There have been forty well-documented cases of 'feral' children (children raised by animals in the wild) in the last few hundred years. Most of these children were either lost or taken by animals when they were only a few months old and have grown up learning the behaviour and customs of the animal that has adopted them. These animals include wolves, monkeys and even an ostrich. The authenticity of these stories, however, has yet to be proved.

In this lesson Ss read about Romulus and Remus and the wolf girls, Kamala and Amala. Through this context they learn various phrasal verbs.

OPTIONAL WARMER

Write: *raising a child* on the board and elicit/teach the meaning. Ask: **Q: What are the most important things you have to think about when you are raising a child?** Ss discuss in pairs. Get feedback from the whole class.

Reading

1 ▶ Focus Ss on the photos and tell them to discuss the question in pairs. Encourage Ss to talk about all the things they know in relation to each photo. Get feedback from the whole group.

Answers: Upper left: Romulus and Remus. They are believed to have founded Rome in Roman mythology. Upper middle: Tarzan, a child brought up by gorillas. Upon discovering he is human, he must decide in which world he belongs. The two most important films of this are Disney's *Tarzan* and the 1984 *Greystoke*. Bottom: Mowgli, main character in *The Jungle Book* by Rudyard Kipling first published in 1893 and first made into a Disney film in 1967. Top right: Kamala and Amala, the two sisters found in the care of a wolf in India in 1920.

2 ▶ Ss read quickly through the text and answer the question. Check with the whole class (four children are mentioned).

3 ▶ Read through the questions with the whole class and then tell the Ss to read the text again and answer the questions with a partner.

Answers: 1 the Roman god Mars 2 by the banks of the River Tiber 3 a wolf 4 a shepherd 5 They built a town in the place where the shepherd found them. 6 Romulus killed Remus. 7 a wolf 8 Their relationship with the other children was very bad. 9 They could see and hear very well. 10 Amala died one year later and Kamala died nine years later.

4 ▶ Ss work in pairs or small groups to discuss the questions. Get feedback from the whole class.

OPTIONAL EXTENSION

If you have access to the Internet, Ss can look at: www. feralchildren.com. They can make notes on a similar story and then tell the rest of the class.

Vocabulary

▶ Ask Ss to brainstorm any phrasal verbs they know already (If Ss struggle to do this you could refer them back to the phrasal verbs in lessons 5.2, 8.1 and 8.2. Get feedback, writing the phrasal verbs on the board and eliciting examples of how they could be used.

5 ▶ Ss work in pairs to match the underlined phrasal verbs in the text with the definitions. Tell them to write the infinitive form of the phrasal verb, as in the text they are in the Past. Check the answers with the whole class.

Answers: 1 to grow up 2 to pick up 3 to look after 4 to bring up 5 to come across 6 to look up to

6 ▶ Ss work in pairs to complete the sentences. Tell them to pay special attention to the form of the verb. Check the answers with the whole class.

Answers: 1 bring up 2 looked up to 3 picked up 4 came across 5 grew up 6 look after

7a ▶ Ss complete the questions in pairs. Tell them to pay attention to the form of the verb.

b ▶ Play recording 10.1 and Ss check their answers.

Answers: 1 Where did you grow up? 2 Who brought you up? 3 As a child, who looked after you when you were ill? 4 As a child, who did you look up to? 5 Have you ever picked up any English from TV or songs? 6 Have you ever come across any money in the street?

Pronunciation

8a ▶ Play recording 10.1 again and Ss underline the words that are stressed. Allow them to check with a partner and then elicit the answers. Point out that with phrasal verbs we usually stress the particle and not the main verb.

Answers: See answers to Ex. 7b

b ▶ Ss ask and answer the questions in pairs. Encourage them to ask follow-up questions where appropriate. Go around the class monitoring their conversations. Get feedback from several Ss.

Lifelong learning

▶ Read through the notes with the class. In pairs, Ss talk about what they normally do and the advantages and disadvantages of each approach. Get feedback from Ss and discuss the different possibilities.

▶ Tell the good idea to have a small vocabulary notebook which they can carry around with them. In this way they can make the most of free moments to have a look at it and test their memories.

OPTIONAL EXTENSION

To practise some of the methods suggested, ask Ss to choose two or three words from the course book which they have learnt. In pairs, they write a definition of one of the words, use another in an example and, in monolingual classes, translate the other.

Ask various Ss to read out their definitions and the other Ss guess the word. Ask other Ss to read out their example sentences and the other Ss must say what the word means. If you have used translation, get some Ss to read out their word in the mother tongue and the other Ss say the word in English.

Listening and speaking

9a▶ Play recording 10.2 and Ss listen to the woman and say which two people most influenced her childhood (her mother and grandmother).

b▶ Read through the statements with the whole class and play recording 10.2 again. Ss decide which statement is false. Allow them to compare with a partner before eliciting the answer (number 4 is false as she says that she didn't take to her teachers and school wasn't easy).

▶ If you feel Ss can cope with more vocabulary, explain the meaning of *take to* (like) and tell Ss to add it to the list of phrasal verbs in Ex. 5. You could also tell them to write an example sentence with this phrasal verb.

c▶ Focus Ss on the How to ... box and read through the notes. Play recording 10.2 again and Ss count the times they hear each phrase.

Answers: I mean ... (2); Well, ... (1); So, anyway ... (1); You see ... (1)

▶ Explain to the Ss that these phrases are very common in normal conversation and help the flow and fluency of what is being said.

10▶ Ss talk about the question in pairs. Go around the class monitoring their conversations and making a note of any mistakes Ss make.

▶ When they have finished, write the mistakes on the board. Ask Ss to try to correct them.

OPTIONAL VARIATION

Refer Ss to the tapescript of recording 10.2 on page 158 and ask them to write something similar about themselves. Tell them to include the expressions from the How to ... box. Make sure Ss realise that this is not normal in writing, but they are doing this to prepare for speaking.
Finally, have them read their pieces of writing in pairs, using the appropriate conversational phrases.

10.2 Zoos: for or against?

For some years now there has been a growing debate about the advantages and disadvantages of keeping animals in zoos. Those who favour zoos argue that animals that are in danger of extinction can be bred in zoos thus preserving the species. Moreover, most zoos now treat animals much better than in the past and are a form of both entertainment and education. Those against zoos maintain that keeping animals in captivity is cruel and shows a lack of respect for both animals and the environment.

In this lesson Ss read some arguments for and against zoos and through this context, look at the grammar of countable and uncountable nouns.

OPTIONAL WARMER

Write *for or against*? on the board and elicit/teach the meaning. Tell the Ss that you are going to say a number of sentences and those who are *for* must stand up and those who are *against* stay sitting down.

Read out the following sentences and elicit reasons for and against from those who stand up and from those who remain sitting down.
The teacher should give more homework. It's fantastic to have a pet. You should never eat fast-food. People shouldn't be allowed to drive their cars in city centres. We should have longer holidays.

Tell the Ss that the next lesson is about arguments for and against zoos.

Reading

1a▶ Ss work in pairs to make a list of advantages and disadvantages of zoos.

b▶ Each pair joins with another pair to compare their ideas. Get feedback from the whole class, writing two columns entitled *advantages* and *disadvantages*) on the board.

▶ Focus the Ss on the photos and ask them:
Q: What can you see in the photos? Does each photo contribute to the arguments for or against zoos?

2▶ Ss quickly read the bulletin board and say if each person is for or against zoos. Check with the whole class.

Answers: against: Chris, Katie and Dave for: Tania

3▶ Read through the questions with the whole class. Ss work in pairs to read the messages again and answer the questions.

Answers: 1 Chris 2 Katie 3 Dave 4 Chris

▶ Ask Ss if there is any vocabulary in the messages that Ss don't understand and encourage other Ss to explain before doing so yourself.

4▶ Ss discuss the question in pairs. Get feedback from the whole class.

Grammar

OPTIONAL GRAMMAR LEAD-IN

Write the following sentences on the board. In pairs, Ss to find two mistakes in each one and correct them.
Much zoos is in a very bad condition.
My moneys are in my pocket.

Elicit the corrections and ask:
Q: Is *zoo* countable or uncountable? (countable)
Explain that this is why the verb must be plural and *much* has to be replaced by *many*.
Q: Is *money* countable or uncountable? (uncountable)
Explain that this is why *money* can't be plural and the verb must be singular.

5a▸ Ss read the sentences and answer the question with a partner. Check with the whole class (*animals* is countable and *information* is uncountable).

b▸ Focus Ss on the words in the box and the Active grammar notes. Ss work in pairs to put the words into the correct column. Draw two columns headed *countable* and *uncountable* on the board. Elicit words to complete them.

Active grammar

countable: holiday, newspaper, job, cheque
uncountable: travel, furniture, work, news, advice, money

▸ Draw a third column on the board with the heading *both*. Explain that some words can be either countable or uncountable. Write *coffee*, *glass* and *hair* on the board.

▸ Give two example sentences with *hair* to demonstrate the difference e.g., *There's a hair in my soup*; *She's got red hair.* In pairs, Ss try to write two example sentences which demonstrate the distinction for *glass* and *coffee*. Get feedback from the whole glass.

▸ Refer the Ss to Reference page 103 and read through the list of uncountable nouns with the whole class.

▸ Give Ss time to read through the rest of the grammar rules and then ask the following questions:
Q: Do we use *a/an* with countable or uncountable nouns? (countable) **Q: Do we use *much* with countable or uncountable nouns?** (uncountable) **Q: Do we use *a bit of* with countable or uncountable nouns?** (uncountable)
Q: What do we usually use in affirmative clauses? (*some*)
Q: What do we usually use in negative and interrogative clauses? (*any*) **Q: When can we use *some* in questions?** (when we expect the person to say yes).

6▸ Ss work in pairs to choose the correct alternative. Elicit answers from various Ss.

Answers: 1 a lot of 2 much 3 some 4 a few 5 a bit of 6 much

7▸ Ss work in pairs to correct the mistakes.

Answers: 1 ... got a new job. 2 ... a few lions. 3 ... a small piece of advice 4 ... a lot of money ... 5 ... a cheque ... 6 ... some great news ...

OPTIONAL EXTENSION

Write the following things on the board: *pollution*; *sports facilities*; *good clubs*; *good food*; *cinemas*; *violence*; *hot weather*; *job opportunities.* In small groups, Ss talk about these factors and say how much or how little there is/are in the town they are in at the moment. Go around monitoring the use of countable/uncountable structures. Finally get feedback.

Writing

8▸ Ss read through the example sentences and choose the correct alternative. Check with the whole class (*although* is followed by a clause). Explain that *although* is used to contrast two opposing ideas. If Ss are finding this difficult give them an extra example e.g., Although she didn't study she passed the exam. Ask Ss to rewrite the sentence putting *although* in the middle.

9▸ Ss write sentences with *although* in pairs. Go around the class monitoring their work as they do this. Check the answers with the whole class.

Answers: 1 We went to the zoo although we've been there before. Although we've been there before, we went to the zoo. 2 This book has been very successful although the author isn't very well-known. Although the author isn't very well known, this book has been very successful. 3 Our staff are getting a pay increase although we can't really afford it. Although we can't really afford it, our staff are getting a pay increase. 4 I want to take up sky diving although it's very dangerous. Although it's very dangerous, I want to take up sky diving. 5 He wants to study Zoology at university although he never reads any books. Although he never reads any books, he wants to study Zoology at university.

10a▸ Ss read the bulletin board in the Writing bank on page 148 and do the exercises. Check with the class.

1▸ Answers: 1 T 2 T 3 F 4 T 5 F

2▸ Answers: 1 it's 2 its 3 its 4 it's

b▸ In pairs, Ss have an imaginary 'online' discussion (on A4 paper) like the one in Ex. 2 by writing their opinions about one of the topics.

c▸ Ss exchange papers with another pair who have written about a different topic. The Ss then respond to the argument, writing their opinions. Papers can be exchanged several times.

OPTIONAL VARIATION

Divide the class into two groups, A and B. Ss in group A think of arguments for the topics in Ex. 10b. Ss in group B think of arguments against. Then put two Ss from A with two from B and they have a group debate. Alternatively, have a whole class debate. In the end, Ss vote for or against, expressing their real opinion.

10.3 Pet TV

The BBC (British Broadcasting Corporation) believes it has a duty to serve minority audiences and in 2004 introduced the new concept of 'pet TV'. 'The sound of running water might attract your fish to the screen, and the sight of fish swimming around a tank might attract your cat' (BBC).

In this lesson Ss read and listen about *Pet TV* and through this context, they analyse the grammar of the definite article.

OPTIONAL WARMER

Write *TV* on the board and ask Ss to brainstorm different types of TV programmes e.g., *documentaries, news, films, soap operas, chat shows, situation comedy, quizzes, sports, cartoons.*
Get feedback from the class and write the words on the board. Now ask:
Q: What type of people do you think normally like each type of programme? Ss talk with their partner and then share their ideas with the rest of the class.
Q: Do you think pets would like any of these programmes? Elicit student response.
Tell Ss that the next lesson is about Pet TV.

Reading and listening

1► Focus Ss on the picture and tell them to answer the questions in pairs, giving reasons for their answers. Get feedback from the whole class.

2► Ss read through the text and answer as many as the questions as they can in pairs. Make sure they understand that they will not be able to answer all the questions. Check the answers with the whole group.

Answers: 1 *Pet TV* 2 next week 3 don't know 4 to find out what animals respond to 5 don't know 6 don't know

3a► Focus Ss back on the list in Ex. 1. Play recording 10.3 and ask them to listen and tick the ones they hear.

Answers: All the things in the list are mentioned.

b► Play recording 10.3 again and Ss answer the rest of the questions from Ex. 2. Make sure they know that they only have to answer questions 3, 5 and 6. Allow them to compare with a partner and then get feedback.

Answers: 3 dogs, cats, birds and fish 5 on the BBC website 6 cats mewing, birds singing, and mice squeaking and images including balls of string, birds and mice. (It is not necessary for Ss to know the exact sounds of the animals, simply saying the sound of a cat is enough.)

4► Ss discuss the questions in pairs. Get feedback from the whole class.

Vocabulary

5► Ss match the beginnings and endings of the sentences in pairs. Check the answers with the whole group.

Answers: 1 c) 2 a) 3 f) 4 h) 5 g) 6 e) 7 d) 8 b)

► Explain to the Ss that these verbs need these dependent prepositions to connect them to the object. Point out that the prepositions do not change the meaning of the verb as happens with phrasal verbs.

6a► Ss complete the questions with a preposition in pairs. Check with the whole class.

Answers: 1 to 2 on 3 for 4 to 5 to 6 about 7 with 8 on

b► Ss ask and answer the questions in pairs. Go around the class making a note of the most important mistakes that they make as they do this. When they have finished the exercise, talk about these mistakes, encouraging Ss to self-correct first.

OPTIONAL EXTENSION

Ss choose one of the verb + preposition combinations and write another question which they would be able to ask other Ss in the class. Ss stand up and mingle, asking and answering each other's questions. Finally, Ss report back on what they have found out.

Grammar

OPTIONAL GRAMMAR LEAD-IN

Write the following sentences on the board and ask Ss to copy them, putting *the* where necessary.
1 *Sam is tallest person in class.* 2 *I like dogs a lot.* 3 *We stayed at a hotel when I was on holiday. Hotel was very expensive but it wasn't very nice.* 4 *What was weather like yesterday?*
Ss compare with a partner. Check the answers.
1 Sam is *the* tallest person in the class. 2 Correct. 3 *The* hotel was very expensive ... 4 What was *the* weather like yesterday?

7► Ss match the examples to the rules. Check with the whole class.

Active grammar

a 2 b 3 c 1

► Refer Ss to Reference page 103 and tell them to read through the notes for this grammar point. Tell them to think about their mother tongue as they do this and compare the English use of *the* with their own language. (Ss with the same mother tongue can do this in pairs.)

► Get feedback from the Ss about the points which differ in English from the rules in their own language. Tell Ss to make a mental note of these points in particular.

8a► Ss complete the sentences in pairs.

b ▶ Play recording 10.4. Ss listen and check their answers.

> **Answers:** 1 the 2 (–) 3 the 4 the 5 (–) 6 the 7 the 8 (–)

▶ Ask the Ss what they notice about the pronunciation of *the*. In all of these sentences *the* is pronounced /ðə/ and it is not stressed. Point out that *the* is pronounced /ðiː/ if it comes before a vowel e.g., *the apple*.

c ▶ Play recording 10.4 again, pausing at the end of each sentence while Ss repeat. Then tell them to practise saying the sentences in pairs.

9a ▶ Read the example sentences with the whole class and put Ss in pairs to find and correct the mistakes. Check the answers together.

> **Answers:** 1 Do you prefer cats or dogs? 2 Correct. 3 Correct. 4 What age do you think children should have to stay at school until? 5 Correct. 6 What's the most beautiful place you have been to? 7 Do you think that money makes you happy? 8 Correct.

b ▶ Ss ask and answer the questions in pairs. Go around the class monitoring their conversations. Finally, get feedback from the whole class.

Speaking

10a ▶ Focus on the How to ... box and read through the different forms of speculating. Ss listen to the advert for cats and then speculate about the sounds in pairs.

▶ Play recording 10.5. Stop after each noise to allow Ss to talk in pairs and note down their speculations.

> **Answers:** As this is speculation, accept any justifiable answers although the actual sounds are as follows:
> 1 snooker ball being hit and falling off a table 2 cat pushing along a toy ball with a bell inside 3 water fountain 4 animal scratching itself 5 birds in a cage 6 rabbit eating lettuce

b ▶ Tell Ss to look at the pictures on page 132 and speculate with a partner as to what they might be. Get feedback from the whole class.

> **Answers:** Again accept any reasonable speculation although the correct answers are: 1 a cat's paw 2 a birdbox in a tree 3 fish in a fish tank 4 a TV remote control 5 a dog's kennel

OPTIONAL EXTENSION

Divide the class into groups. One student from each group is blindfolded. Other Ss in the group make noises so that the student can speculate what it is e.g., *slamming the door, stamping their feet*
Extend this to other senses e.g., smell and touch. Blindfolded Ss feel or smell different things and guess what they are. As preparation, tell Ss to bring in food items like crisps or spices, or do this yourself.

Communication: Animal protection

In this lesson Ss read information about various charities that are involved in protecting animals. They also plan a contribution to this movement of their own.

Write *animals in danger* on the board and ask Ss to talk in pairs about what things people do to help animals in danger. Get feedback from the whole class.

1 ▶ Read through the questions with the whole class and put Ss in pairs to read the information and answer the questions. Check together.

> **Answers:** 1 the RSCPA 2 the Monkey Sanctuary Trust 3 WWF (the World Wildlife Fund) 4 the Monkey Sanctuary Trust 5 WWF (the World Wildlife Fund) 6 the RSCPA

▶ Ask the Ss if there are any words they don't understand and encourage other Ss to explain before doing so yourself.

OPTIONAL EXTENSION

Ask Ss to work in pairs to write three more questions as in Ex. 1 about the charity information. Ss then swap questions with another pair and answer them.

2a ▶ Read through the situation with the whole class and tell Ss to think for a minute about what they would do with the £1,000 and why.

b ▶ Put Ss in groups of four and Ss discuss their ideas and draw up a list of things they could spend their money on. Finally, they make a decision about how to spend the money.

3 ▶ Each group chooses a spokesperson who presents their ideas to the rest of the class.

Review and practice

1▶

Answers: 1 (–) 2 (–) 3 (–) 4 a 5 (–) 6 (–) 7 an

2▶

Answers: 1 a/a/the 2 a 3 the 4 (-) 5 the 6 (–) 7 the

3▶

Answers: 1 much 2 a lot 3 piece 4 some 5 little 6 many 7 a lot of

4▶

Answers: 1 few 2 of 3 many 4 a 5 piece

5▶

Answers: 1 on 2 to 3 with 4 on 5 for 6 about 7 to 8 to

6▶

Answers: 1 depends 2 up 3 rat 4 after 5 cat 6 up 7 fish 8 mouse 9 up 10 grew

Notes for using the Common European Framework (CEF)

CEF References

10.1 Can do: talk about people who influenced you

CEF B1 descriptor: can convey information and ideas on abstract as well as concrete topics, check information and ask about or explain problems with reasonable precision (CEF page 83)

10.2 Can do: write a short contribution for a bulletin board

CEF B1 descriptor: can produce continuous writing which is generally intelligible throughout (CEF page118)

10.3 Can do: speculate about sounds and pictures

CEF B1 descriptor: can explain why something is a problem, discuss what to do next, compare and contrast alternatives (CEF page 79)

CEF quick brief

The Common European Framework suggests that learners need more than language knowledge to communicate successfully in a language. They also need 'communicative competences' which empower the learner to actually use their knowledge. The How to ... boxes in Total English are designed to develop communicative competences.

Portfolio task

Download the Total English Portfolio free from www.longman.com/totalenglish.

Objective: to reinforce student autonomy in updating the Portfolio.

This task can be done in Ss' L1.

1▶ For homework, ask Ss to update the Passport section of their Portfolio. They might like to reassess their abilities in the different skills areas or add to their list of language learning and intercultural experiences.

2▶ Ask Ss to bring their Passport sections in and show them to other Ss.

11 Travel

Overview

Lead-in	**Vocabulary:** transport
11.1	**Grammar:** Present Perfect Simple with *just, yet, already*
	Vocabulary: holidays
	Can do: find out if someone would be a good travel companion
11.2	**Grammar:** verbs with two objects
	Vocabulary: greetings and presents
	Can do: make generalisations about customs
11.3	**Grammar:** Past Perfect Simple
	Can do: write about a place you've travelled to
Com. Focus	Single or return?
Reference	
Practice	

Summary

Lesson 1: Ss discuss what problems you can have with travel companions and read an extract from a diary, in which Lucy complains about her travel companion, Andy. Then they listen to a conversation in which Lucy tells Andy that she doesn't want to travel with him anymore.

Lesson 2: Ss complete sentences about customs in different countries. Then half the Ss read a text offering advice to business travellers on giving gifts to people from different cultures and the other half read a text about cultural differences in forms of address, personal space and physical greetings.

Lesson 3: Ss listen to an interview with a travel writer in which she talks about her childhood, how she got into travel writing and the difficulties she faces.

Communication Focus: Ss listen to four conversations about travelling on different types of transport. Then they role-play buying a ticket at the train station.

Film bank: Gill's wild world (3'19")

A short film about the life of a travel writer

Gill Williams is the travel editor for a British newspaper and makes travel programmes about various destinations. We find out how she feels about travelling all the time and what places she would still like to visit.

Possible places to use this short film are:

▶ before the Lesson 3 as an introduction to the topic of travel writers

▶ after Lesson 3 to extend the topic of travel writers

▶ at the end of the unit to round up the topic and language

For ways to use this short film in class, see Students' Book page 143 and Teacher's Book page 194.

Lead-in

▶ Introduce Ss to the topic of travel. Write *travel* on the board and ask: **Q: How often do you travel? Q: Where do you usually travel to?**
Q: What types of transport do you usually take? If Ss only answer with regard to their holidays ask: **Q: What type of transport do you use in the city?**
Q: Do you like travelling? Encourage Ss to answer with regard to both holidays and day-to-day travelling.
Q: If *travel* is a verb, what is the noun and who is the person who travels? Elicit or teach *trip* (although *travel* can sometimes be used as a noun e.g., *on my travels* or as a collective noun, it isn't common and it's better to concentrate on *trip* at this level). The person is *traveller*.

1▶ Ss work in pairs to find the words in the word search. Check they understand the meaning of *across* and *down*. Get feedback from the whole group, having individual Ss pronounce the words.

▶ Point out the difference between a motorbike and a moped (a moped is small and has a low-powered engine whereas a motorbike is bigger and has a high-powered engine) and coach and bus (coach is normally between cities and bus within a city).

Answers: across: motorbike, coach, ferry, bicycle, train, van, plane down: car, moped, taxi, bus, lorry

2a▶ Ss match the words and forms of transport in pairs.

b▶ Play recording 11.1 and have Ss check their answers.

Answers: go by: bus, coach, ferry, train, plane, motorbike, taxi or car
get on/off: a bus, coach, ferry, train, plane, motorbike, moped or bicycle
get into/out of: a taxi, van or car
catch: a bus, coach, ferry or train
take: a bus, coach, ferry, plane, train or taxi
miss: a bus, coach, ferry, plane or train
ride: a motorbike, moped or bicycle

3a▶ Ss work in pairs to correct the sentences. Get feedback from different Ss.

Answers: 1 by 2 riding 3 on 4 take 5 off 6 missed

b▶ Ss ask and answer the questions in pairs. Get feedback from the whole class.

EXTEND THE LEAD-IN

Write *train, coach, car, plane, motorbike* on the board. Tell Ss to imagine they are going to travel to a place about 200 km away. In small groups, Ss rank, from most to least, the five types of transport according to the categories: safest, most comfortable, cheapest, most enjoyable. Get feedback from the class. Then ask which type of transport they would choose.

11.1 Travel companions

Travelling is not always easy and it's not surprising that travel companions often get on each other's nerves. Some companies like e–travel, now give advice on choosing a travel companion. They suggest that before your trip you speak openly about the activities you want to do, the type of accommodation preferred, and the money situation as well as considering each other's personality traits.

In this lesson Ss read a diary extract about a difficult travel companion and through this context consider the grammar of *just*, *yet* and *already*.

OPTIONAL WARMER

Introduce the topic of holidays and travelling by asking: **Q: When did you last go on holiday? Where did you go? Who did you go with? Do you prefer to travel with other people or alone?**
Ask Ss to brainstorm in pairs the advantages and disadvantages of travelling with other people. Get feedback and write the two lists on the board.

Reading

1▶ Ss discuss the questions with a partner. Get feedback, focusing particularly on question 2.

2▶ Focus Ss' attention on the photo and ask them what they can see (a woman on holiday, backpacking).

▶ Ss read the diary extract quickly and say which annoying habits are mentioned (he talks a lot, snores and complains). Tell them not to worry about any words they don't understand at this stage.

3▶ Tell the Ss they are going to listen to a summary of Lucy's diary but with three mistakes. Play recording 11.2 and Ss listen. Allow them to compare with a partner and then play the recording again if necessary. Check the answers with the whole class.

Answers: 1 The recording says that Lucy is worried about travelling with Andy but in the beginning she thinks it's a good idea. 2 The recording says they are travelling by train but they are travelling by bus. 3 The recording says that on Tuesday afternoon Andy is shouting and annoying Lucy but he is singing to himself.

▶ Ask Ss if there is any vocabulary in the diary extract that they still don't understand and encourage other Ss to explain before doing so yourself.

4a▶ Ss write out a dialogue in pairs in which Lucy tells Andy that she doesn't want to travel with him anymore. Go around the class monitoring and picking up any mistakes.

b▶ Ss practise their dialogue. Ask for volunteers to role play their dialogue for the rest of the class.

c▶ Play recording 11.3. After they have listened, Ss comment on the dialogue in pairs, saying in what ways it was different from theirs. Get feedback from the class.

Grammar

OPTIONAL GRAMMAR LEAD-IN

Write the following mixed up sentences on the board. Ss work in pairs, with books closed, to try to order the sentences. Check with the whole class and write the correct sentences on the board.
1 *just he asleep has fallen* (He has just fallen asleep).
2 *already Andy me to annoy started has* (Andy has already started to annoy me).
3 *stopped yet he has talking not* (he has not stopped talking yet).
Ask Ss what tense is being used (Present Perfect). Underline the words *just*, *already* and *yet* and tell the Ss that they are going to study the use of the Present Perfect with these words.

5▶ Focus Ss on the Active grammar box. Tell them to read through the grammar notes and complete the rules with *just, yet* or *already.* Check with the whole class.

Active grammar

a) *Just* means a short time ago.
b) *Already* shows that something happened sooner than expected.
c) *Yet* shows that the speaker expected something to happen before now.

▶ Tell Ss to look at Reference page 113. Give them a few minutes to read through the information and then ask:
Q: Where do you usually put *just* in the sentence? (between *has/have* and the Past Participle)
Q: Where do you usually put *already* in the sentence? (between *has/have* and the Past Participle or at the end of the sentence)
Q: Where do you usually put *yet* in the sentence? (at the end) **With what type of sentences do we usually use *yet*?** (negative and interrogative)
▶ If Ss are having problems with these structures, give them more examples e.g., *We have just completed the Active grammar box*; *We have already studied units 1–10; We haven't finished the course book yet.*

6▶ Ss write *just*, *yet* or *already* in the correct place in pairs. Check the answers with the whole class.

Answers: 1 Simon's already left the party. 2 Diana hasn't phoned yet. 3 I've already spent all my money. 4 Have you written any postcards yet? 5 My parents have just come back from holiday.

Pronunciation

7a▶ Ask Ss to pronounce *yet* and *just* in pairs. Play recording 11.4 and Ss check the pronunciation.

b▶ Ss practise saying the sentences with a partner. Go around the class checking pronunciation as they do this.

8▶ Ss turn to page 132. Focus them on the words in the box and check they understand all the words. In pairs, they make sentences using *just* and *yet* and the words in the box. Get feedback from the whole class.

Answers: 1 She has just folded her clothes. 2 She hasn't packed her bag yet. 3 She has just washed her hair. 4 She hasn't dried her hair yet. 5 She hasn't made the bed yet. 6 She has just brushed her teeth. 7 She has just had a shower. 8 She hasn't written her postcards yet.

Vocabulary

9a▶ Focus on the photos. Ss say what type of holiday they can see in pairs. Get feedback from the class.

Answers: Pic A: camping holiday Pic B: sightseeing holiday Pic C: skiing holiday Pic D: beach holiday

OPTIONAL EXTENSION

In pairs, Ss think of a place they would recommend for each type of holiday, giving reasons for their choice.

b▶ Ss match the opposites. Check the answers with the whole class.

Answers: 1 d) 2 a) 3 f) 4 c) 5 g) 6 b) 7 e)

10▶ Put Ss in pairs. Tell one of the two to close their books while the other tests them on three or four of the new expressions. Ss then change roles.

11▶ Focus on the How to ... box and read through the notes with the Ss. Tell Ss that they are going to describe a really good holiday they have had. Give them a few minutes to plan what they are going to say and make notes.

▶ Ss tell each other about their holidays in pairs. Monitor conversations and note errors. Finally, write the errors on the board and encourage Ss to self-correct.

Speaking and writing

12a▶ Play recording 11.5. Ss listen and write the questions they hear. Allow them to compare with a partner and play the recording again if necessary.

Answers: See transcript on page 158.

b▶ Ss write two more questions in pairs.

13a▶ Ss change partners and ask and answer their questions, making a note of each other's answers. After a few minutes, tell Ss to stop, change partners again and repeat the exercise. Do this a number of times.

b▶ Eventually Ss go back to their original partner and tell each other who is the best travel companion for them and why. Get feedback from various Ss.

c▶ Ss write about that travel companion.

Lifelong learning

▶ Read through the suggestion with the whole class and ask how many Ss normally do this. In pairs, Ss think of three or four pairs of opposites. They then test other Ss in the class by saying one word and eliciting the opposite.

11.2 Customs worldwide

Successful communication between people from different cultures depends in part, on an intercultural understanding of customs and ways of behaving. Failure to comprehend factors such as customs when greeting a stranger, hospitality or certain forms of body language can cause grave problems and embarrassment.

In this lesson Ss read some advice for business travellers and through this context consider the grammar of verbs with two objects.

OPTIONAL WARMER

Write *intercultural differences* on the board and elicit/teach the meaning (the differences between different cultures in ways of behaving and customs).

In small groups, Ss brainstorm some intercultural differences that they have noticed between their own culture and other cultures e.g., when travelling. Get feedback from the whole class.

Vocabulary

1▶ Focus Ss on the photos and tell them to discuss with a partner what they can see, using the words in the box. Get feedback from the whole class and ask them in which cultures they think this behaviour is common.

2a▶ Ss complete the sentences in pairs with the words in the box.

b▶ Play recording 11.6 and Ss listen and check their answers.

Answers: 1 wave 2 shake hands 3 bow 4 kiss

c▶ Ss discuss the question. Get feedback from the whole class.

Reading

3▶ Divide the class into two groups A and B. As look at the text on page 108 and Bs look at the text on page 129.

▶ Ss read through the text quickly to see which of the things in Ex. 2 are mentioned. Tell them not to worry about any vocabulary they don't understand at this stage. Get feedback.

Answers: Student A's text mentions giving gifts and student B's text mentions shaking hands and bowing.

4a▶ Ask Ss to read the text again in pairs and to make a note about the significance of the things listed in the box. Tell them to help each other with any difficult vocabulary or to ask you.

b▶ Pair student As and Bs. Student A asks student B about their text. Encourage Ss to answer the questions using their own words rather than reading from the text.

c▶ Following the same procedure student B asks student A about his/her text.

▶ Tell Ss to close their books and check the answers with the whole class.

Answers: Student A's text: 1 at the end of a visit 2 a pen or something not available in Japan 3 No, it's unlucky. 4 No, because the word for *clock* is similar to the word for *death*. 5 Because many of the best leather products come from South America. 6 No, because they are sometimes associated with romance.
Student B's text: 1 No, they normally use surnames. 2 in the Middle East 3 Because they feel uncomfortable if you stand too close. 4 No, you shouldn't. 5 Yes, sometimes when greeting Westerners. 6 No, they don't.

5▶ Tell Ss to answer the first question with a partner and get feedback from the class. (This is a traditional English saying which means that when we are in a different country/region we should adopt the habits and customs of the local people).

▶ Now ask Ss to discuss the second question and get feedback. This needs to be handled with some sensitivity so don't prolong the discussion if some Ss are likely to be offended by the opinions of others.

OPTIONAL EXTENSION

In pairs, Ss write a humorous mini-dialogue which demonstrates a cultural misunderstanding. The dialogue should be between people of different nationalities in a specific situation. As they write the dialogues go around the class monitoring Ss' work. When they have finished Ss act out the situation for other Ss.

Grammar

OPTIONAL GRAMMAR LEAD-IN

Write the following stem sentences on the board. In pairs, discuss ways of completing them.
1 *When you are invited to somebody's house for dinner it's a good idea to take the host/hostess ...*
2 *When somebody is ill in hospital, you should give them ...*
3 *If it is your teacher's birthday, you could bring her/him ....*
Get feedback from the class and complete each sentence on the board with one example e.g., 1 a bottle of wine. 2 grapes. 3 a big present.

Underline the direct and the indirect object in the second part of the sentence (the host/a bottle of wine; them/grapes; her/him/a big present).

In pairs, Ss discuss which one of the objects underlined in each sentence is direct and one is indirect. Check the answers with the whole class (in each case the first object is indirect and the second is direct).

6▶ Ss read through the Active grammar box and write *to* where necessary in the example sentences.

Active grammar
1 It is polite to bring your host flowers.
2 It is polite to bring flowers *to* your host.

▶ Ask the Ss:
Q: Which structure is more common in English?
(number 1)

▶ Ss should feel quite comfortable with this structure, but if not refer them to Reference page 113 and go through some more examples with the whole class.

7a▶ Ss correct the mistakes in pairs.

b▶ Play recording 11.7. Ss listen and check their answers.

Answers: 1 Our company offers you more choice. 2 I lent him €20 about three weeks ago. 3 Could you bring me that book when you come? 4 He sent her a huge bunch of flowers. 5 Would you like to tell me anything? 6 We must give our hosts a special gift.

Person to person

8a▶ Read through the example questions with the whole class. In pairs, Ss write five more similar questions using the verbs at the end of the Active grammar box.

▶ As Ss write the questions go around the class monitoring their work. Encourage Ss to self-correct mistakes before correcting yourself.

b▶ Reorganise the class so that Ss are working with a different partner. Ss ask and answer each other's questions.

▶ Ask some pairs to repeat one of their questions (with answer) for the whole class.

OPTIONAL VARIATION

Instead of each pair writing five new questions, ask individual Ss to write one question using one of the verbs from the Active grammar box. Ss stand up and mingle, asking their question and getting answers from all their classmates. After a few minutes, Ss sit down and report back to the whole class about the answers they have been given.

Speaking

9a▶ Ss spend a few minutes thinking about customs in their country or in a country they know well in relation to the topics shown in the box. You could group Ss from the same country together.

b▶ Read through the notes in the How to ... box with the class. Pair Ss from different countries, if possible. They tell each other about the topics given in Ex. 9a using the structures given in the How to ... box.

11.3 A dream job?

In recent years, travel writing has become big business. There are dozens of travel magazines and guidebooks to destinations all over the world. However, although being a travel writer may seem like a dream job, competition is fierce and making money is not easy.

In this lesson Ss listen to a woman talking about being a travel writer and through this context, they analyse the grammar of the Past Perfect Simple.

OPTIONAL WARMER

Ask Ss: **Q: What is your dream job? Why would you like to do this job? Can you think of any disadvantages of this job?** Ss discuss these questions with a partner get feedback from the whole class. Tell Ss that the next lesson is called 'A dream job?'.

Listening

▶ Focus Ss on the pictures and ask them to discuss in pairs what they think each book is about.

1▶ Ss discuss the question in pairs. Get feedback from the whole class. Ask the Ss which of the three travel books illustrated they would most like to read.

2a▶ Tell the Ss they are going to listen to an interview with a travel writer. Give them time to read through the topics. Check they understand what they have to do.

▶ Play recording 11.8 and Ss tick they topics they hear. Get feedback from the whole class.

Answers: She talks about numbers 1, 2 and 4.

▶ Write the interviewer's question *What was your first break as a travel writer?* on the board. Elicit/teach the meaning of *break* in this context (important opportunity).

b▶ In pairs, Ss look at the questions and discuss the answers from what they remember from listening the first time to the recording.

▶ Play recording 11.8 again. Allow the Ss to discuss the answers again and then get feedback.

Answers: 1 She started travelling with her family. 2 She wrote a diary. 3 A friend asked her to write a travel guide about Turkey.

3a▶ Read through the four points with the whole class and tell the Ss that they must put them in order. Play recording 11.9. Ss compare answers. Check them together.

Answers: 1 d 2 c 3 a 4 b

b▶ Allow Ss time to read through the questions with a partner and see if they remember any of the answers.

▶ Play recording 11.9. Ss compare their answers in pairs before you check with the whole class.

Answers: 1 the language 2 deciding what to include and what to leave out 3 Bill Bryson 4 Read as many travel books as you can, take a lot of notes when travelling and go for it.

▶ Check that Ss understand the expression *go for it* (don't spend time worrying about what might happen, just try to do it with all your energy).

4▶ Ss discuss the questions with a partner. Get feedback from the whole class.

Grammar

OPTIONAL GRAMMAR LEAD-IN

Write the following disordered sentences on the board. Ss rewrite them with the words in the correct order.
Peter when started had class the arrived. (The class had started when Peter arrived).
I learnt by I time had to the read four was (By the time I was four I had learnt to read).

Get feedback and write the sentences on the board. Underline the Past Perfect Simple in each. Ask Ss:
Q: What tense is this? Elicit/teach Past Perfect Simple.
Q: When do we use it? Allow the Ss to suggest answers to this question in order to see how much they know, but don't explain yourself at this point.

5a▶ Focus Ss on the sentences and play recording 11.10. Allow Ss to compare what they have written with a partner before checking with the whole class.

Answers: 1 had visited 2 hadn't been 3 Had you written

b▶ Focus Ss on the Active grammar box. Ss read through the notes and choose the correct alternative in pairs.

▶ As they do this, copy the timeline on the board. Elicit the correct answer (before) and demonstrate using the timeline. (NB: If the sequence of actions is clear from the context, it is not necessary to use the Past Perfect Simple e.g., I got up and then I went to work).

c▶ Ss look at the tapescript on page 159 and underline two more examples with a partner. Check the answers with the whole class.

Answers: ... I had seen and experienced.
I had lived in Turkey for about two years.

▶ Tell Ss to look at Reference page 113. Give them a few minutes to look the notes and ask:
Q: Does the Past Perfect change with the person e.g., *he*, *we* or *they*? (No)
Q: When is the Past Perfect common? After verbs of saying and thinking and after *when*.
Q: How do we form the negative? Elicit both the contracted and full form: *hadn't* and *had not*.
Q: How do we form the interrogative? (*Had* + subject + Past Participle.)

6▶ Ss choose the best alternative in pairs. Check the answers with the whole class.

Answers: 1 had begun 2 had run 3 went 4 hadn't 5 had gone 6 had 7 hadn't been 8 had arranged

7▶ In pairs, Ss put the verbs in the correct tense.

Answers: 1 arrived/had left 2 asked/had lost 3 got/hadn't packed 4 decided/had been 5 wanted/had forgotten 6 realised/had met

Pronunciation

8a▶ Play recording 11.11 and Ss listen to the pronunciation of *had* in context. Point out that in affirmative sentences the weak form /həd/ is usually pronounced. In negatives and interrogatives the strong form /hædnt/ or /hæd/ is pronounced.

b▶ Ss repeat the sentences in Ex. 7 in pairs, paying attention to pronunciation. Go around monitoring.

Person to person

9▶ Ss describe what they can see in each picture, asking you for any vocabulary items they don't know. Ask a few Ss to describe each picture for the class.

▶ Ss discuss what had happened previously, using the Past Perfect. Ask them to think of as many explanations as possible. Elicit suggestions from the whole class.

Writing

▶ Write *Cuba* on the board in pairs. Ss discuss what they know about Cuba. Get feedback from the whole class.

10a▶ Now ask Ss to read through the text quickly and say which of the topics in the box are mentioned (all of them except the countryside).

b▶ Ss read through the text again, noting down senses and adjectives and what they describe in pairs. Get feedback. Write the adjectives and nouns on the board.

Answers: 1 really interesting – the city; old – cars, buildings; friendly – people; hot – weather; yellow – door; unpainted – buildings; fantastic – coffee, food; taste delicious – coffee; sound of trumpets, drums.
2 I had never tasted such delicious coffee before. Used to describe something that the writer had never experienced previously.

▶ In pairs, Ss think of more adjectives that could be used to describe each noun. Get feedback and write the adjectives on the board. Ss can use them in their writing.

11▶ Read through the instructions with the whole class. Give them plenty of time to think about the place they have chosen and make notes.

▶ In pairs, they tell each other about the place. Ensure Ss ask each other questions to stimulate more ideas for the writing. Ss note the things their partner asks them. Before they write, remind Ss of the travel writer's advice: Choose carefully from your notes about what to include as you want the writing to be as interesting as possible.

Communication: Single or return?

In this lesson Ss listen to four conversations related to travelling by train, plane, bus and coach. Then they role-play buying tickets.

1a▶ Ss work in pairs to describe the four pictures. Get feedback from various Ss.

b▶ Play recording 11.12 and Ss listen and match the dialogues to the pictures. Get feedback.

Answers: 1 B 2 C 3 D 4 A

2a▶ Ss work in pairs to complete the dialogues with the words from the box.

b▶ Play recording 11.12 again and Ss listen and check their answers.

Answers: Dialogue 1: I'd like a return/That's £18.50
Dialogue 2: pieces of luggage/pack your suitcase
Dialogue 3: One pound
Dialogue 4: I'd like to book/like to pay

▶ Ask the Ss if there are any words or phrases that they don't understand and encourage other Ss to explain before doing so yourself.

c▶ Ss practise reading the dialogues in pairs.

▶ Then only one student (the one who speaks first in each dialogue) looks at the book while the other tries to remember/improvise.

3▶ Put the Ss in pairs, A and B. Student A looks at page 127 and student B looks at page 129. Give them plenty of time to read through the instructions and check they are clear about what to do.

▶ Ss role-play the two situations. If you have time, ask for volunteers to role-play a situation for the rest of the class.

Review and practice

1▸

Answers: 1 already 2 yet 3 just 4 yet 5 just 6 already 7 yet

2▸

Answers: 1 She hasn't phoned me yet. 2 Natalia has just brought them. 3 Have you moved in yet? 4 I've just painted it. 5 Have you finished it yet? 6 She's already gone home. 7 I haven't asked him yet.

3▸

Answers: 1 I told him all my secrets. 2 Juan owes me a lot of money. 3 Can I offer you some tea? 4 He promised me a pay rise this month. 5 My grandmother always gives me really good advice. 6 I sent some flowers to the nurse who looked after me. 7 Could you bring us the bill please?

4▸

Answers: 1 wanted/had seen 2 arrived/had missed 3 closed/had left 4 had eaten/felt 5 saw/hadn't studied 6 tired/had forgotten

5▸

Answers: I went to the ticket office to buy my train ticket. When I tried to pay for the ticket, I realised I didn't have my wallet. I remembered that when I had got of the bus, someone had pushed past me. I realised that this person had taken my wallet.

6▸

Answers: 1 shake 2 get 3 had 4 rented 5 waved 6 going

Notes for using the Common European Framework (CEF)

CEF References

11.1 Can do: find out if someone would be a good travel companion

CEF B1 descriptor: can enter unprepared into conversation on familiar topics, express personal opinions and exchange information on topics that are familiar, of personal interest or pertinent to everyday life (e.g. family, hobbies, work, travel and current events) (CEF page 74)

11.2 Can do: make generalisations about customs

CEF B1 descriptor: can express his/her thoughts about abstract or cultural topics such as music, films (CEF page 77)

11.3 Can do: write about a place you've travelled to

CEF B1 descriptor: can write a description of an event, a recent trip – real or imagined (CEF page 62)

CEF quick brief

There are hundreds of Can do statements in the Common European Framework, which can make it difficult for a learner to assess their level. To simplify matters, The CEF contains a 'self-assessment grid' containing brief descriptions of what a learner can do at each of the six major levels. This grid is in the Total English Portfolio.

Portfolio task

Download the Total English Portfolio free from www.longman.com/totalenglish.

Objective: to reinforce student autonomy in updating the Portfolio.

This task can be done in Ss' L1.

1▸ For homework, ask Ss to update the Biography section of their Portfolio. They might like to reassess their language learning aims, history or significant experiences. They might also like to go over the Can do statements again and tick the new objectives at A1 and A2 level that they can now achieve.

2▸ Ask students to bring their Biography sections in and show them to other Ss.

12 Money

Overview

Lead-in	**Vocabulary:** money
2.1	**Grammar:** Second Conditional
	Vocabulary: money
	Can do: say what you'd do in a hypothetical situation
2.2	**Grammar:** reported speech
	Vocabulary: education
	Can do: report what someone said to you
2.3	**Grammar:** *both, neither, either*
	Vocabulary: verb + prepositions (2)
	Can do: describe similarities/differences
Com. Focus	Excuse me, but ...
Reference	
Practice	

Summary

Lesson 1: Ss read a text about how a big newsagent's in England, WHSmith, has decided to allow people to buy their newspapers by simply leaving the correct money in an 'honesty box'. Ss then discuss questions about money.

Lesson 2: Ss consider the meaning of words related to education and then talk about their own education. Then they listen to a radio broadcast about a school in Bristol that has given £11,000 to it's A-level students for getting good grades.

Lesson 3: Ss read a text about a court case which was held in the USA over who was the owner of a baseball, worth $1 million, which had been hit into the crowd of spectators by Barry Bonds of the San Francisco *Giants* as he completed his 73rd home run of the season.

Communication Focus: Ss discuss various problems that customers have in a restaurant, clothes shop, bookshop and a train station. Then they role play one of the conversations.

Film bank: The Ladykillers (4'11")

An extract from a classic British film

The Ladykillers is one of the most famous 'Ealing Comedies' – a series of films made in the studios in Ealing, London. In this film a group of criminals pretend to be musicians in order to rob a bank. Their biggest problem proves not to be the police but Mrs Wilberforce, the sweet old lady whose house they are staying in.

Possible places to use this short film are:

- ▶ before Lesson 1 to introduce the topic of honesty and money
- ▶ after Lesson 1 to extend the topic of crime and money
- ▶ at the end of the unit to round up the topic and language

For ways to use this short film in class, see Students' Book page 144 and Teacher's Book page 194.

Lead-in

▶ Write *money* on the board and tell Ss to work in pairs to brainstorm words related to the topic. Give them a few minutes and then get feedback from the whole class. Write the words on the board.

1▶ Tell the Ss to look at the photos in pairs and say what they can see. Get feedback from the whole class and write the new words on the board.

> **Answers:** Pic 1: coins Pic 2: a piggy bank Pic 3: a cashpoint machine Pic 4: a shop which has a sale on

▶ Ask some questions to the whole group to practise some of the new words:

Q: What is the name of the coins in your country? And in Britain?
Q: Do you have a piggy bank? What are you going to do with the money you have in it?
Q: Do you use cashpoint machines? When?
Q: At what time of year do they normally have sales in your country? Do you go to them?

2a▶ Ask some questions to check that Ss understand the words in the box.

Q: What verb do we use with money when we talk about our jobs? (earn) **And when we get money from a competition?** (win)
Q: What verb do we use for the action of taking money from a cashpoint machine? (withdraw).

▶ Ss work in pairs to complete the sentences.

b▶ Play recording 12.1 and get them to check their answers.

> **Answers:** 1 lending 2 borrowing 3 save 4 spending 5 earn 6 withdraw 7 cost 8 won

c▶ Ss ask and answer the questions in pairs. Get feedback from the whole class.

EXTEND THE LEAD-IN

Play a game of categories to revise vocabulary from this unit and other units throughout the book.

Draw eight columns on the board with the headings: *money*, *travel*, *animals*, *work*, *body*, *places*, *food*, *music*.

Divide the class into small groups and tell one Ss from each group to copy the chart. Call out a letter and Ss have to write one word beginning with that letter in each category as quickly as they can.

When a group/pair finishes they shout *stop* and all other Ss have to stop writing. If after a couple of minutes no group has finished, stop them yourself (there may not always be a word for each category). Ss tell you their words and score a point for each correct answer.

Continue with other letters. The winners are those with the most points at the end.

12.1 Is honesty the best policy?

An 'honesty box' is a box at public locations like airports or stations where people are asked to deposit their money (unsupervised) in exchange for a newspaper which is placed on a rack next to the box. The experiment was started in March 2004 by WHSmith, the British newsagent, at Heathrow Airport and has been so successful that Smith has extended it to thirty locations throughout England. Similar honesty boxes are quite common in the USA.

In this lesson Ss read about honesty boxes and through this context extend their money vocabulary and consider the grammar of the Second Conditional.

OPTIONAL WARMER

Write *honesty* on the board and ask Ss what part of speech it is (a noun). Elicit/teach the adjective and the prefix to form the opposite of both (*honest*; *dishonest*; *dishonesty*). Ask Ss to discuss *honesty* in pairs by asking: **Q: When you are given too much change in a restaurant or shop, what do you do?**

Reading

1▶ Ss discuss what they can see in the picture with a partner. Get feedback from the whole class.

2▶ Tell Ss to read through the text quickly and answer the question. Tell them not to worry about any words they don't understand at this stage. Get feedback (C is correct).

3▶ Focus the Ss on the example sentence and elicit the correct form ('Honesty boxes' are for people who want to buy newspapers). Ss read the text again and correct the sentences with a partner.

Suggested answers: 1 You put the money directly into the 'honesty box'. 2 David McRedmond already knows that the 'honesty boxes' have been a success. 3 A TV programme organised an 'honesty survey'. 4 The pretend cashpoint gave customers ten pounds too much. 5 Most of the customers didn't give the extra money back to the bank. 6 People seem to have a different attitude towards big organisations and small shops.

▶ Ask the Ss if there is anything in the text that they still don't understand and encourage other Ss to explain before doing so yourself.

4▶ Ss discuss the question with a partner. Get feedback from the whole class.

Vocabulary

5a▶ Ss work with a partner to discuss the meaning of the underlined words. Get feedback from the whole class. If Ss have dictionaries, encourage them to use them.

b▶ Ss match the two columns in pairs. Check the answers together.

Answers: 1 d) 2 f) 3 a) 4 b) 5 c) 6 e)

6a▶ Tell Ss to cover the table and try to complete the questions from memory. Allow them to look back at the table if they can't remember or to check when they have finished.

Answers: 1 tip 2 cash 3 interest 4 tax 5 pension 6 salary

b▶ Ss discuss the questions with a partner. Go around the class monitoring their work and making a note of any mistakes you hear.

▶ Get feedback about the questions and then write the mistakes you noted on the board. Encourage Ss to correct them if they can. If not, correct them yourself.

OPTIONAL EXTENSION

Ask Ss to discuss the following questions in pairs:

1 What products do you think should and shouldn't be taxed?
2 What other people do we tip apart from waiters?
3 How much interest does the bank pay you for money you have saved?
4 Do you think it's necessary to have a private pension?
5 What do you think the minimum salary should be?
6 What are the advantages and disadvantages of paying by credit card and not in cash?

Grammar

OPTIONAL GRAMMAR LEAD-IN

Write the following stem sentences on the board:
If a cashpoint gave me too much money, I would ...
If I won the lottery, I would ...
Ss complete the sentences individually and then compare with a partner. Get feedback from a few Ss and then elicit/teach the name of this grammatical structure (Second Conditional).
Ask Ss how to form the First Conditional and write an example on the board (e.g., *If it is expensive, I won't buy it*). Elicit the use of this structure (to talk about a possible situation in the future).

7▶ Focus Ss on the Active grammar box. Read through the example sentences with the whole class.

▶ Tell Ss to read through the notes and choose the correct alternatives. Check the answers together.

Active grammar

1 The Second Conditional refers to imaginary situations.
2 The Second Conditional refers to present and future time.
3 The *if* clause comes first or second.
4 Use *might* if you are less certain.

▶ Elicit/teach the abbreviation of *I would* (*I'd*) and tell Ss that this is most common in spoken English.

▶ Remind Ss that when the *if* clause comes second, there is no comma.

▶ Write the following sentence on the board:
If I were rich, I'd travel around the world.
Explain to the Ss that *were* is normally used instead of *was* in Second Conditional sentences with *I* and *she/he/it* (although in spoken English both can be used). This is what is sometimes referred to as the Subjunctive Mood.

8▶ Ss work in pairs to put the words in the right order. Check the answers with the whole class.

Answers: 1 If you had a dog, you would get more exercise. 2 He would pass his exams if he worked harder. 3 She would be much happier if she left her boyfriend. 4 If I spoke German, my job would be much easier. 5 If I had a car, I would drive to work.

9a▶ Read through the example sentences with the Ss and check they understand what to do. Ss then work in pairs rewriting the sentences.

b▶ Play recording 12.2 and Ss check their answers. They also count how many times the contracted form is used (in all the sentences).

Answers: See transcript on page 159.

Person to person

10a▶ Ss discuss the picture with a partner and say what they would do if they saw this happening. Get feedback from various Ss.

b▶ Ss turn to page 132 and discuss with a partner what they would do in each situation.

c▶ In pairs, Ss write two more situations. These don't necessarily have to be related to money.

▶ Ss then stand up and mingle, asking each other what they would do in these situations.

▶ Ss sit down and compare answers with their original partner. Finally, they report back to the rest of the class.

OPTIONAL EXTENSION

Write 'If this person were a country, which country would they be?' on the board.

Explain that you are going to play a game.
Choose a student but don't tell the class who you have chosen. Now Ss have to ask you questions, like the one above in order to guess that student.

In each question *country* is substituted for words such as *food*, *colour*, *type of music*, *famous actor/actress*, *film*, *book*, *clothes*, *animal*.

When somebody guesses, it is their turn to choose a person and the game begins again.

12.2 The price of success

In order to increase student motivation, many schools offer prizes and awards for good achievement. This idea has been taken one step further by a school in Bristol where students are being given quite large sums of money for meeting their targets. While teachers and students seem to like the idea, others are critical of the 'commercial' values it conveys.

In this lesson Ss listen to a radio news report about this school and through this context they analyse the grammar of reported speech.

OPTIONAL WARMER

Write *education* on the board. Ss brainstorm words related to the topic in pairs. Get feedback from the whole class and write the words on the board.

Vocabulary

1▶ Ss work in pairs to complete the sentences with the words in the box. Point out that they may have to change the form of the verb.

▶ Check the answers with the whole class. Explain to Ss that A-levels are the final state exams that Ss take before going to university. Acceptance at a university normally depends on the grades you get in these exams.

Answers: 1 failed 2 passed 3 take 4 got 5 retake

2a▶ Ss discuss the difference in meaning with a partner. Go around the class monitoring their conversations but don't give them the correct answers yet.

b▶ Ss underline the stress in each word with a partner.

c▶ Ss check their answers on page 132. Give them plenty of time to read through the differences and check the stress of the words.

▶ Tell Ss to turn back to page 118. Ask different Ss to pronounce each word for the rest of the class and explain the difference in meaning in their own words.

3▶ Ss discuss the questions with a partner. Get feedback from the whole class.

Listening

4a▶ Focus Ss on the picture. Ss talk about what they think is happening in pairs. Get feedback from the class.

b▶ Play recording 12.3 and tell Ss to listen to see if they were right. Allow Ss to share with a partner the things they have heard. Then elicit information from the class.

5a▶ Read through the questions with the whole class and allow them to discuss in pairs any answers they remember from the first time they listened.

▶ Pre-teach *bribery* (when you give somebody money to make them do or not do something) and *laptop computer* (portable computer).

▶ Play recording 12.3 again and Ss listen, check any answers they already have and answer the rest of the questions in pairs. Check the answers with the class.

Answers: 1 £11,000 2 £500 3 head of sixth form education 4 Because it rewards everyone for doing well, not just the best students in the year. 5 She is generally negative. She says it feels a bit like bribery and students should work hard for exams because they want to do well, not for money. 6 He is generally positive because more students had got places at university than ever before. 7 She is generally positive because it made her work harder and she earned a lot of money, with which she is going to buy a laptop computer.

b▶ Ss discuss the scheme in pairs first and then with the rest of the class.

OPTIONAL EXTENSION

Ss to make a list of other ways of motivating Ss to study hard. Get feedback and write the list on the board. Then Ss put the things in order of how effective they think they are. Discuss their ideas together.

Grammar

OPTIONAL GRAMMAR LEAD-IN

Write the following disordered sentences on the board. Ss rearrange the words in pairs.

1 *told The teacher was exam not us difficult the* (The teacher told us the exam was not difficult).
2 *had My exam failed she sister her said* (My sister said she had failed her exam).

Ask Ss: **Q: What's the name of this grammatical structure?** (Reported speech).
Q: What do you think each person actually said?
Ss to discuss this in pairs then get feedback.
1 'The exam is not difficult.' 2 'I have failed my exam.'

6▶ Focus Ss on the Active grammar box and read through the direct speech in points 1–3. Play recording 12.4 and Ss complete the gaps in the reported speech. Check with the whole class.

Active grammar

1 had got 2 thought/was 3 was going to buy

▶ Focus Ss on the rest of the grammar notes. Give them a few minutes to read through the information. Then ask:
Q: What's the difference between using *say* and *tell*? *Tell* needs an indirect object e.g., him or me. *Say* doesn't need a indirect object.
Q: What do we change the Present to in reported speech? Past.
Q: What do we change the Past and the Present Perfect to? Past Perfect. **And *will* or *can*?** *Would* or *could*.

▶ Give an example to show how the pronoun might change: '*I* live in England'. Ss write the reported form in pairs (She said/told us that *he* lived in England). Check with the class, pointing out the change of pronoun.

▶ Explain that if you know that what is being reported is still true, the tense can stay the same e.g., She said/told us that he *lives* in England.

If Ss still seem unsure of this grammar point, refer them to Reference page 123 and go through more examples.

7▶ Ss work in pairs to correct the incorrect sentences. Check with the whole class.

Answers: 1 I told Simon ... 2 Correct. 3 ... they had known ... 4 ... told me to ... 5 ... she was living ... 6 ... he couldn't help ...

8▶ Ss work in pairs to report the sentences. Check with the whole class. Point out that *that* can be omitted and often is in spoken English.

Answers: 1 Anna said (that) she preferred studying in the evenings. 2 Anna told Pete (that) she was working at the local university. 3 Anna said (that) Mark had seen Terry in the bookshop. 4 Anna told Pete (that) they hadn't lived there for long. 5 Anna said that her revision notes had been on the table. 6 Anna said she was going to speak to the Professor of Economics.

Speaking

9▶ Focus Ss on the How to ... box. Explain that it's sometimes difficult to answer a question. Read through the three reasons and the example sentences together. Tell Ss to use these structures in the next activity.

▶ Refer Ss to the table and tell them they have to ask each question to a different student, and to follow each question with: 'Why?'

▶ Ss stand up and mingle, asking and answering questions and making a note of the answers they hear.

OPTIONAL VARIATION

Before Ss mingle, tell them to work in pairs to add three or four questions to this table. Tell them to make the questions difficult to answer. Ss ask all the questions when they mingle.

10▶ Read through the example sentences with the whole class. Ss then sit in small groups and talk about their tables, using reported speech.

Writing

11a▶ Refer Ss to the formal letter on page 146 and give them time to do the exercises.

1▶ Answers: 1 For more information
2 course dates; number of students, who arranges accommodation.

2▶ Answers: 1 firstly, to begin with, to start with
2 secondly, next, I'd also like to know, as well as this
3 lastly, finally

b▶ Read through the advert with the class. Ss write a formal letter to the university, using the prompt, to ask for further information.

12.3 The $1 million baseball

It is thought that baseball is based on the British game of rounders (a simple bat and ball game played in schools). The first American league was created in New York in 1857 and it is now the most popular sport in the USA.

In this lesson Ss read about a million dollar baseball and through this context analyse the grammar of *both, neither* and *either*.

OPTIONAL WARMER

Play twenty questions with sports. Tell Ss that you are thinking of a sport and that they have to guess that sport by asking *yes/no* questions e.g., *Do you play inside*? When Ss have guessed, they then play the game in small groups.

Reading

1▶ Ss discuss the questions in pairs. Get feedback from the whole class.

Answers: 1 baseball 2 The aim of the game is to get more runs than the opposing team. A run is scored when a batter hits the ball and then runs around the four bases before the opposing team reach a base with the ball. 3 Ss' own answers

2▶ Read the question with the class and Ss read quickly through the text to find the answer. Tell Ss not to worry about any vocabulary they don't understand at this stage.

▶ Elicit the correct answer (The argument was about who owned the record-breaking baseball).

3▶ Read through the questions with the whole class and tell Ss to read the text again and answer the questions with a partner. Check with the whole class.

Answers: 1 the number of home runs of the season 2 Because it was the ball that broke the record. 3 Popov 4 Fans knocked it out of his hands. 5 a certificate to say the ball was his 6 He took Hayashi to court. 7 four months 8 that the ball belonged to neither of them

4▶ Ss find the words in the text and using the context, discuss the meanings with a partner. Check the answers together.

Answers: 1 the place where spectators stand or sit 2 to score a point by running around all the bases before the other team get the ball back 3 to possess something 4 somebody who works at the stadium 5 to say that something is true 6 the money you pay for service 7 to disagree with a judge's decision and ask for another court case

▶ Ask Ss if there is any more vocabulary that they don't understand in the text and encourage other Ss to explain before doing so yourself.

5▶ Ss discuss the question in pairs. Get feedback.

Vocabulary

OPTIONAL VOCABULARY LEAD-IN

Write the following verbs on the board: *depend, appeal, agree, respond, apply, spend, worry, listen*. Remind Ss that you studied these verbs in lesson 10.3 and that each one has a dependent preposition. Ask Ss to try to remember their dependent prepositions in pairs. (depend on, appeal to, agree with, respond to, apply for, spend on, worry about, listen to)

6▶ Focus Ss on the verbs in the box and tell them to look back at the text in order to find the dependent preposition. Check the answers with the whole group.

Answers: play for, agree with, belong to

▶ Explain to Ss that these verbs are often followed by these prepositions, but that some verbs may be followed by more than one preposition in different contexts.

▶ Write on the board and teach/elicit the difference between: *play for a team* (*for* is used before the group you belong to) and *play with your dog* (*with* is used before your partners in the game).

7▶ Ss work with a partner to complete the sentences. If you have dictionaries, allow the Ss to consult them where necessary. Check the answers with the whole class.

Answers: 1 with 2 with 3 at 4 for 5 to 6 for 7 for 8 on

8▶ Ss ask and answer the questions with a partner. Get feedback from several Ss.

OPTIONAL EXTENSION

In pairs, Ss write similar questions with two or three of the verbs (+ preposition) not used in Ex. 8, i.e., *argue with, look at, depend on, agree with, belong to*. Ss ask each other their questions in new pairs.

Grammar

OPTIONAL GRAMMAR LEAD-IN

Write the following questions on the board. In pairs, Ss answer them, looking back at the text if necessary.

1 *What did both Popov and Hayashi believe*? (That the ball belonged to both of them)
2 *Who said it belonged to neither of them*? (The judge)
3 *Do you think either of them was right*? (Ss' own answers)

Get feedback about the answers and then underline *both, neither* and *either* and tell Ss this is the grammar point you are going to study.

9▶ Read through the example sentences with the whole class. Now tell Ss to read the rest with a partner and complete the gaps. Check the answers with the class.

Active grammar

a) Use *either* with a singular noun.
b) Use *both* with a plural noun.
c) Use *neither* with a singular noun.

▶ Point out the two possible structures at the end of the Active grammar box and the fact that *both* and *neither* are usually used in affirmative sentences whereas *either* is usually used in negatives or interrogatives.

▶ Write further examples on the board if Ss are unsure of this point. Make them relevant to Ss in the class.

e.g., *Both* Pablo and Maria are Spanish. *Both* of them are Spanish.
Neither Pablo nor Maria is English. *Neither* of them is English.
Do you live with *either* Pablo or Maria? Do you live with either of them?
I don't live with *either* Pablo or Maria. I don't live with *either* of them.

10▶ Ss correct the mistakes in pairs. Check with the whole class.

Answers: 1 We can eat at either the Italian or the French restaurant tonight. I don't mind. 2 Correct. 3 Neither of the boys likes swimming very much. They prefer football. 4 Correct. 5 I'm away on both of those days. 6 Correct.

11a▶ Ss complete the sentences in pairs.

b▶ Play recording 12.5. Ss listen and check their answers.

Answers: 1 both 2 either 3 Neither 4 Both 5 both

Pronunciation

12a▶ Play recording 12.5 again and Ss listen to the pronunciation of *both*, *neither* and *either* in context. Ask Ss to repeat the sentences with good pronunciation.

b▶ Ss change some part of the sentences so that they are true for them. Ss compare sentences in pairs.

Speaking

13a▶ Focus Ss on the words in the box. Ss discuss these things in pairs to find four things they have in common.

b▶ Ss swap partners and tell each other what they found out with their original partner using *both* and *neither*. Get feedback from the whole class.

Lifelong learning

▶ Read through the Lifelong learning box with the class. Ss make a list in pairs of what they are going to do. Get feedback, encouraging Ss to make realistic plans and take on board other Ss' suggestions.

Communication: Excuse me, but ...

In this lesson Ss listen to three dialogues in which customers make complaints before practising the dialogues themselves.

1a▶ Focus Ss on the pictures and tell them to discuss what they think is happening in each one in pairs. Get feedback from the whole class.

Answers: Pic A: They have been overcharged./The bill is too expensive. Pic B: The woman has been given the wrong change. Pic C: There is something wrong with the sweater he bought.

b▶ Ss discuss what they would do and say in each situation.

2▶ Ss read through the sentences with a partner and match them to one of the pictures, giving reasons where there are disagreements. Don't give out the answers yet.

3▶ Play recording 12.6 and Ss check their answers. Check with the whole class.

Answers: Dialogue 1: sentences 2, 4 and 7
Dialogue 2: sentences 1, 5 and 9
Dialogue 3: sentences 3, 6 and 8

4a▶ Divide the class into three groups, A, B and C. Play recording 12.6 again and the Ss in group A make notes about dialogue 1, those in group B make notes about dialogue 2 and those in group C make notes about dialogue 3.

▶ Allow Ss to compare with a partner from the same group.

b▶ Rearrange the class so that a student A is working with a student B and a student C. Each one reports their dialogue to the others. Get feedback from various Ss.

5▶ Put Ss in pairs. Tell them to practise acting out the situations with the waiter/assistant being first friendly and then unfriendly.

▶ Ask confident Ss to role-play a situation for the rest of the class.

Review and practice

1 ▶

Answers: 1 I'd do things differently if I had my life again. 2 I'd buy a dog if I didn't live in a city. 3 What would you do if you saw an accident in the street? 4 If Karla studied more she might pass her exams. 5 If I had Pete's address, I'd send him a birthday card. 6 People would understand me more easily if my English was better. 7 What would you take if you were going on a cycling holiday in France? 8 If you had more time, would you read more?

2 ▶

Answers: 1 had/would buy 2 would be/spoke 3 got/wouldn't be 4 would feel/phoned 5 didn't work/wouldn't be 6 would do/had 7 found/would take 8 failed/would retake

3 ▶

Answers: 1 tell 2 told 3 say 4 said 5 say 6 told 7 tell

4 ▶

Answers: 1 I thought you said you weren't going home soon. 2 I thought you said you wouldn't see Steve and Jim tomorrow. 3 I thought you said you had a lot of time at the moment. 4 I thought you said they hadn't borrowed your car for the weekend. 5 I thought you said you hadn't talked to Tara.

5 ▶

Answers: 1 Both men were wearing long black coats. 2 Neither hotel has a swimming pool. 3 Correct. 4 Correct. 5 I'm afraid the Maths teacher has had problems with both of your sons. 6 I don't think I like either of her brothers. 7 Correct.

6 ▶

Answers: 1 pension 2 argue 3 reward 4 borrow 5 depends 6 tax

Notes for using the Common European Framework (CEF)

CEF References

12.1 Can do: say what you'd do in a hypothetical situation

CEF B1 descriptor: can describe events, real or imagined (CEF page 59)

12.2 Can do: report what someone said to you

CEF B1 descriptor: can collate short pieces of information from several sources and summarise them for somebody else (CEF page 96)

12.3 Can do: describe similarities/differences

CEF B1 descriptor: can give straightforward descriptions on a variety of familiar subjects within his/her field of interest (CEF page 58)

CEF quick brief

One of the implications of the Common European Framework and the Can do statements is that students are assessed in terms of how well they can achieve a communication objective. The aim is not to perform the task with perfect accuracy but to perform well enough at that particular reference level. The Can do statements set appropriate objectives for each reference level.

Portfolio task

Download the Total English Portfolio free from www.longman.com/totalenglish.

Objective: to reinforce student autonomy in updating the Portfolio.

This task can be done in Ss' L1.

1 ▶ For homework, ask Ss to update the Dossier section of their Portfolio. They might like to add another piece of work to their folder or choose another task to work on with the aim of adding it to their Biography.

2 ▶ Ask Ss to bring their Biography sections in and show them to other Ss.

photocopiable worksheets

contents

24-hour quiz

Student A

1 Go for a walk
2 Three hundred and sixty-five
3 Chat
4 Lunch
5 Go clubbing
6 Get up
7 Nine o'clock
8 Week
9 Quarter past five

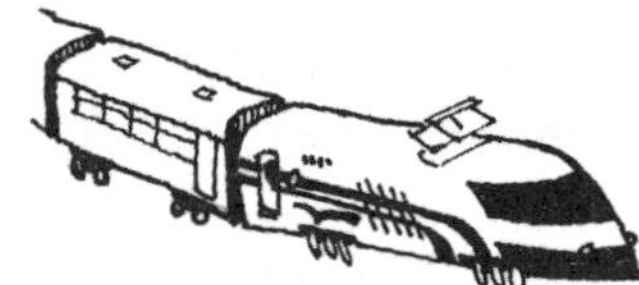

Answer the questions with words from above, 1–9.

a What do seven days make? ________
b How many days are there in a year? ________
c What can you do with your dog? ________
d What's a different way of saying five fifteen? ________
e What can you do with friends on the phone or the Internet? ________
f What meal do the British usually eat at 12.30? ________
g What's the opposite of 'go to bed'? ________
h What time do the British often start work? ________
i What do you do if you want to dance? ________

Now listen to your partner's questions and complete the words a–i.

a E _ _ _ _
b D _ N _ _ _ _ _ _
c W _ _ _ _ _ _
d F _ _ _ _ -T _ _
e C _ _ _ _
f E _ _ _ _ _ _ _
g H _ _ _ P _ _ _ T _ _ _ _
h B _ _ _ _ _ _ _ _
i C _ _ _ _ Y _ _ _ _ _ _ _ _ _

Student B

1 Do nothing
2 Early
3 Check your emails
4 Catch
5 Exercise
6 Half past three
7 Breakfast
8 Fifty-two
9 Weekend

Answer the questions with words from above, 1–9.

a What is the opposite of late? ________
b If you don't work, study or play, what do you do? ________
c What is the same as Saturday and Sunday together? ________
d How many weeks are there in a year? ________
e What other verb means 'to take' a train or bus? ________
f What can you do at the gym? ________
g What's a different way of saying three thirty? ________
h What meal do we eat in the morning? ________
i What do you do to read messages on your computer? ________

Now listen to your partner's questions and complete the words a–i.

a W _ _ _
b T _ _ _ _ H _ _ _ _ _ _ A _ _ S _ _ _ _ -F _ _ _
c G _ F _ _ A W _ _ _
d Q _ _ _ _ _ _ P _ _ _ F _ _ _
e C _ _ _
f L _ _ _ _
g G _ _ U _
h N _ _ _ O' _ _ _ _ _
i G _ _ _ _ _ _ _ _ _

How well do you know your partner?

absolutely love	really like	quite like
keen on	don't mind	not very keen on
don't like	can't stand	really hate

a	b	c	d
e	f	g	h
i	j	k	l

Right (✓) or Wrong (X)

1 I ____________ listening to heavy rock music.
2 I ____________ going to parties.
3 I ____________ doing English homework.
4 I ____________ snakes.
5 I ____________ fast food.
6 I ____________ sunbathing.
7 I ____________ staying in bed late.
8 I ____________ doing sport.
9 I ____________ babies.
10 I ____________ smoking in public places.
11 I ____________ following fashion.
12 I ____________ speaking in public.

I think you really hate listening to heavy rock.

No, you're wrong. I absolutely love it, especially ACDC early in the morning.

How often ... ?

1

Find somebody who:
never reads a newspaper.
usually reads in bed.
sometimes reads in English.
NAME(S)

2

Find somebody who:
a) hardly ever goes to the cinema.
b) often goes to the theatre.
c) never watches DVDs or videos.
NAME(S)

3

Find somebody who:
a) never goes shopping for clothes.
b) usually buys food at a supermarket.
c) sometimes shops on the Internet.
NAME(S)

4

Find somebody who:
a) hardly ever meets friends at the weekend.
b) never goes to a club.
c) usually eats in a restaurant.
NAME(S)

5

Find somebody who:
a) always does sport at the weekend.
b) never watches sport on TV.
c) sometimes listens to sport on the radio.
NAME(S)

6

Find somebody who:
a) usually eats fast food.
b) never drinks alcohol.
c) hardly ever eats breakfast.
NAME(S)

7

Find somebody who:
a) often wears a hat.
b) usually wears a dress.
c) hardly ever wears jeans.
NAME(S)

8

Find somebody who:
a) often travels by plane.
b) always walks to school/work.
c) hardly ever rides a bike at weekends.
NAME(S)

9

Find somebody who:
a) usually stays at home during the holidays.
b) never goes abroad.
c) hardly ever sunbathes.
NAME(S)

10

Find somebody who:
a) is hardly ever tired.
b) is always happy.
c) is often angry.
NAME(S)

What are you doing in London?

Part 1

You are an actress/actor.
Where are you from?
You are making a film in London.
What is it called and who are you working with?
Are you having a fantastic/good/bad/terrible time at the party? Why?

You are a writer.
Where are you from?
You are writing a book in London.
What is it called and what is it about?
Are you having a fantastic/good/bad/terrible time at the party? Why?

You are a singer.
Where are you from?
You are making a new record in London.
What's it called and what type of music is it?
Are you having a fantastic/good/bad/terrible time at the party? Why?

You are a film director.
Where are you from?
You are making a film in London.
What is it called and who are you working with?
Are you having a fantastic/good/bad/terrible time at the party? Why?

You are a famous sports man/woman.
Where are you from?
You are training for a competition in London.
Which competition and where is it going to be?
Are you having a fantastic/good/bad/terrible time at the party? Why?

You are a TV presenter.
Where are you from?
You are making a TV programme in London.
What is it and what is it about?
Are you having a fantastic/good/bad/terrible time at the party? Why?

Part 2

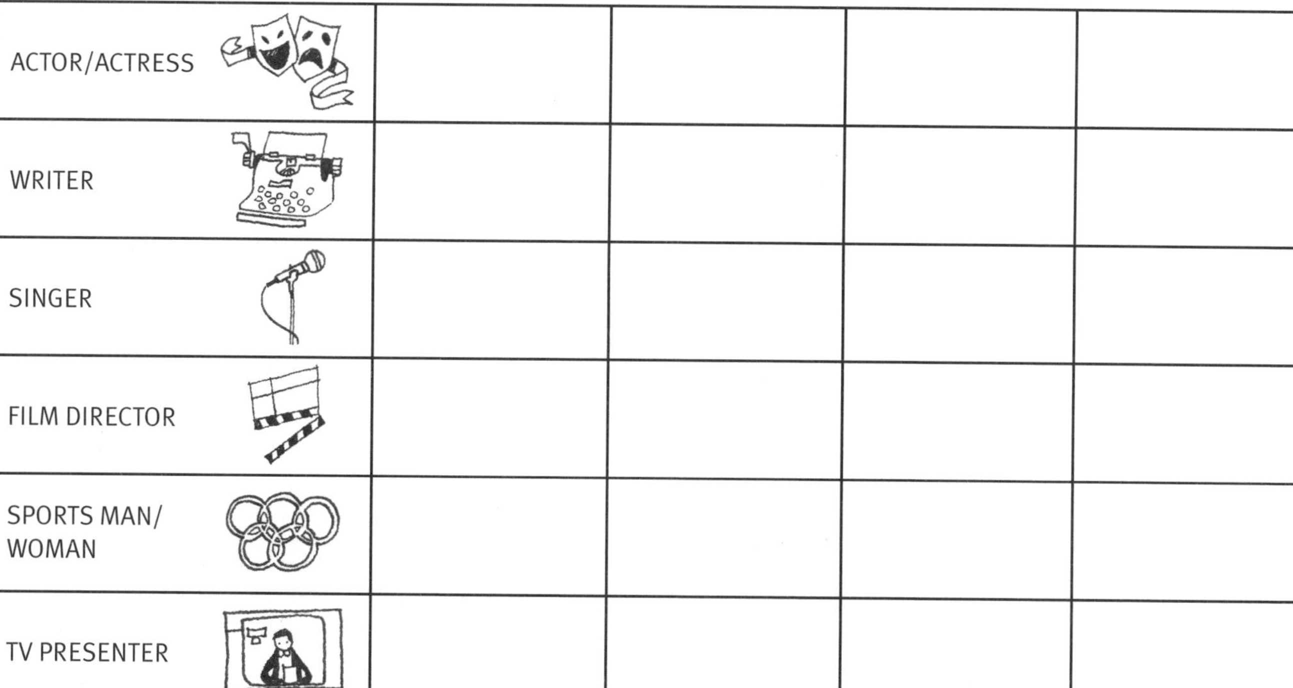

ACTOR/ACTRESS				
WRITER				
SINGER				
FILM DIRECTOR				
SPORTS MAN/ WOMAN				
TV PRESENTER				

Are you the perfect student?

Student A

1 When you come to English class, what do you usually think?
  a Fantastic! I absolutely love English classes. Studying English is my favourite activity.
  b It's OK, but I sometimes prefer a drink with friends.
  c How boring! I really hate them.

2 In my opinion, English is:
  a Impossible, I never understand anything.
  b Really, really easy.
  c Sometimes difficult, but I can improve.

3 How often do you speak your first language in the class?
  a Never. That's a terrible thing to do.
  b Not usually but sometimes I forget and speak my first language.
  c When the teacher is not listening, always!

4 Do you know why you're studying English?
  a I think so. More or less.
  b No idea, but everybody does it, so do I!
  c Yes, definitely. It's good for all parts of my life; travelling, my job, my studies, communicating with others ...

Student B

1 What do you do in class?
  a I always work very hard and do my best.
  b I usually work hard but sometimes I'm tired and it's difficult.
  c I think about my boyfriend/girlfriend, what I am having for lunch or anything else really.

2 When you learn a new word, what do you do?
  a Write it in a notebook and forget it until just before the exam.
  b Think 'fantastic!' and try to use it all the time.
  c Forget it completely!

3 Outside of class, what do you do?
  a Always look for opportunities to practise English – the Internet, books, chatting to tourists.
  b I sometimes practise English when I have the opportunity.
  c Outside of class? English doesn't exist for me.

4 If you're not very good at speaking, for example, what should you do?
  a Practise speaking more in English.
  b Always ask the teacher first when I have to speak to check that my sentence is correct.
  c Speak in my first language.

Are you really into music?

Ask your partner the following questions.

1 When you are at home, do you:

a Listen to some kind of music most of the time?

b Sometimes listen to a CD or the radio?

c Hardly ever play CDs or listen music on the radio?

2 Which of the following best describes you?

a I'm very talented musically. I can play more than one instrument and I can read music and play by ear.

b I can play an instrument quite well, but I'm no pop star!

c Music! What's that?

3 What does the word 'garage' mean to you?

a It's a type of music, of course. I know some clubs that play that type of music.

b I'm not really sure but I think it's a modern type of music.

c It's a place where you park your car, of course.

4 How often do you go to live concerts?

a As often as I can. I absolutely love listening to live bands.

b I sometimes go when I have the opportunity.

c Never. There are too many people and you often have to stand up for hours.

5 Which of the following do you agree with?

a There aren't enough music programmes on the TV. I wish there were more.

b I think there are exactly the right number of music programmes on the TV.

c Music programmes are boring. I never watch them.

6 Do you know what records are in the top ten at the moment?

a Sure. I think I probably know most of them.

b I think I can remember two or three.

c At the moment? No idea.

7 What type of music did Louis Armstrong play?

a Classical

b Jazz

c Rock

8 Who is the lead singer of *Coldplay*?

a Chris Martin

b Liam Gallagher

c Paul McCartney

Add up your partner's points. Score three points for every a, two points for every b, and 1 point for every c.

Results

19–24

You are really into music, aren't you? What about forming a band or becoming a DJ? But remember, there are other things in life.

13–18

You know something about music, but you're not completely crazy about it. You have other interests too.

8–12

'If music is the food of life' then you have problems. Maybe you can't stand most music or maybe other things are just more important for you!

Historical fact or fiction?

Student A

Read the following sentences and think of a question to ask to find the missing information.

1 The White House was originally grey before they painted it white.

2 The French revolution started in ____________.

3 The first modern Olympic Games were in Athens in 1796.

4 Concorde ______________ in 1969.

5 Christmas became a national holiday in the USA in 1790.

6 Until 1965, people drove on the left of the road in __________.

7 The Islamic prophet Muhammad was born in 469 AD.

8 __________ was the first man to travel into space.

9 Workers first discovered Neanderthal man in France.

10 Gandhi studied in _______ when he was a young man.

11 Christopher Columbus first arrived in America in 1392.

12 Mozart grew up in __________.

Which six sentences do you think are false?

Student B

Read the following sentences and think of a question to find the missing information.

1 The White House was originally ____________ before they painted it white.

2 The French revolution started in 1788.

3 The first modern Olympic Games were in Athens in _________.

4 Concorde started flying in 1969.

5 Christmas became a ______________ in the USA in 1790.

6 Until 1965, people drove on the left of the road in Sweden.

7 The Islamic prophet Muhammad was born in _______ AD.

8 Yuri Gagarin was the first man to travel into space.

9 Workers first discovered ____________ in France.

10 Gandhi studied in England when he was a young man.

11 Christopher Columbus first arrived in America in __________.

12 Mozart grew up in Austria.

Which six sentences do you think are false?

So does she!

a

b

c

d

e

		AGREE	DISAGREE
1	I *have/haven't* got a dog.		
2	I *can/can't* play the guitar.		
3	I *am/am not* reading a book at the moment.		
4	I *love/don't love* listening to jazz.		
5	I *am/am not* tired at the moment.		
6	I *grew up/didn't grow up* in a city.		
7	I *have/haven't* got a bike.		
8	I *can/can't* speak French.		
9	I *won/didn't win* a competition when I was young.		
10	I *am/am not* studying at the university.		
11	I *hate/don't hate* hamburgers.		
12	Last summer I *went/didn't go* to the beach.		
13	Yesterday I *ate/didn't eat* pasta.		
14	I *can/can't* swim very well.		

f

g

h

i

j
k

l
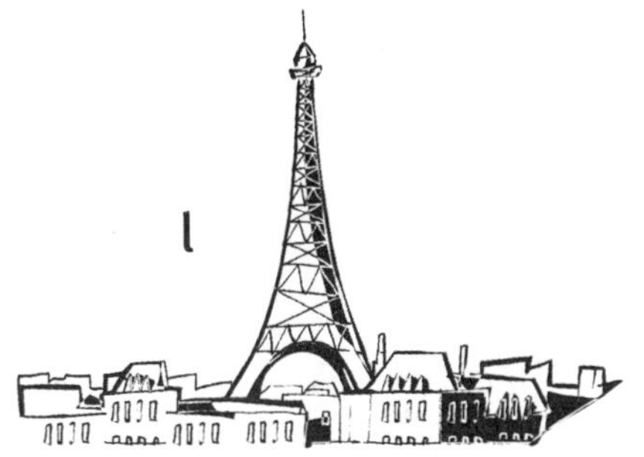
m
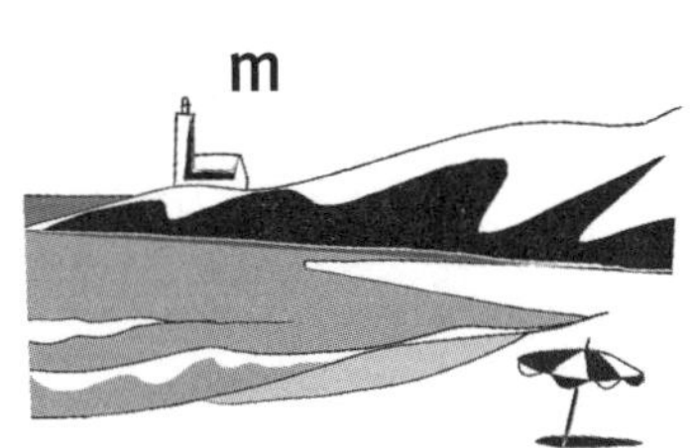
n

How many of the class have ... ?

1 How many people in the class have been abroad?

Which country do they like the most?

2 How many people have seen the film *Titanic*?

What did they think of it?

3 How many people have argued with a teacher?

What did they argue about?

4 How many people have had a snack today?

What did they have?

5 How many people have met a famous singer?

Who was it?

6 How many people have bought something today?

What was it?

7 How many people have sung in public?

Where did they sing?

8 How many people have been to the cinema this month?

What did they see?

9 How many people have broken a part of their body?

Which part did they break?

10 How many people have had more than one job?

What did they do?

What are they going to do?

It's a place where ...

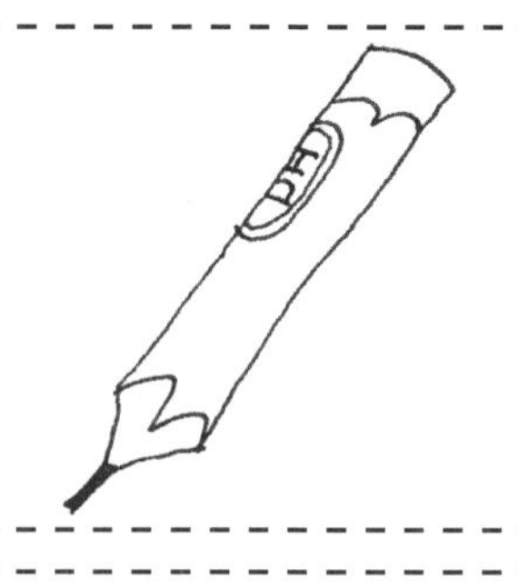

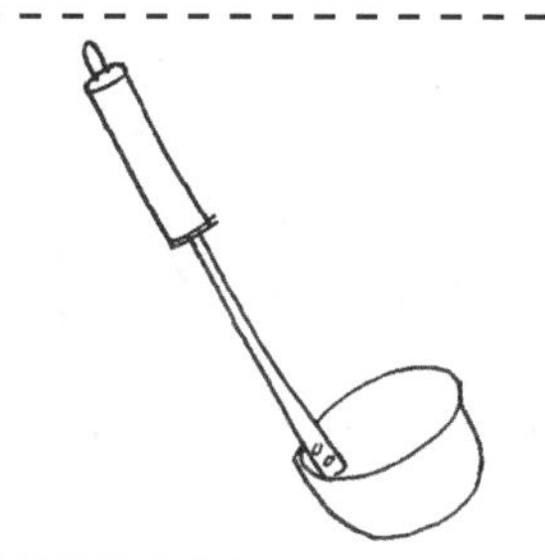

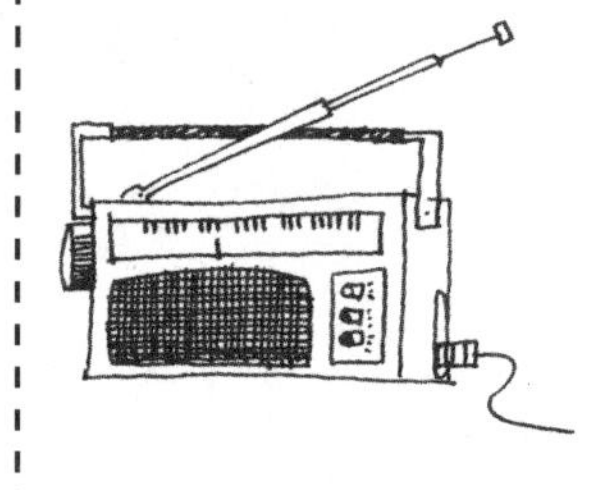

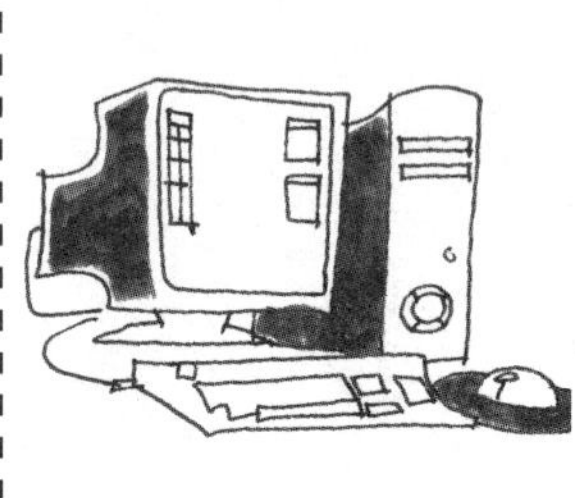

A perfect weekend!

Arrange a perfect weekend with your partner. Complete eight squares in your diary, choosing from the box below and using your own ideas. e.g., *having dinner with Britney Spears or playing tennis with Peter.* Leave seven spaces free.

Having breakfast/lunch/dinner (what type of restaurant?)
Playing a sport (what type?)
Going to the cinema/theatre/opera to see (what?)
Meet a famous person (who?)
Going to a place (where?)
Having a lie-in or a nap
Going to a live concert (what band?)
Going clubbing (where?)
Visiting an art gallery/historical building (which?)
Going shopping (for what?)
Doing nothing
Studying (what?)
Playing a game (what?)
Going for a walk (where?)

	FRIDAY	SATURDAY	SUNDAY
9a.m.			
12.30p.m.			
4p.m.			
7p.m.			
10p.m.			

Now talk to other members of the class. Try to persuade one more person to do the activities you have chosen with you and your partner. Write his or her name next to the activity. If somebody persuades you to do something in your free squares, write down the activity.

A: Why don't you come for a walk in the mountains with me and Lola at 9 o'clock on Sunday morning?

B: No, thank you. I like sleeping at 9 o'clock in the morning.

A: What are you doing at 9 a.m. on Friday?

B: Nothing. Why?

Which restaurant do you prefer?

Student A

Gino's Restaurant

Open every day except Tuesday, 12.30p.m.–3p.m. and 7p.m.–1a.m.

Specialities of the house include:

Extra large pizzas

Fresh pasta

Rice

Traditional Italian desserts

Set 3 course meal £30

Come and enjoy your meal in an imaginative atmosphere with a surprise singer every night

You can find us at 23 Silver Street in the centre of Leeds

The White Horse Restaurant

Open every day except ________,

12p.m.–__p.m. and ____–8p.m.

Specialities of the house include:

Traditional British _______

Roast beef and _________

Roast ________ and chips

Strawberry ______ and ______

Set 3 course meal £_____

Come and enjoy your meal in a ________ atmosphere with ______ music on Saturdays

You can find us at ___________ in the centre of Manchester

Which restaurant do you prefer?

Student B

The White Horse Restaurant

Open every day except Monday,

12p.m.–4p.m. and 6–8p.m.

Specialities of the house include:

Traditional British lamb

Roast beef and vegetables

Roast chicken and chips

Strawberry cheesecake and cream

Set 3 course meal £25

Come and enjoy your meal in a family atmosphere with live music on Saturdays

You can find us at 14 Massey Court in the centre of Manchester

Gino's Restaurant

Open every day except _______, 12.30p.m.–__p.m. and ____–1a.m.

Specialities of the house include:

__________ pizzas

Fresh ________

____

Traditional Italian _________

Set 3 course meal £_______

Come and enjoy your meal in an _________ atmosphere with an _____________ on Fridays

You can find us at __________ in the centre of Leeds

Agreeing and disagreeing

Write a number next to the sentences below to show if you agree or disagree.

1 = strongly agree
2 = partially agree
3 = depends
4 = partially disagree
5 = strongly disagree

1 Mental strength is more important than physical strength in today's world.

2 Men always have more physical strength than women.

3 Women usually have more mental strength than men.

4 Men usually control their fear better than women.

5 You can learn to control your fear.

6 You can always rely on your family more than your friends.

7 It's better not to rely on your partner too much.

8 The most important thing in life is to achieve your goals.

9 If you work a lot you can always achieve your goals.

10 It's more important to have new challenges every day than to have a relaxing life.

I strongly agree with number 2. That's nature.

Don't be silly! Look at me!

The comparison challenge

START	TRAIN/ BUS (comfortable)	?	YOU/ TEACHER (tall)	?	MOUNTAIN CLIMBING/ SWIMMING (dangerous)	LONDON/ TOKYO (big)
EXAM/ PARTY (bad)	?	BERLIN/ MOSCOW (FROM LONDON) (far)	?	LION/ MOUSE (dangerous)	?	ICE CREAM/ FRUIT (delicious)
SNAKES INSECTS (disgusting)	RUNNING/ SLEEPING (energetic)	?	OPERA/ JAZZ (relaxing)	?	THEATRE/ CINEMA (expensive)	?
MEAT/ VEGETABLES (cheap)	SATURDAY/ MONDAY (good)	BREAKFAST/ LUNCH (early)	?	EVENING/ AFTERNOON (late)	?	BOOK/ TABLE (small)
?	PASTA/ RICE (nice)	?	ENGLISH/ YOUR LANGUAGE (difficult)	?	MATHS/ HISTORY (easy)	FINISH

RULES

Throw a dice and move that number of squares.
If the square has words, make a comparative sentence. If the square has a ?, your partner asks you a question.
If you get it right, stay where you are. If you get it wrong go back two squares.

Student A

1 What's the comparative of *good*? (*better*)
2 What's the comparative of *far*? (*further*)
3 Right or wrong? Peter is more tall than me. (wrong – *taller*)
4 How do you spell the comparative of *hot*? (*h-o-t-t-e-r*)
5 What's the missing word? She arrived later me. (*later **than** me*)
6 What's the missing word? I am beautiful than my sister (*more **beautiful** than*)
7 Can you name a meal later than lunch? (*dinner* or *supper*)
8 What's the opposite of *longer*? (*shorter*)

Student B

1 What's the comparative of *bad*? (*worse*)
2 How do you spell the comparative of *happy*? (*h-a-p-p-i-e-r*)
3 Right or wrong? This book is more boring than that one. (right)
4 What the comparative of *crazy*? (*crazier*)
5 What's the missing word? She isn't intelligent as me. (*as **intelligent** as*)
6 What's the missing word? We are better at sport them. (*sport **than** them*)
7 Can you name an animal smaller than a cat? (e.g., *bird*)
8 What's the opposite of *more expensive*? (*cheaper*).

World records

1 Which is ______________ (long) river in the world?

a Thames ❐
b Amazon ❐
c Nile ❐

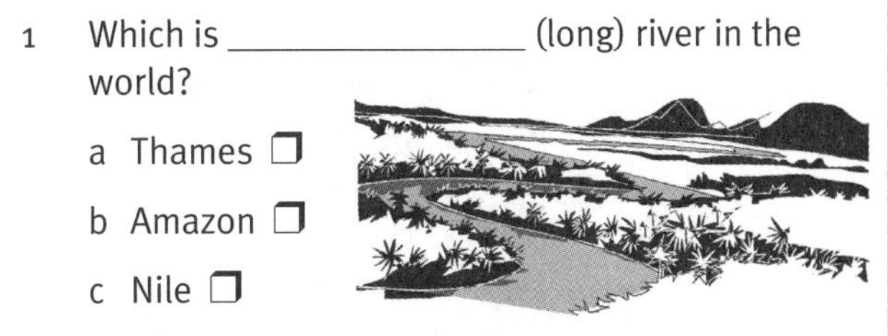

2 Which is ______________ (high) mountain in the world?

a K2 ❐
b Everest ❐
c Kanchengjunga ❐

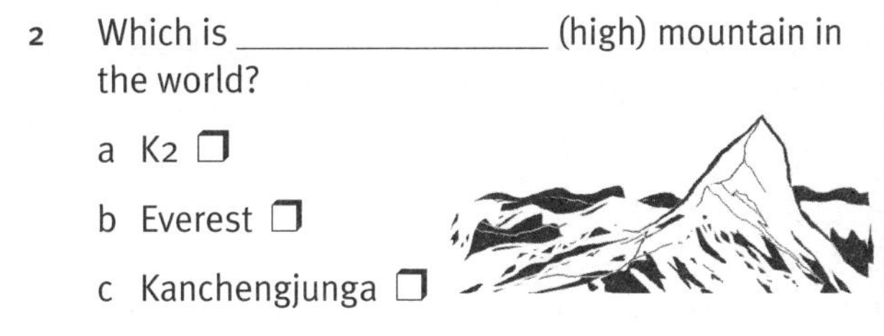

3 Which is ______________ (far) planet from the sun?

a Pluto
b Mars
c Earth

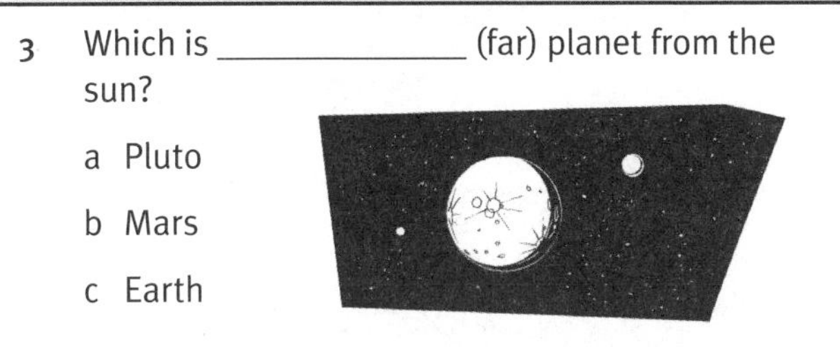

4 Which is ______________ (populated) country in the world?

a China ❐
b USA ❐
c India ❐

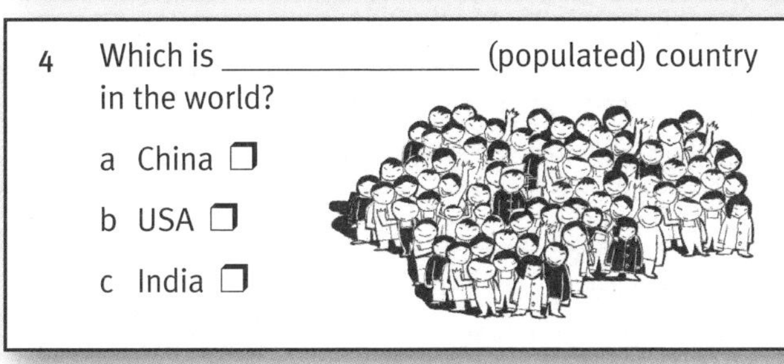

5 Which is the ______________ (small) country in the world?

a Monaco ❐
b Lichtenstein ❐
c Vatican City ❐

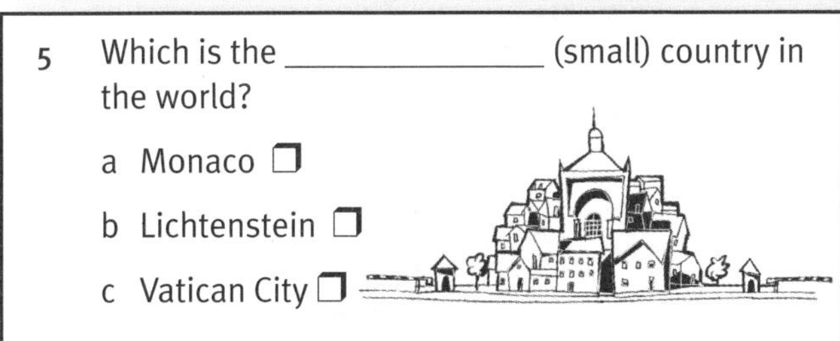

6 Which is ______________ (fast) land animal in the world?

a Lion ❐
b Horse ❐
c Cheetah ❐

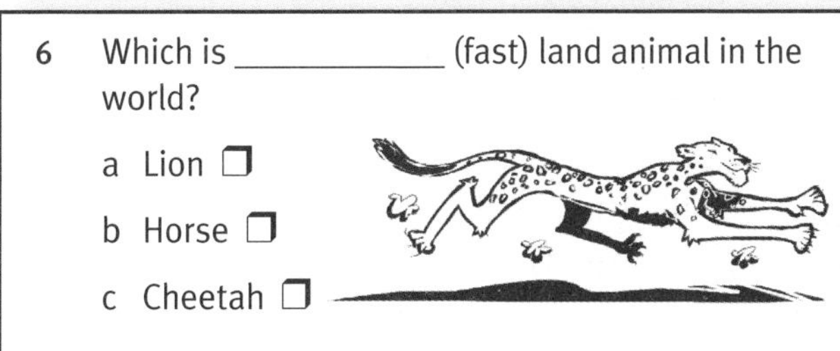

7 How much does ______________ (expensive) hotel room in the world cost?

a $1000 ❐
b $15,000 ❐
c $33,000 ❐

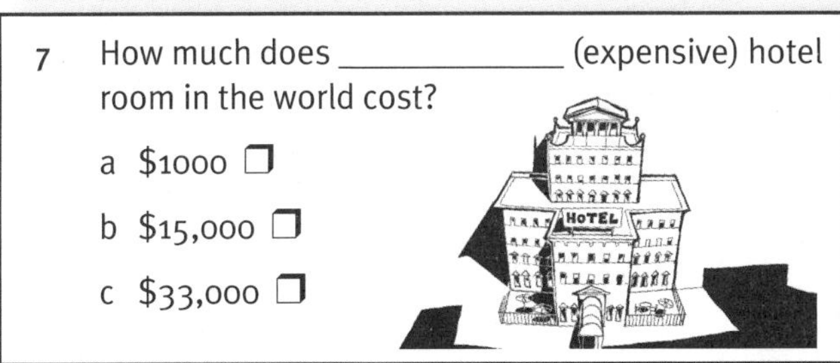

8 When was ______________ (early) colour TV transmission?

a 1898 ❐
b 1928 ❐
c 1948 ❐

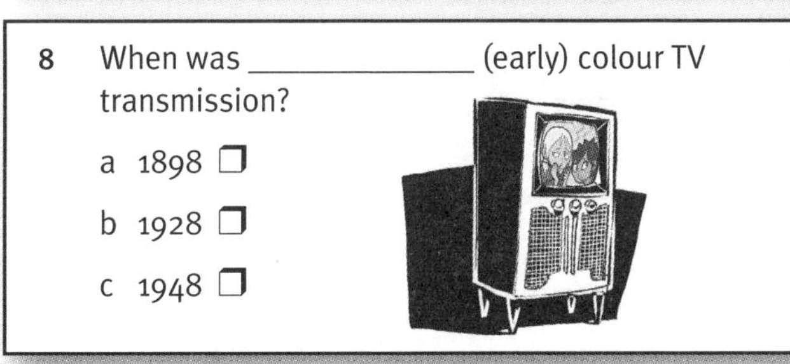

9 Which is ______________ (polluted) city in the world.

a Mexico City ❐
b London ❐
c New Delhi ❐

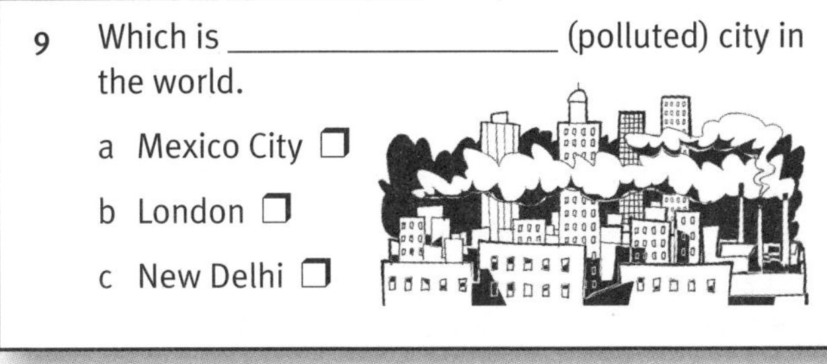

10 Which country has been ______________ (popular) tourist destination ever?

a Spain ❐
b Italy ❐
c France ❐

11 Which fruit has ______________ (high) number of calories?

a Strawberry ❐
b Avocado ❐
c Banana ❐

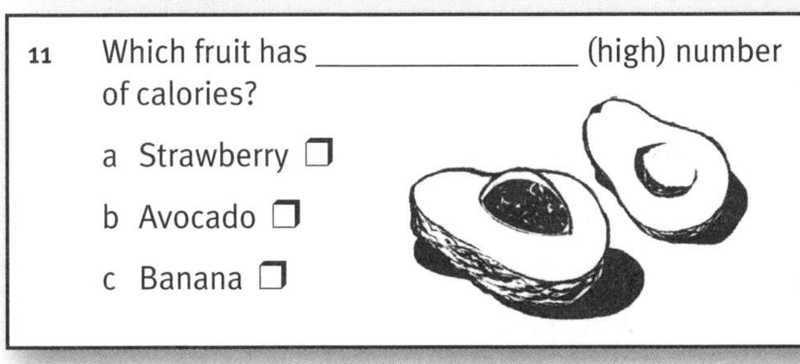

12 How much did ______________ (heavy) man in the world weigh?

a 635kg ❐
b 400kg ❐
c 205kg ❐

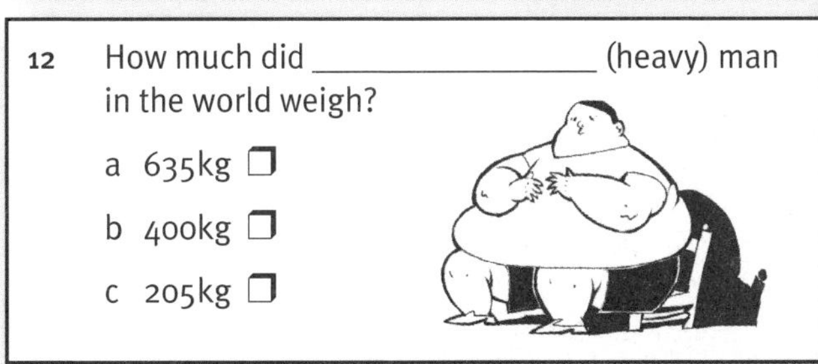

Ask politely.

You are a secretary at Queen's College Language School.
You have to give the following information to new students:

Language Courses

1 month = £300

3 months = £750

Classes are in the morning from 9 o'clock until 12.30, or in the afternoon from 2 o'clock until 5.30.

Maximum number of students per class is 15.

Extra activities, e.g., visits to art galleries, cinema trips, and parties in the evenings (£8 each).

Student placement tests every Monday morning.

You want to study at Queen's College Language School. Go to the office and ask the secretary **POLITELY** for some information. You want to know.

1 How much do the courses cost?
2 How many hours a day do you study?
3 What time do the classes start and finish?
4 Is there a limit to the number of students per class?
5 Are there any organised trips or activities in the evenings?
6 Have you got to do a placement test? When?

When you have all the information (ask extra things if you like), decide which course you want to take.

You are staying in London at the Royal Park hotel. Go to the office and ask the secretary **POLITELY** for some information. You want to know.

1 What time is breakfast served?
2 Is there any access to Internet in the hotel?
3 What is the international dialling code?
4 How far is it to the nearest underground station?
5 How do you get to the swimming pool and gym?
6 How do you get to Buckingham palace from the hotel?

When you have finished thank the receptionist and ask her/him to give you an early morning call to wake you.

You are a receptionist at the Royal Park hotel, London. You often have to answer clients' questions. Give the following information to your partner, the client.

1 Breakfast 7.30–10 am.
2 Internet can be used in every room at a cost of £2 per hour.
3 There is also a swimming pool and a gym for client's use on the fifth floor.
4 The international dialling code is 00.
5 The hotel is in central London so there are two underground stations about 5 minutes' walk from the hotel. Buckingham Palace is at the end of the street, on the left.

Find the difference.

Student A

Find the difference.

Student B

The rebellious grandmother

look after	graduate from university	first kiss
get married	get a job	teenager
toddler	have children	born
get engaged	earn a good salary	learn to drive a car
rebel against	get a place of you own	

Tell the story of Alice, the rebellious grandmother, with a partner. You must use all the words in the box.

In 1930, baby Alice ...

When Alice was a child ...

In 1947, Alice ...

One year later ...

In her early twenties, Alice ...

In her twenties, thirties, and forties Alice ...

In her early sixties, Alice ...

In her late sixties, Alice ...

In her early seventies, Alice ...

What do you think Alice will do when she retires?

Rules around the world

Discuss the following rules with a partner and choose the verb form that makes it true.

1 You *can/can't* drive through the centre of London without paying a special tax.

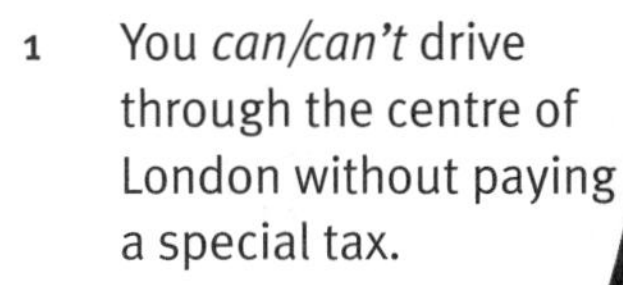

2 In Spain, you *should/shouldn't* stretch in class.

3 In Sweden you normally *have to/don't have* to take off you shoes before entering a house.

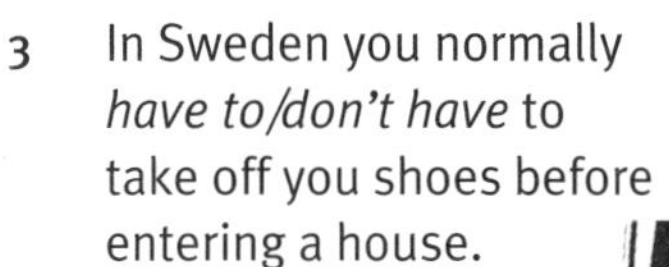

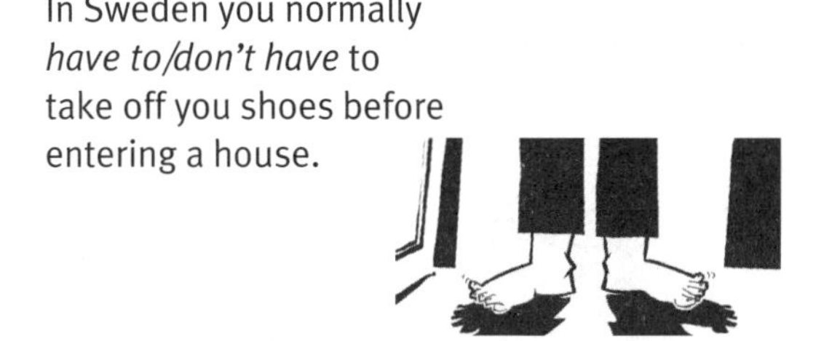

4 In the California USA, you *can/can't* smoke in enclosed public spaces.

5 You *should/shouldn't* wash yourself very well before you get into a public bath in Japan.

6 In Finland you *have/ don't have* to say hello to somebody that you don't know very well when you meet them in the street or a lift

7 In England, you *have/ don't have* to tip the waiter in bar or restaurant.

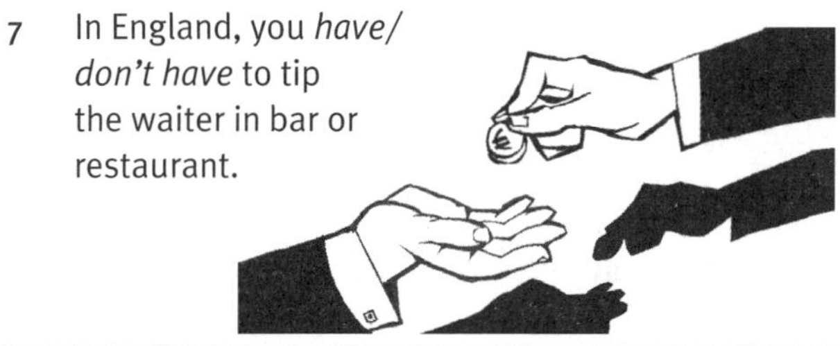

8 If you are given a present in Japan, you *should/shouldn't* open it until later.

9 If you want to give a Chinese person a present, you *should/shouldn't* give them a clock.

10 You *have/don't have* to stay at school until the age of 16 in Mexico.

11 You *can/can't* get married legally until the age of 18 in India.

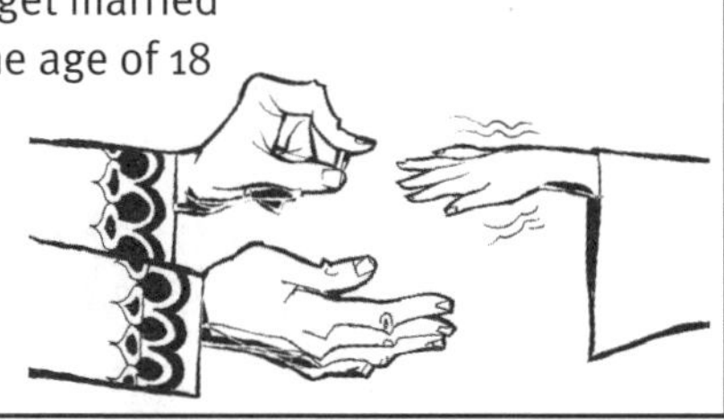

12 If you are invited to have dinner at somebody's house in Senegal, you *should/shouldn't* eat with the first three fingers of your left hand.

How can you change these rules to make them true for your country?

How long have you ... ?

1 **How many people have got a computer?**
Who has had their computer for the shortest and longest period of time?

2 **How many people live in a flat?**
Who has lived there for the shortest and the longest period of time?

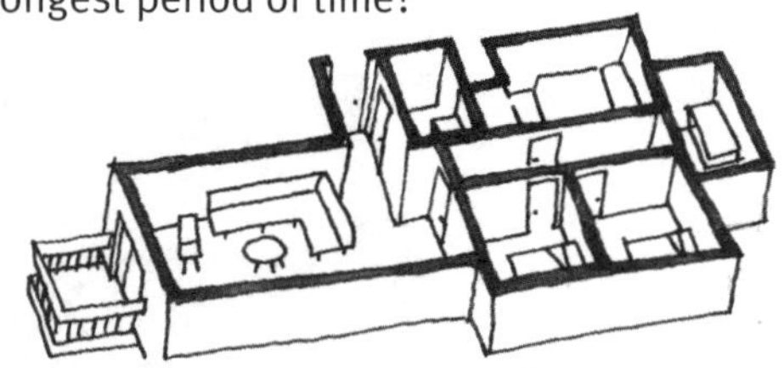

3 **How many people have a hobby?**
Who has had their hobby for the shortest and longest period of time?

4 **How many people have got a best friend?**
Who has known their best friend for the shortest and longest period of time?

5 **How many people are at university?**
Who has been at university for the shortest and longest period of time?

6 **How many people work?**
Who has had their present job for the shortest and longest period of time?

7 **How many people can ski?**
Who has been able to ski for the shortest and longest period of time?

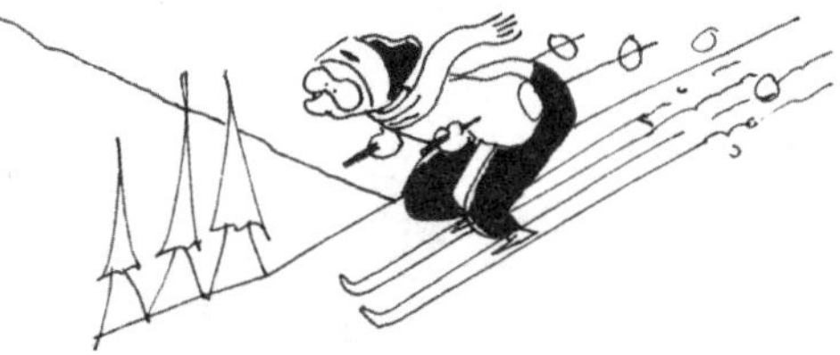

8 **How many people have a favourite band or singer?**
Who has liked that band or singer for the shortest and longest period of time?

9 **How many people have got a pet?**
Who has had their pet for the shortest and longest time?

10 **How many people know how to drive?**
Who has known how to drive for the shortest and longest period of time?

What did life use to be like before ... ?

Student A

Work with your partner to complete the sentences below. Try to think of at least two ideas for each invention.

1 Before the invention of the plane
People used to ________________.
People didn't use to ________________.

2 Before the invention of electricity
People used to ________________.
People didn't use to ________________.

3 Before the invention of clocks
People used to ________________.
People didn't use to ________________.

4 Before the invention of money
People used to ________________.
People didn't use to ________________.

5 Before the invention of the wheel
People used to ________________.
People didn't use to ________________.

What did life use to be like before ... ?

Student B

Work with your partner to complete the sentences below. Try to think of at least two ideas for each invention.

1 Before the invention of the TV
People used to ________________.
People didn't use to ________________.

2 Before the invention of the computer
People used to ________________.
People didn't use to ________________.

3 Before the invention of fast food
People used to ________________.
People didn't use to ________________.

4 Before the invention of the telephone
People used to ________________.
People didn't use to ________________.

5 Before the invention of motorways
People used to ________________.
People didn't use to ________________.

Whose life is this?

place of birth	year of birth	appearance
present home	marital status	studies job
hobbies	important stages in career	successes in life

?

1
NAME: Brad Pitt
YEAR AND PLACE OF BIRTH: 1963 in Oklahoma, USA
LIVES IN: California, USA.
MARITAL STATUS: Divorced from a famous actress.
STUDIES: Journalism at university.
JOB: Actor.
HOBBIES: Playing the guitar and gardening.
IMPORTANT STAGES IN CAREER: Films include *Thelma & Louise*, Ocean's *Eleven* and *Troy*.
SUCCESSES IN LIFE: Nominated for an Oscar in *Twelve Monkeys*.

2
NAME: Madonna
YEAR AND PLACE OF BIRTH: 1958 in Detroit, USA.
LIVES IN: London, England.
MARITAL STATUS: Married (for the second time) to a film director.
STUDIES: Finished school at 18 with good grades.
JOB: Singer, actress and writer.
HOBBIES: Yoga
CAREER: Songs include *Material Girl* and albums include *Ray of Light*
SUCCESSES IN LIFE: Created her own record company called 'Maverick' and starred as Evita Perón in a musical film.

3
NAME: Paul McCartney.
YEAR AND PLACE OF BIRTH: 1952 in Liverpool, UK.
LIVES IN: Rye, England
MARITAL STATUS: Married (for the second time) to a model.
STUDIES: Left school early to start playing in a band.
JOB: Singer and musician.
HOBBIES: Music.
CAREER: Songs include *She Loves You* and films include *A Hard Day's Night*.
SUCCESSES IN LIFE: Given the title of 'Sir' by the Queen of England.

4
NAME: Penélope Cruz
YEAR AND PLACE OF BIRTH: 1974 in Madrid, Spain
LIVES IN: California, USA.
MARITAL STATUS: Single
STUDIES: Left school early to concentrate on ballet and dance.
JOB: Actress
HOBBIES: Listening to classical music.
CAREER: Films include *All About My Mother* and *Vanilla Sky*.
SUCCESSES IN LIFE: Became famous in Hollywood.

5
NAME: Jennifer López
YEAR AND PLACE OF BIRTH: 1969 in New York, USA.
LIVES IN: Miami, USA.
MARITAL STATUS: Married (for the third time) to a famous actor.
STUDIES: High school graduate.
JOB: Singer and actress.
HOBBIES: She was very good at sport at school and writes songs.
IMPORTANT STAGES IN CAREER: Films include *Selena* or *The Wedding Planner*. Dancing for Janet Jackson. Created her own perfume.
SUCCESSES IN LIFE: Voted twice as sexiest woman in the world. Highest paid Latin actress.

6
NAME: Jude Law
YEAR AND PLACE OF BIRTH: 1972 in London, England.
LIVES IN: London, England.
MARITAL STATUS: Divorced.
STUDIES: Left school young to play a part in TV series *Families*.
JOB: Actor.
HOBBIES: Football.
IMPORTANT STAGES IN CAREER: Films such as *Gattaca, The Talented Mr Ripley* and *Cold Mountain*.
SUCCESSES IN LIFE: Nominated for several prizes in the theatre and has his own production company.

Around the world quiz

Answer the questions in groups.

1. What's the capital of Canada?
2. What's the capital of Switzerland?
3. Which country is bigger: Brazil or Canada?
4. Which country is smaller: Italy or Spain?
5. Which country is situated in North America: Columbia or Mexico?
6. Which country is situated in both Europe and Asia?
7. Where are the remains of the 'Hanging Gardens of Babylon'?
8. Where are the remains of Stonehenge?
9. Which countries in Europe are completely surrounded by water?
10. Which country, Italy or China, do you think was the most popular tourist destination in the world in 2003?
11. In which country can we find the region known as 'Brittany'?
12. Which country's landscape can you see in the film The Lord of the Rings?
13. Which European country has a white eagle as its national symbol?
14. Which nationality is famous for its sausages?
15. Which country does the dish of raw fish called 'sushi' come from?

What will happen to Peter's Bay?

Peter's Bay is a small fishing village in the north of Scotland. It's a very beautiful place situated on the coast. The local community is very close and everybody knows and helps each other. Until now, they have never had many visitors. However, the Easytravel holiday company have made a proposal to the villagers. They want to make Peter's Bay into a new, modern tourist destination. They are planning to build hotels, restaurants, fun areas and souvenir shops. To do this they need to buy land from the residents, and they are offering a lot of money. Tonight there is a meeting in the Village may to discuss the matter.

A You are the director of Dreamworld. You have to convince the people that your plan is a good idea. Think about the positive things that will happen, e.g., more jobs, more choice for shopping, more modern things like Internet cafés, more cosmopolitan atmosphere.

B You are the owner of a very small hotel. You don't like the idea because you attract people to your hotel because the place is peaceful and an alternative destination for tourists. Think about the negative things that will happen e.g., you will lose business, more pollution, more noise, ugly buildings, more crime.

C You are a mother/father of two small children. You like where you live because you think it is a good place to bring up children. Think about the negative things that will happen e.g., more pollution, more noise, ugly buildings, more crime, danger for the children.

D You are a young man/woman who has just finished a tourism course. You love your village but you'd like it to change. Think about the positive things that will happen, e.g., more jobs, more choice for shopping, more modern things like Internet cafés, more cosmopolitan atmosphere, more money for the villagers and you of course.

Too, too much, too many or not enough?

Part A

Part B

Discuss the following topics with a partner using *too much, too many* and *not enough*.

Job opportunities in your country

Free time in your life

Good programmes on TV in your country

Traffic in the place where you live

English homework on this course

Parks in the place where you live

Places where you can smoke in your country

Sports facilities in the place where you live

Pollution in the world

Guess the *like* question.

Write your answers to the questions in the boxes below. Don't do it in order.

1 Which countries would you like to visit?

2 What do you look like?

3 What was the weather like yesterday?

4 What do you like doing in your free time?

5 What does your best friend look like?

6 What is your city/town/village like?

7 What type of music do you like?

8 What job would you like to do in the future?

9 What food do you like the most?

10 Who do you look like in your family?

11 What do you like doing in summer?

12 What is English like?

FOLD

A perfect holiday!

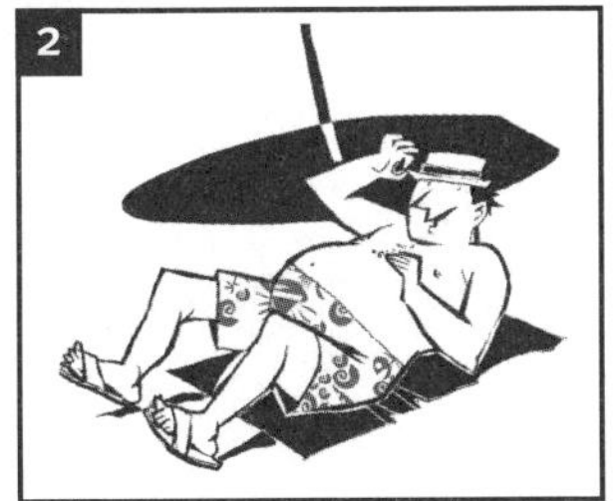

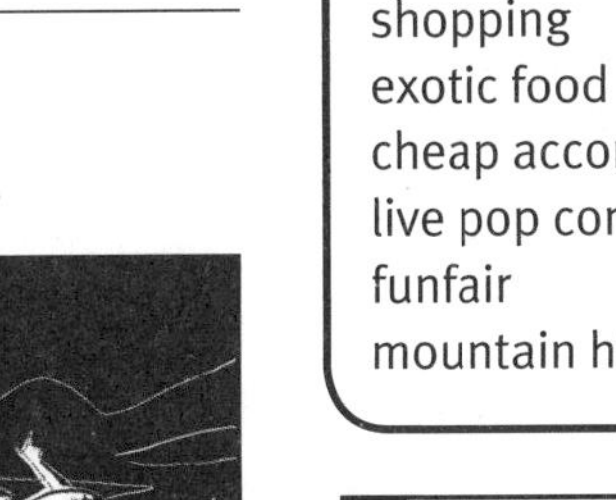

busy nightlife	romantic restaurants
high temperatures	sunbathing
shopping	sightseeing
exotic food	museums and galleries
cheap accommodation	cafés
live pop concerts	theatre
funfair	all night beach parties
mountain hiking excursions	water park

Decide in pairs which of these things the following people would like on holiday.

- a A couple who have just got married.
- b A group of university students.
- c A old retired couple, in their seventies.
- d A family of mother and father in their thirties and two children aged five and eight.
- e You.
- f Your partner.

Find the word.

T	O	E	S	A	E	L	B	O	W
H	L	J	H	D	O	B	S	D	A
U	C	M	O	U	T	H	T	D	N
M	O	E	U	X	V	I	R	I	K
B	C	D	L	I	P	S	E	E	L
A	H	I	D	W	R	I	S	T	E
U	E	C	E	A	E	W	S	O	I
K	E	I	R	I	X	S	E	A	R
C	K	N	S	S	Q	E	D	I	Z
U	S	E	S	T	O	M	A	C	H

1 You use this part of your body to say OK without speaking. It's part of your hand.

2 It joins you hand to your arm.

3 It's where you would wear a belt.

4 You have ten of them on your feet.

5 You have two of these, one at the top of each arm.

6 You use this to talk.

7 If you eat something bad or too much, this part of your body aches.

8 If you have too much work you will probably feel like this.

9 It's in the middle of your arm.

10 What a lot of people go on when they have put on weight.

11 You need one of these in order to listen.

12 Women often paint these with make-up. They are a part of your face.

13 This is something we take when we are ill.

14 The thing that joins you foot to your leg.

15 These may turn red when you're hot.

Advertising promises

courses in management	washing powder	vitamins
perfume	slimming aid	high energy drink
flight company	dating agency	car insurance

What will be the result if you use these products? Invent an advertising slogan for each product with your partner.

If you use Flash, ...

Invent a new product and then write your slogan.

What type of person?

Student A

Read the following questions and write the correct form of the verb.

1 Do you ever avoid ________________ (do) the housework?

2 Do you hope ________________ (have) a lot of children in the future?

3 Do you normally offer ________________ (help) old people or people who are having difficulties when you meet them in the street or on the bus?

4 Have you ever considered ________________ (live) in another country?

5 Can you imagine ________________ (be) a famous artist, singer or musician one day?

6 Do you often promise ________________ (do) things and then not do them?

7 Do you enjoy ________________ (organise) your papers, notes and other personal items?

8 Do you want ________________ (travel) to lots of foreign countries?

Now ask your partner the questions. Ask follow-up questions. What is she/he like?

What type of person?

Student B

Read the following questions and write the correct form of the verb.

1 Do you expect ________________ (cry) when you watch a sad or romantic film?

2 Have you ever considered ________________ (change) the thing you are studying or your job?

3 Can you afford ________________ (go) out every night?

4 Do you want ________________ (be) rich one day?

5 Do you avoid ________________ (do) energetic activities and sports?

6 Which people do you miss ________________ (see) when you are away from home?

7 Do you always enjoy ________________ (be) with lots of people, at parties for example?

8 What type of person do you think you seem ________________ (be) to others when they first meet you?

Now ask your partner the questions. Ask follow-up questions. What is she/he like?

What's my problem?

1
PROBLEM: You can't sleep.
You have this problem because ...

GIVE ADVICE AND EXPLAIN RESULT: You should/Why don't you ... so
Or EXPRESS PURPOSE: to/in order (not) to/so that ...

2
PROBLEM: You don't understand your English teacher.
You have this problem because ...

GIVE ADVICE AND EXPLAIN RESULT: You should/Why don't you ... so
Or EXPRESS PURPOSE: to/in order (not) to/so that ...

3
PROBLEM: You can't find a job.
You have this problem because ...

GIVE ADVICE AND EXPLAIN RESULT: You should/Why don't you ... so
Or EXPRESS PURPOSE: to/in order (not) to/so that ...

4
PROBLEM: Your boyfriend/girlfriend pays more attention to your best friend than to you.
You have this problem because ...

GIVE ADVICE AND EXPLAIN RESULT: You should/Why don't you ... so
Or EXPRESS PURPOSE: to/in order (not) to/so that ...

5
PROBLEM: You failed all your exams.
You have this problem because ...

GIVE ADVICE AND EXPLAIN RESULT: You should/Why don't you ... so
Or EXPRESS PURPOSE: to/in order (not) to/so that ...

6
PROBLEM: Your neighbours make a lot of noise all night.
You have this problem because ...

GIVE ADVICE AND EXPLAIN RESULT: You should/Why don't you ... so
Or EXPRESS PURPOSE: to/in order (not) to/so that ...

7
PROBLEM: You're always tired.
You have this problem because ...

GIVE ADVICE AND EXPLAIN RESULT: You should/Why don't you ... so
Or EXPRESS PURPOSE: to/in order (not) to/so that ...

8
PROBLEM: Your baby cries all night.
You have this problem because ...

GIVE ADVICE AND EXPLAIN RESULT: You should/Why don't you ... so
Or EXPRESS PURPOSE: to/in order (not) to/so that ...

9
PROBLEM: You're addicted to the Internet.
You have this problem because ...

GIVE ADVICE AND EXPLAIN RESULT: You should/Why don't you ... so
Or EXPRESS PURPOSE: to/in order (not) to/so that ...

10
PROBLEM: You're afraid of flying but need to travel a lot.
You have this problem because .....

GIVE ADVICE AND EXPLAIN RESULT: You should/Why don't you ... so
Or EXPRESS PURPOSE: to/in order (not) to/so that ...

Stressful situations

1 What do you think are the top causes of stress in today's society? Make a list of ten things with your partner.

2 Do you think there is more stress in some countries than others? Write three countries where you think the stress is very high and three countries where you think the stress is very low.

3 Do you think men and women react differently to stress? In what ways?

The speed quiz

1 What was the top speed of the Rolls-Royce Phantom III car, built between 1936 and 1939?

a 85 km/h ❐
b 148 km/h ❐
c 198 km/h ❐

2 Some of the newer motorways in Italy have a maximum speed limit of

a 135 km/h ❐
b 150 km/h ❐
c 180 km/h ❐

3 The speed limit is written in miles per hour in which of the following countries?

a UK and Australia ❐
b UK and Germany ❐
c UK and the USA ❐

4 How fast can a rabbit run?

a 12 km/h ❐
b 38 km/h ❐
c 56 km/h ❐

5 When carrying passengers, Concorde usually travels at a speed of

a 1,900 km/h ❐
b 2,400 km/h ❐
c 2,700 km/h ❐

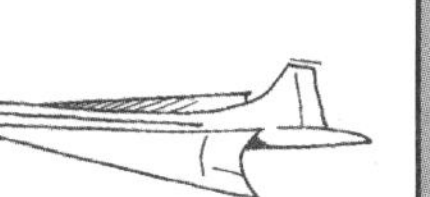

6 What, until 2003, has been the fastest selling consumer electronic product in history.

a The DVD ❐
b The TV ❐
c The radio ❐

7 Speed cameras were invented by a Dutch company founded by the rally driver, Maurice Gatsonides in

a 1950s ❐
b 1970s ❐
c 1990s ❐

8 In which city was there a terrorist attack with sarin gas on the underground during rush hour in 1995?

a New York ❐
b Tokyo ❐
c Moscow ❐

9 If you are travelling at 60 km/h and you see this sign with a blue background and white letters on the road, what should you do?

a Stop ❐
b Speed up ❐
c Slow down ❐

10 If you are in New York and it's 10.30, how many hours would you have to change your clock to catch up with the people in London?

a 3 hours ❐
b 5 hours ❐
c 7 hours ❐

Passive playtime

Student A

1 What/pasta/make/from? (flour)

2 Where/Moussaka/traditionally/eat? (Greece)

3 How much of the earth/cover/by water? (70–75%)

4 Who/a newspaper/run by? (an editor)

5 Where/the city of Prague/situate? (The Czech Republic)

6 How many calories/use/playing tennis for an hour? (380–460)

7 How much/customers/charge for service in USA? (15%)

8 What letter/not pronounce/in the word answer? (w)

Student B

1 What/olive oil/make/from? (olives)

2 Where/gazpacho/traditionally/eat? (Spain)

3 How much of Antartica/cover/by ice? (about 98%)

4 Who/a school/direct by? (head teacher/master/mistress)

5 Where/the city of Santiago/situate? (Chile)

6 How many calories/use/walking for an hour? (180–240)

7 How much/people/charge for driving through central London? (£5)

8 What letter/not pronounce/in the word science? (c)

How well do we know each other?

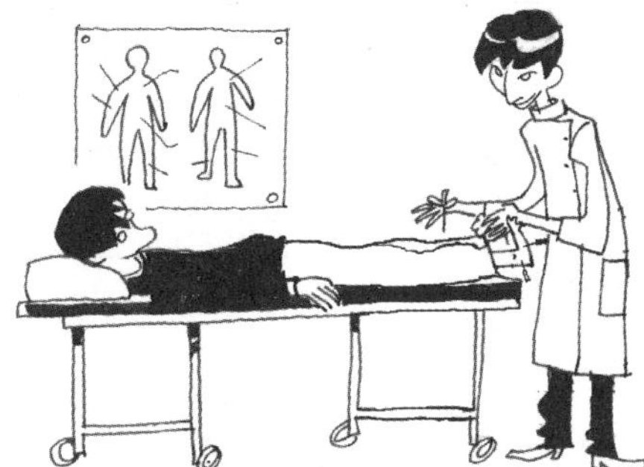

1 __________ has three brothers and sisters.

2 __________ went to the cinema last week.

3 __________ has been to England.

4 __________ would like to be famous.

5 __________ can play a musical instrument very well.

6 __________ finds it easy to ask somebody out.

7 __________ enjoys his/her job or studies very much.

8 __________ went away last weekend.

9 __________ has broken the speed limit when driving.

10 __________ used to hate school when he/she was small.

11 __________ came here by car.

12 __________ is going out tonight.

13 __________ is good at cooking.

14 __________ has never failed an exam.

15 __________ is sensitive.

16 __________ eats a lot of junk food.

17 __________ is going to get married in the near future.

18 __________ has tried acupuncture.

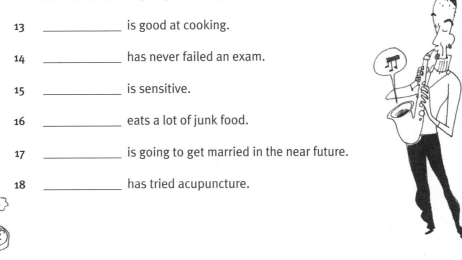

Who did it?

Last Saturday at 7 o'clock in the evening a famous actress was murdered in her mansion in Beverly Hills. Now you are at a party and you know that the murderer is here. The other people at the party were doing one of the things listed in the table below. Ask questions to the different people and try to guess who the murderer is. Start with: *What were you doing last Saturday at 7 o'clock.*

Somebody was watching a film at the cinema	Somebody was playing a sport
Somebody was shopping	Somebody was having a dance class
Somebody was having a meal	Somebody was driving somewhere
Somebody was studying French	Somebody was watching a play at the theatre
Somebody was practising in a band	Somebody was killing the actress

You were watching a film. Think about:
1 Where?
2 What film?
3 With who?

You were playing a sport. Think about:
1 Where?
2 What sport?
3 With who?

You were shopping. Think about:
1 Where
2 What for?
3 With who?

You were having a dance class. Think about:
1 Where?
2 What type of dancing?
3 With who?

You were having a meal. Think about:
1 Where?
2 What did you eat?
3 With who?

You were driving somewhere. Think about:
1 Where?
2 What for?
3 With who?

You were studying French. Think about:
1 Where?
2 What did you learn?
3 With who?

You were watching a play at the theatre. Think about:
1 Where?
2 What play?
3 With who?

You were practising in a band. Think about:
1 Where?
2 What type of music?
3 With who?

You were murdering the actress, but pretend you were doing something else from the list in the table.

Discussion time

Mark one of the columns with X for the ten statements you hear.

	TOTALLY AGREE	PARTIALLY AGREE	DEPENDS	PARTIALLY DISAGREE	TOTALLY DISAGREE
1					
2					
3					
4					
5					
6					
7					
8					
9					
10					

Statements

1 It's extremely rude not to arrive on time to meet friends.

2 We shouldn't allow children to eat fast food.

3 It should be legal for bosses to check their employees personal emails.

4 It's a good idea to charge people for driving through city centres.

5 Real human communication is deteriorating because of computers.

6 Couples split up more these days because they make the decision to get married too quickly.

7 It's not acceptable for a woman to ask a man out.

8 Going out with a new boyfriend or girlfriend is the best way to get over splitting up with your old partner.

9 The Internet is a good way to find a boyfriend or girlfriend.

10 People today work harder and faster than they did one hundred years ago.

What's my job?

inside/outside	difficult/easy	easy/difficult to get promoted
uniform	private company/state	dangerous
work from home	with people/food/animals, etc.	travel
university/special training	high/low salary	a lot/ a little responsibility
dirty/clean	long/short hours	with hands/mind
alone/in a team	special equipment	at night/during the day

Which candidate, which job?

MARINE HOTEL is looking for a manager. Our hotel is small and friendly and has 10 rooms. It is situated very near to the beach and attracts mainly national and local tourists although occasionally we get people from abroad. We have a small but fantastic restaurant, a tennis court and swimming pool. We'd like to organise extra activities and excursions for our guests in the future.

CITY TOURS are looking for a tour guide to take people around the city. The job involves walking around the city explaining the history and importance of the monuments to tourists. The guide will also have to accompany the tourists at lunch and resolve any problems they have during their visit. We generally get tourists from all over the world and visits can be morning, afternoon or evening.

Candidate 1

NAME: Marie Holmes

AGE: 21 years old

QUALIFICATIONS: Graduate in tourism.

WORK EXPERIENCE: Saturdays in a clothes shop.

LANGUAGES: English, French, Spanish and a little German.

DRIVING LICENCE: No

INTERESTS: Reading, sport and travelling

Candidate 2

NAME: Peter Falmer

AGE: 55 years old

QUALIFICATIONS: Courses in computing, business and administration at the local college.

WORK EXPERIENCE: 10 years as a bus driver. 20 years managing own transport business.

LANGUAGES: English and a little French.

DRIVING LICENCE: Yes

INTERESTS: Computers, travelling and cooking.

Candidate 3

NAME: Susana Pérez

AGE: 32 years old

QUALIFICATIONS: Graduate in history. Courses in cooking and wine tasting.

WORK EXPERIENCE: Assistant Spanish teacher and waitress.

LANGUAGES: English and Spanish.

DRIVING LICENCE: Yes

INTERESTS: Archaeology, dancing and art.

Candidate 4

NAME: John Schmidt

AGE: 36 years old

QUALIFICATIONS: Graduate in business and management.

WORK EXPERIENCE: Administrative assistant in Germany for 10 years.

LANGUAGES: English and German.

DRIVING LICENCE: Yes

INTERESTS: Football, travelling and economics.

Abilities: past, present and future

buy a house	ski	climb a mountain
play chess	speak on the pone in english	use a computer
do nothing	read stories to your grandchildren	pay by credit card
drive a car	play the guitar	stay up all night

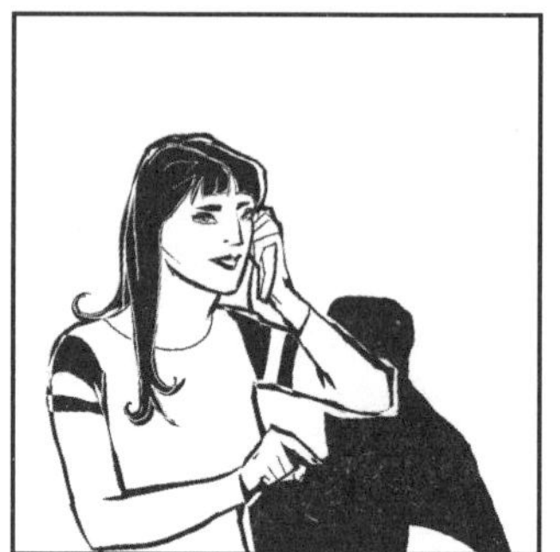

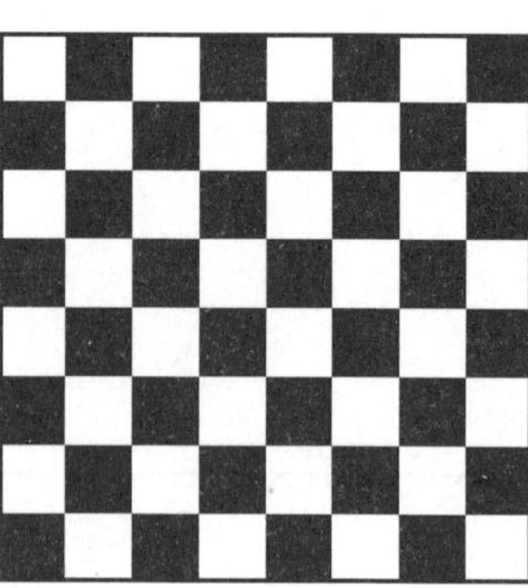

Talk to your partner about the pictures and your abilities in the past, present and future.

I can't drive at the moment because I haven't passed my test, but I think I'll be able to drive next year because I'm going to take lessons soon.

Oh, I could drive when I was 18, but not very well. I had two accidents.

What, where and when?

1 Penicillin __________ (discover) by (LXRNEDAEA NMLFGIE) __________

2 (ARBAMHA NLINOCL) __________ (be) president of the United States between 1861 and 1865.

3 The famous painting known as (HTE NOMA ILAS) __________ (steal) in 1911.

4 Hollywood actress (NWAINO YREDR) __________ (arrest) for stealing from a shop. She __________ (say) she was preparing for a part in a film.

5 The Magic Flute and the Turkish March__________ (write) by __________ (FGNGAOWL DAMUESA ZRTMOA).

6 One of the greatest British writers of all time (LWIALMI EPSKEASHARE) __________ (die) in Stratford upon Avon in 1603.

7 The film (ROLD FO HET SIGRN) __________ (give) the most Oscars in 2004.

8 Radioactivity __________ (discover) by __________ (AMEIR RCEIU), who was the first person who __________ (win) two Nobel prizes.

9 (NIKRDGNI CALHOLO) __________ (make) illegal in the USA between 1913 and 1933.

10 (RELADNXEA LBEL) __________ (invent) the first telephone in 1876.

11 One of the most beautiful pieces of architecture in the world, (HET JTA ALAMJ) __________ (build) in honour of Shah Jehan's wife in the first half of the 17th century.

12 (BRALTE TSIENNIE) __________ (be) one of the most important scientific thinkers of the early 20th century. He __________ (recognise) internationally around 1905 for his special theory of relativity.

13 On January 28th 1986, the space shuttle (LNGHACERLE) __________ (explode) killing all seven astronauts on board.

14 The (NDLONO EEY) __________ (open) to celebrate the Millennium in Great Britain.

15 East and West Germany __________ (unite) after the collapse of the (NBIREL LAWL) __________ in 1989.

Negotiated solutions

Student A

Read the following situations. Talk to your partner and try to negotiate a solution.

1 You are the mother/father of a 16-year-old boy/girl. Your child's marks from school have not been very good recently and you think that he/she should study more. You've decided that he/she can only go out with friends once a week (at weekends) and must be home by 11p.m.

2 You share a flat with another person who, in your opinion, is very lazy. You like the flat to be very tidy and clean every day. Your flatmate, however, never does anything and leaves his/her things everywhere. You don't like this situation and have decided to have a serious talk about responsibilities.

3 Next summer you are going on holiday with your best friend. You'd like to go to the beach. You have been studying really hard this year and all you want to do is relax and lie by the swimming pool. You really want to escape from the city as you spend all year there. Talk to your friend to plan the holiday.

4 You are planning to start a business with a partner. You have decided that it should be a restaurant. You think that the best idea is to start a fast food restaurant as there are a lot of students in you town and there is only one other fast food restaurant. You also think that you could make a lot of money because people eat quickly and then leave so there are a lot of customers in one day. Discuss your plans with your partner.

Negotiated solutions

Student B

Read the following situations. Talk to your partner and try to negotiate a solution.

1 You are a 16-year-old boy/girl. Next Thursday your favourite group are playing a concert in your city. The concert starts at 10 o'clock and most of your friends are going. You know that your parents are not going to like the idea, especially as your marks at school have not been very good recently. Try to persuade your mother/father to let you go.

2 You share a flat with another person who, in your opinion, thinks about cleaning too much. You are very busy and have an important job and don't have much time for cleaning although you do some things like washing up. Recently you've noticed that your flatmate is always angry.

3 Next summer you are going on holiday with your best friend. You'd like to travel around the country visiting different cities as you are very interested in history and would like to visit monuments and museums. You like to do lots of activities when you are on holiday and learn new things at the same time. Talk to your friend to plan the holiday.

4 You are planning to start a business with a partner. You have decided that it should be a restaurant. You think that the best idea is to start a sophisticated, expensive restaurant with very special food and an elegant atmosphere. You think this would be a very interesting job and satisfying. You also know that each customer will pay a lot of money so you could earn a lot of money from the business. Discuss your plans with your partner.

Animal crossword

Student A

Give your partner a clue for the words given in the crossword.

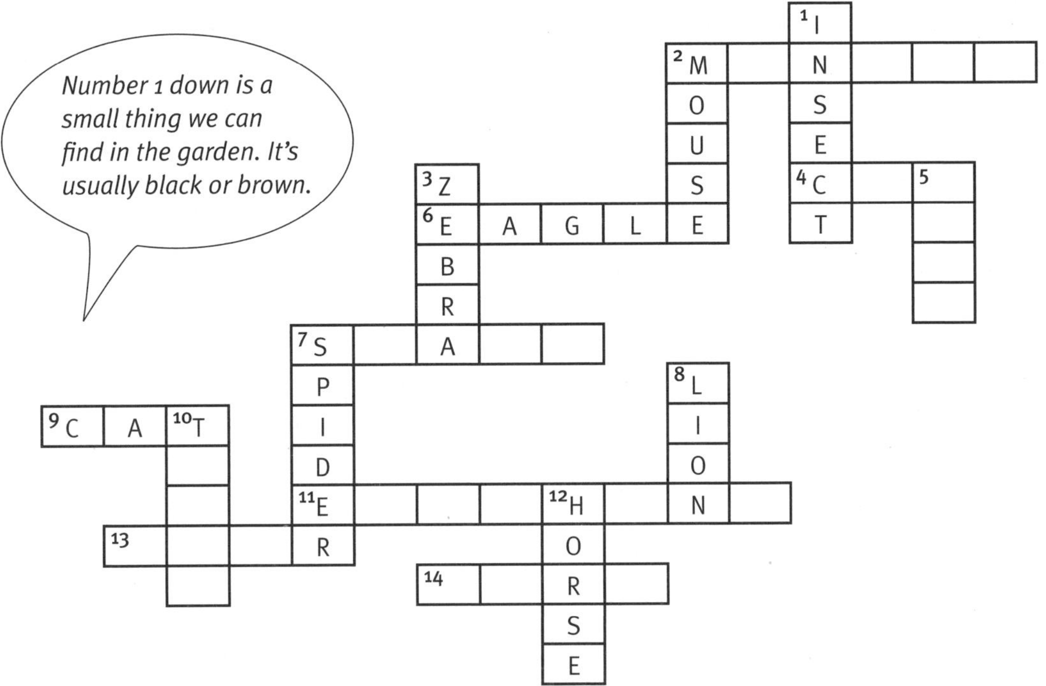

Animal crossword

Student B

Give your partner a clue for the words given in the crossword.

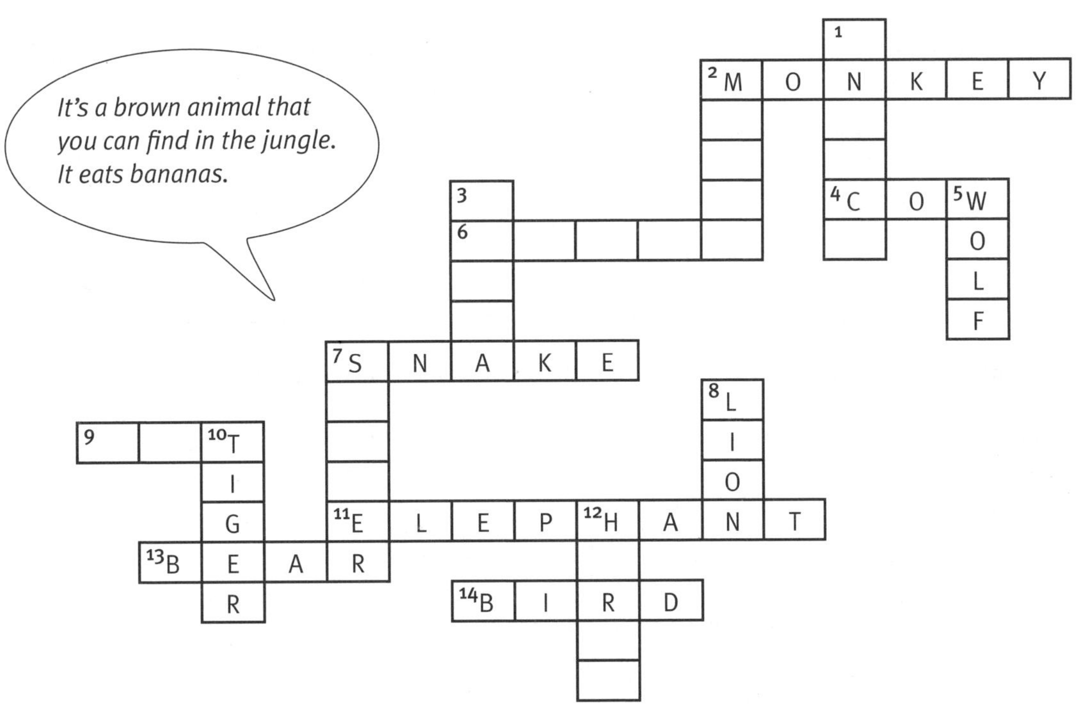

Phrasal verb question time

Student A

Choose a verb from the first box and a preposition from the second box to make a phrasal verb. Complete the sentences with correct form of these verbs.

pick	look
grow	look
come	get

after	on with
up	up
across	up to

1 Do you think girls tend to ____________ more quickly than boys or vice versa?

2 Do you think it's possible to ____________ a language simply by living in the country or do you think formal classes are necessary?

3 Have you ever ____________ somebody you know in an unexpected place?

4 Do you ____________ any particular person in your family?

5 Do you ____________ classmates/workmates?

6 Do you think you will have to ____________ your parents when they are very old?

✂- -

Phrasal verb question time

Student B

Choose a verb from the first box and a preposition from the second box to make a phrasal verb. Complete the sentences with correct form of these verbs. In question 2, repeat the same phrasal verb.

look	get
grow	bring
come	take

to	on with
up	after
across	up

1 Do you think it's better for children to ____________ in the countryside or in a city? Why?

2 What sports did you ____________ when you were younger? And which didn't you ____________?

3 Have you ever ____________ somebody famous?

4 Do you think women know naturally how to ____________ children?

5 Do you always ____________ the people you live with?

6 Do you ever have to ____________ young children or animals?

Find the difference

Student A

Find ten differences between your picture and your partner's picture. Use the words in the box.

some	any	many	much	a few
a little	a bit	a piece of	a lot of	

Student B

Find ten differences between your picture and your partner's picture. Use the words in the box.

some	any	many	much	a few
a little	a bit	a piece of	a lot of	

Noughts and crosses

1	2	3	4
5	6	7	8
9	10	11	12
13	14	15	16

Instructions

- Choose a square and listen to your partner's sentence.
- Is it right or wrong? If it's wrong, correct it. If you choose correctly put a cross or a nought in the square.
- Now it's other team's turn.
- The winner is the one with most noughts or crosses at the end. You get an extra point for three noughts or crosses in a row.

Sentences A

1 My brother's the younger than me. (✗ – no the)
2 This is the one that I want. (✓)
3 I'm going to apply on a job. (✗ – apply for)
4 The old people should be respected. (no the)
5 I'd like to be a pilot in the future (✓)
6 She's tall and the hair is curly. (✗ – my hair).
7 Can I have a milk please. (✗ – some milk)
8 She agrees the other person. (✗ – agrees with)
9 Peter is a old friend. (✗ – an)
10 Pacific ocean is very big. (✗ – The)
11 I know the family sitting over there. (✓)
12 Everest is a very high mountain. (✓)
13 Will you pass me butter. (✗ – the butter)
14 I am worried about my exams. (✓)
15 The Spanish are usually dark. (✓)
16 I don't like the cats at all. (✗ – no the)

Sentences B

1 The man on my left is a doctor. (✓)
2 My brother works as fire fighter. (✗ – a fire fighter)
3 The lake Geneva is very beautiful. (✗ – no the).
4 She's the tallest girl in the class. (✓)
5 I've been listening the radio. (✗ – listening to).
6 Susan is at university at the moment. (✓)
7 It will be difficult to climb the mountain. (✓)
8 I went out with the friend last night. (✗ – a friend).
9 Do you want the lunch now? (✗ – no the)
10 There's a in centre. (✗ – the centre)
11 I usually spend a lot on clothes. (✓)
12 Pollution is a big problem. (✓)
13 I stayed at a hotel in south of Italy. (X – the south)
14 It depends of the teacher. (✗ – depends on)
15 I like the oranges best. (✗ – no the)
16 Last weekend she studied a lot. (✓)

A danger to animals?

Match three words from the box to each picture.

hunting	cut down	factory	kennel
capture	pollution	abandon	gun
farming	roads	smoke	holidays

Questions

1 What is happening in each picture?

2 Why are these things dangerous for animals?

3 How can these problems be solved?

4 If you were given the opportunity to help animals in some way, which of these problems would you choose to work with and why?

Transport race

1 It can be for mountains or racing and has two wheels. (7)

____

2 In London they are black and in New York they are yellow. (4)

____

3 Some say that a Harley Davidson is the best one of these. (9)

____

4 You can do this to a motorbike, moped and bicycle and even to a horse. (4)

____

5 Concorde is the fastest kind of these. (5)

____

6 This form of transport is also the word for the person who helps sports men and women prepare for competitions. (5)

____

7 In London they are red and have an upstairs and a downstairs. (3)

____

8 If you arrive at the bus stop late, this will happen. (4)

____

9 You can take your car from England to France if you catch one of these. (5)

____

10 It's not a car and it's not a lorry but something in between. (3)

____

11 It runs on a track and the first steam one was invented by George Stephenson. (5)

____

12 You have to wait until the bus, plane or train stops completely before you do this. (3, 3)

____

13 We do it to a ball but also to a bus (and it begins with an animal that purrs). (5)

____

14 Similar to what you say when you do something wrong but changing the s for an l. (5)

____

15 The opposite of give and you can do it to a taxi, a plane or a train. (4)

____

16 In 1990 there were almost 500 million of these things that you can park in a garage and fill with petrol. (3)

____

Already done it?

Find out

1 Find out how many students in the class have given somebody a present recently. Find out who to and what it was.

2 Find out how many students were promised rewards for doing the housework, helping their parents or doing homework when they were children. Find out what rewards they were promised.

3 Find out how many students have lent something to somebody recently. Find out what is was.

4 Find out how many students have written somebody an email today. Find out who to and what about.

5 Find out how many students have sent a letter or card to somebody recently. Find out who to and why.

6 Find out how many students have told somebody some important information recently. Find out what it was.

7 Find out how many students have taught somebody something recently. Find out who to and what it was.

8 Find out how many people have bought somebody something recently. Find out what it was and who it was for.

9 Find out how many students have shown somebody some photographs recently. Find out what they were and who to.

10 Find out how many students have offered somebody some help recently. Find out what it was and who to.

Explain that!

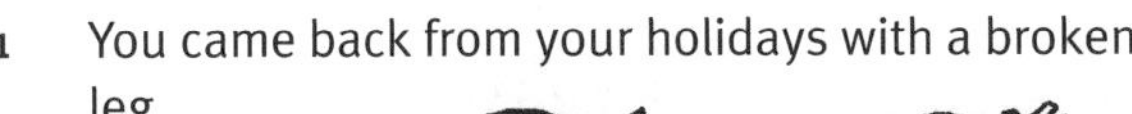

1 You came back from your holidays with a broken leg.

2 You were in shop in Greece stealing bread.

3 You arrived home completely wet on a sunny day.

4 You were speaking English to a French person.

5 You were walking down the street with Tom Cruise.

6 You threw your food at the waiter in an expensive restaurant.

7 You were jumping up and down without stopping.

8 You were driving on the wrong side of the road.

9 You resigned from your job.

10 You invited and paid for the whole class to go to Australia on holiday.

11 You sent the American president a letter.

12 You were riding an elephant through London city centre.

13 You were camping in the garden of your house.

14 You gave your English teacher a big kiss.

Travel options

Student A

Ask your partner questions in order to complete the missing information about the coach service.

TRAIN EXPRESS LONDON–LEEDS

TIMETABLE

Monday–Friday Every 2 hours (6a.m.–10p.m.)

Saturdays 11a.m., 4p.m., 8p.m.

Sundays 11a.m., 6p.m.

TRAVEL TIME 2hrs 15min

PRICES

Single £28

Return £39.50

LUGGAGE LIMITATIONS None

COACH EXPRESS LONDON–LEEDS

TIMETABLE

Monday–Friday ____________

Saturdays ____________

Sundays ____________

TRAVEL TIME ____________

PRICES

Single ____________

Day Return ____________

LUGGAGE LIMITATIONS ____________

What's the best way to travel in your opinion? What does it depend on? Are the coach and bus services similar in your country?

Travel options

Student B

Ask your partner questions in order to complete the missing information about the train service below.

COACH EXPRESS LONDON–LEEDS

TIMETABLE

Monday–Friday 10a.m., 3p.m., 8p.m.

Saturdays 11p.m., 11p.m.

Sundays 2p.m., 10p.m.

TRAVEL TIME 3hrs 45mins

PRICES

Single £11.50

Return £19

LUGGAGE LIMITATIONS 2 suitcases or big bags + 1 handbag

TRAIN EXPRESS LONDON–LEEDS

TIMETABLE

Monday–Friday ____________

Saturdays ____________

Sundays ____________

TRAVEL TIME ____________

PRICES

Single ________

Return ________

LUGGAGE LIMITATIONS ______

Do you think it's better to travel by train or by coach? What does it depend on? Is it better to travel by coach or train in your country?

The money game

START

FINISH

1 You get a good job and e_______ a lot of money. Go forward 3 squares.

2 You w_____ the lottery. **Go forward 5 squares.**

3 MONEY MAKES THE WORLD GO ROUND.

Do you agree?

4 You buy some cheap things in the January s_____. **Go forward 2 squares.**

5 FOOTBALLERS EARN TOO MUCH.

Do you agree?

6 In which country is the currency called 'rupis'?

7 IT'S ESSENTIAL TO SAVE FOR THE FUTURE.

Do you agree?

8 You l_____ some money to a person you never see again. **Go back 4 squares.**

9 What can you see in picture number 1?

10 IT'S BETTER NEVER TO BORROW MONEY.

Do you agree?

11 You w____ £30 in a competition. **Go forward 2 squares.**

12 What can you see in picture 2?

13 You s_______ all your salary in the first 3 days of the month. **Go back 7 squares.**

14 In which country is the currency called 'lire'?

15 MONEY CAUSES PROBLEMS IN MANY FAMILIES.

Do you agree?

16 You w_______ __ £200 from the cash-machine and spend it all. **Go back 4 squares.**

17 Your new car c_______ half the normal selling price. **Go forward 3 squares.**

18 What can you see in picture 3?

19 You s_____ over half of your salary this month. **Go forward 2 squares.**

20 MONEY CAN'T BUY HAPPINESS.

Do you agree?

21 In which country is the currency called 'yen'?

22 What can you see in picture 4?

23 You b______ some money from a friend but can't pay it back. **Go back 7 squares.**

The Money Game

Hypothetical questions

How do you think your life would be different if you were a member of the opposite sex?

Imagine your house or flat was on fire, all the people you live with had already escaped and you could save one possession. What would you save and why?

If you could change one thing in the world simply by wishing it, what would you change and why?

In what ways do you think the world would be different if women had all the important political and economic positions of power?

If money wasn't a problem and you had a maximum of two months in which to travel, where would you go on holiday?

If you suspected that your sister's husband was having an affair, would you tell her?

If you were going for an interview for a job that you really wanted, would you lie in your CV?

If you had a teenage son and you thought that he was taking drugs, what would you do?

If scientists invented a type of medicine that stopped you from feeling hungry, would you take it?

If you had enough money to live without a salary, would you stop working? If yes, what would you do with your time?

If you were given the opportunity to travel to another planet, would you go?

If you could be an animal, which animal would you be, and why?

What did you say?

Student A

Ask your partner the following questions. Do not write the answers but try to remember them.

1 What's your favourite animal?

2 What do you like doing in your free time?

3 What did you do last night?

4 What's the most beautiful place you have ever visited?

5 Do you think you will be rich one day?

6 How many brothers and sisters have you got?

7 Can you drive?

8 What was the last film you saw?

9 How often do you play sport?

10 What are you going to do tonight?

Now tell a different partner what you have heard using reported speech.

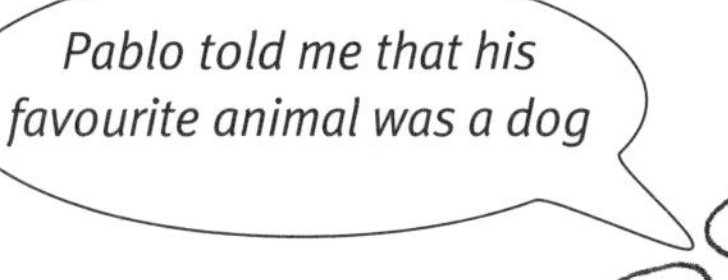

Pablo told me that his favourite animal was a dog

Student B

Ask your partner the following questions. Do not write the answers but try to remember them.

1 What's your favourite food?

2 What do you usually do on Saturday night?

3 What did you do last summer?

4 What's the most frightening experience you have ever had?

5 Where do you think you will live when you are old?

6 How many good friends have you got?

7 Can you ski?

8 What was the last thing you ate?

9 How often do you go out with your friends?

10 What are you going to do next weekend?

Now tell a different partner what you have heard using reported speech.

Julia told me that her favourite food was fish.

Which pair said that?

NAME ____

Find answers for each category that are true for you and your partner.

1 You like this actor/actress. ___________________
2 You don't like this actor/actress. ________________

3 You would like to visit this country. _________________
4 You wouldn't like to visit this country. ________________

5 You can play this sport. ________________
6 You can't play this sport. ________________

7 You ate this yesterday. ______________
8 You didn't eat this yesterday. ______________

9 You have seen this film_________________
10 You haven't seen this film _________________

11 You liked this subject at school. ________________
12 You didn't like this subject at school. ______________

13 You like this singer/group. _____________
14 You don't like this singer/group. ______________

15 You normally do this on Saturdays. ___________
16 You don't normally do this on Saturdays. _________

17 You admire this famous person. ______________
18 You don't admire this famous person. ________________

19 You like to wear this colour. ________________
20 You don't like to wear this colour. _____________

Listen to your classmates read out the information and guess which pair of students they are describing. If you are not sure, check by asking questions.

Have either of them got blond hair?
Are either of them wearing jeans?

Problems, problems, problems!

Student A

Read the following and act out the situation with a partner.

1 You work in an expensive clothes shop. You don't often have problems with customers because the things you sell are excellent quality. If a customer does have a problem, you can exchange the item for something else if they have a receipt. You never give refunds.

2 You are in a restaurant with a friend. You ordered one salad to share, fish and chips and a lasagne. When the bill comes you realise there is a mistake because they have charged you for two salads when you only ordered one. Complain to the waiter and ask him to change the bill.

3 You are a taxi driver. You have just taken a client somewhere and the clock says £7.50 but you are going to charge £12.50 because he/she had two suitcases (£1 each) and it is after midnight which means you charge an extra £2.

4 You have just bought a book which was £5.80 and you think you give the shop assistant a £20 note. He/she only gives you £4.20 change. Complain.

Problems, problems, problems!

Student B

Read the following and act out the situation with a partner

1 Last week you bought a very expensive jacket and when you got home you found a hole in it. You go back to the shop to complain. What you really want is a refund as you have seen a nicer jacket in another shop. You also have a little problem – you have lost the receipt.

2 You are a waiter in a restaurant. A customer is going to complain about the bill because you have charged for two salads not one. This is not a mistake, however, because when two customers order one salad you always give them a big salad containing two portions.

3 You are in a taxi. You have just arrived at your destination and on the clock the price says £7.50. Pay the taxi driver. You have only got £11.40.

4 You are a shop assistant in a book shop. You charge a customer for a book which costs £5.80 and you think she gives you a £10 note. You give her £4.20 change.

Teaching notes

Unit 1 Vocabulary
24-hour quiz

Procedure

Divide the class into two groups, A and B. Give a copy of worksheet A to group A, and give a copy of worksheet B to group B.

Tell students to answer the questions with a partner from the same group, choosing words from the first column. Go around the class helping students with any problems and checking they have the right answers.

Put the students in small groups, so that two students from group A and two from group B are working together. Tell the students to ask and answer each other's questions, writing their answers in the second column. Each team gets one point for each correct answer.

Unit 1 Grammar 1
How well do you know your partner?

Procedure

Divide the class into pairs. It is a good idea to check that none of the pairs know each other too well (e.g., best friends, family members etc.). If they do, rearrange the class a little.

Give each member of the class a copy of the worksheet and tell them to match the pictures and the activities, writing the correct number (1–14) next to each picture. When they have finished, check the answers with the class.

Now tell the students to complete the sentences as if they were their partner. This part is done in silence with students using their knowledge and their imagination.

Now have the students check their answers, ticking or crossing the last column and correcting any which were wrong. Encourage them to speak as much as possible about their likes and dislikes, as in the example given.

Get feedback from the whole class and their correct or incorrect guesses.

Answers

a 4 b 7 c 8 d 11 e 10 f 12 g 2 h 1 i 3 j 5 k 9 l 6

Unit 1 Grammar 2
How often ...?

Procedure

Pre-teach: *abroad*, and check any other vocabulary you think the students may have problems with.

Give one survey card to each student and tell them to ask the other members of the class the question *How often ... ?*. Students answer the question using adverbs of frequency. When they find a student who corresponds to a sentence they write their name in the space provided. Students can write more than one name if they have time.

Before you begin, check students know how to form the correct question. Point out that on the cards the sentences are written in third person singular and the question must be formed in second person singular. Pay special attention to the student who has card ten as here the verb to be is used and the question structure is slightly different.

The students mingle in order to ask and answer questions.

Get feedback from the students about their findings, having them make sentences about their classmates in the third person singular or plural (if they have found more than one person).

Unit 1 Grammar 3
What are you doing in London?

Procedure

Tell the students they are going to a VIP party in London. Give each student a role card and tell them to read and complete the information using their imagination.

Now give them a copy of the table which appears on the second half of the worksheet. If there are six or more students tell them they have to find a person for each category (actor, singer, etc.) and complete the information. If there are fewer than six students, have the students complete their own information first in the table before looking for the other students.

Check the students know which questions to ask before they begin.

Tell students to mingle, getting as much information as possible from their classmates in order to complete the table.

When they have finished get feedback from the class, having them report back in the third person singular and using both the Present Simple and Continuous.

Unit 1 Communication
Are you the perfect student?

Procedure

Divide the class into two groups, A and B. Give a copy of worksheet A to group A, and give a copy of worksheet B to group B.

Have the students work in small groups of two or three. Tell them to read through the questions and choose the option that most corresponds to the way they think or behave. Tell them to help each other with any difficult vocabulary and circulate in order to deal with any difficulties.

Write any difficult words on the blackboard and talk with the whole class about the meaning of these words before going on to the second part.

Rearrange the students so that a Student A is with a Student B. Have each student ask the questions to their partner, making a note of the option chosen.

Now have A and B work together to decide what the perfect student's answer would be and if either of them have chosen this option. The correct option is not always clear and the idea of the 'perfect' student is over-exaggerated anyway.

Get feedback from the class, using this discussion in order to establish learning goals and strategies for the rest of the course. This may also give you a clearer picture of students' needs and motivations.

As a follow up you could ask students to give points for each option (3 = the best answer, 2 = the second best, and 1 = the worst) and calculate their own scores according to this marking system. Students could write a report about their behaviour and aims for the course.

UNIT 2 Vocabulary

Are you really into music?

Procedure

Pre-teach: *live concert* and *top ten* (the records that have sold the most that week)

Give each student a copy of the worksheet and tell them they are going to interview their partner to find out how much they like and know about music.

Students interview each other, asking the questions in turn and noting down the other person's answer. When one student is reading the question, you can ask the other not to look at the sheet in order to increase their listening practice.

When the students have finished, tell them to calculate their partner's score (the answer to question 7 is B, and question 8 is A) and read the analysis of the results. Get feedback from the students about their partners.

UNIT 2 Grammar 1

Historical fact or fiction?

Procedure

Divide the class into two groups, A and B. Give a copy of worksheet A to group A, and give a copy of worksheet B to group B.

Tell the students to read through the sentences in groups of two or three, checking any vocabulary they are unsure of with you. Tell them to write a question for each alternate sentence, in which some of the information is missing.

Rearrange the students so that a Student A is with a Student B. Tell the students to ask the questions to their partner, completing the sentences with the information given.

When the students have finished, read through all the sentences as a class, checking that the students understand and have the correct completed sentences.

Now tell the students that six of the sentences are false. Have them decide with a partner which ones they are. Get feedback from the class, asking the students to correct the false information if they can.

Answers

The false sentences are: number **2** (it started in 1789) number **3** (it was 1896) number **5** (it became a national holiday in 1890) number **7** (he was born in 569) number **9** (it was in Germany) number **11** (it was in 1492).

UNIT 2 Grammar 2

So does she!

Procedure

Give one copy of the worksheet to each student. In pairs, have them identify the illustrations using the words from sentences 1–14. Get feedback from the class.

Now tell the students to circle one of the verb forms so that the sentence is true for them.

Tell students they have to find one person who agrees and one person who disagrees with them for each sentence and write the name in the correct column. Tell them to mingle. One student reads out a sentence and the other responds using *neither*, *so* or a short sentence. e.g., A: *I can't swim very well B: I can* or *Neither can I.*

When they have finished, get feedback from the whole class.

UNIT 2 Grammar 3

How many of the class have ...?

Procedure

Give one card to each student and tell them to read the information.

Explain that students have to find out how many people in the class have done the thing that is written on their card by asking the question: *Have you ...?* Point out that with some of the questions students may have to use *Have you ever ...?* If a student has done this thing, extra information must be requested, this time in the Past Simple.

Tell the students to mingle and ask the questions. Students can either make a note of the answers or they can try to remember.

When they have finished, get feedback from different members of the class. If there are more than ten students, you can put students with the same card together so that they can compare information before the feedback session.

UNIT 2 Communication
Feelings

Procedure

Give each student or pair of students a copy of the worksheet. Focus their attention on the pictures and the words in the box. Tell them to match the words with the pictures in pairs. Get feedback from the class.

Now tell them to answer a question to their partner e.g., 'How do you feel when you see a clown?' Encourage them to explain why they feel this way. If you feel it is necessary you can brainstorm feelings and write them on the blackboard before starting the activity, e.g., *make(s) me feel sad, angry, happy, excited, bored, energetic, tired, afraid* or *make(s) me cry, smile, laugh etc.*

Get feedback from the class and then focus their attention on the second activity. Read the example with the class and then tell them to make similar sentences in pairs, choosing relevant pictures (They don't need to speak about all of them).

UNIT 3 Vocabulary
All about food

Procedure

Divide the class into two groups, A and B, and give a copy of worksheet A to group A and of worksheet B to group B.

Have the students check they understand all of the words written in their crossword in pairs, helping them with any problems they might have.

Now rearrange the students so that one Student A is with one Student B. tell them not to look at each other's paper. Focus the students' attention on the example sentence and tell them to give each other clues for the rest of the words. Write *down* and *across* on the blackboard so that students can identify the direction of the words.

When students have finished get feedback about all the words, checking for pronunciation.

UNIT 3 Grammar 1
What are they going to do?

Procedure

Give a copy of the worksheet to each student or pair of students. Tell them to discuss what they think the people are going to do in each picture.

Go around the class helping with any vocabulary they might need and checking that students are using the tense correctly.

When they have finished tell the students they are going to play a memory game. Student A looks at the worksheet, holding it so that Student B can't see it and asks: *In picture 3, are they going to make a cake?* The other student answers: *yes, they are* or *no, they aren't*. The student asks five questions and then they change roles.

Finally, have the students talk about their own future plans with reference to the pictures.

Answers

Suggested answers

1 They are going to rob the bank. 2 He's going to jump into the pool. 3 They are going to go on holiday. 4 He's going to make a cake. 5 She's going to learn to drive. 6 She's going to do an exam. 7 They're going to play football. 8 She's going to see a film. 9 It's going to eat the chicken. 10 He's going to give up chocolate 11 She's going to buy a new car. 12 They're going to go fishing.

UNIT 3 Grammar 2
It's a place where ...

Procedure

1 Divide the class into groups of four (five or six if numbers demand it) and within each group have them form two teams, each consisting of at least two students.

2 Give each group a pile of cut-up pictures (one whole worksheet) and tell them to out them face down. Have the teams toss a coin or throw a dice to see who goes first. One student takes a picture and explains it to the other members of his or her team, using defining relative clauses e.g., *It's a person who ... It's a place where ... It's a thing which ...* within a time limit of 30 seconds. If the team member guesses correctly, they keep the card. If not, it is put on a separate used pile. Then a member of the other team has a go. This continues until all the cards have been used.

3 The winning team is that which has the most cards at the end.

UNIT 3 Grammar 3
A perfect weekend!

Procedure

Give a copy of the worksheet to each student and tell them to work with a partner to make arrangements for a perfect weekend. Encourage them to discuss the options and to come to a compromise about what they are going to do. The students write these things down in the diary, leaving seven spaces free.

Now have the students mingle with other classmates. Tell them to try to persuade one student to do each activity with them and write the name in the diary next to that activity. They also complete their free spaces with activities they have been persuaded to do.

The first person to find somebody to do all the activities with them is the 'winner'.

UNIT 3 Communication

Which restaurant do you prefer?

Procedure

Divide the class into two groups, A and B, and give a copy of worksheet A to group A and of worksheet B to group B.

Tell the students to look at the second restaurant advert and think of questions they could ask in order to find out the missing information. Go around the class helping with the questions. If the students are having difficulty, get them to write them down.

Rearrange the students so one Student A is with one Student B. tell them to ask the questions and complete the missing information.

When they have finished, have the students discuss which restaurant they would prefer and why?

UNIT 4 Vocabulary

Agreeing and disagreeing

Procedure

Give each student a copy of the worksheet and tell them to look at the box, which shows different degrees of agreement and disagreement. Read through the different expressions, checking that the students understand them.

Tell them to read the sentences below and write a number next to each sentence to express their opinion e.g., if they strongly agree with the first sentence they write number 1 next to it. Go around the class helping the students with any problematic sentences.

Give an example to the whole class by expressing your opinion about one of the sentences, giving reasons for why you think what you do. Now have the students compare their answers in small groups of three or four. Encourage them to give reasons for their opinions.

UNIT 4 Grammar 1

The comparison challenge

Procedure

Cut the worksheet into three sections as indicated and give a copy of the board game and a dice to each pair of students. Give a copy of Student A questions to one of each pair and a copy of Student B questions to the other.

Focus their attention on the rules and go through them, making sure that the students know how to play the game.

The students shake the dice to see who goes first, then move around the board making comparative sentences with the words provided and answering their partners' question when they land on a ? square. If the students answer all eight of these questions they no longer have to do anything on the ? square. The winner is the first to reach finish.

UNIT 4 Grammar 2

World records

Procedure

Give a copy of the worksheet to each pair of students. Tell them to complete each question by forming the correct superlative form. Then tell them to discuss the three options and choose which answer they think is correct.

When they have finished, have the students exchange their papers with another pair of students so that they can correct each other's. Get individual students to read the question and their answer and discuss the correct answer with the whole class.

Answers

1 c 2 b 3 a 4 a 5 c 6 c 7 c (in a hotel in Switzerland) 8 c 9 a 10 c 11 b 12 a

UNIT 4 Grammar 3

Ask politely.

Procedure

Divide the class into pairs and give a copy of the language school receptionist role card to one of the two and the language school student role card to the other. Tell the students to read the information and go around the class helping with any difficulties.

Tell the students to act out the situation. Remind the student to use indirect questions and encourage them to elaborate the dialogue in any way they want.

Ask for volunteers to act out the situation for the rest of the class. Correct any problems with the indirect questions when they have finished.

Now do the same with the hotel role cards, making sure that the secretary now plays the role of client and the student now plays the role of the receptionist so that all students have a chance to practise indirect questions.

Unit 4 Communication

Find the difference.

Procedure

1 Divide the class into pairs and give a copy of worksheet Student A to one of the pair and Student B to the other. Tell the students not to look at each other's paper.

2 Focus their attention on the example and tell them to describe their pictures in a similar way or ask questions in order to find ten differences. Go round the class as they do this helping with vocabulary and correcting any mistakes.

3 When they have finished, have each pair look at both pictures together and have different students report back on the differences.

Answers

1 number of tents 2 number of blankets 3 size/age of boy with torch 4 number of spades 5 girl eating chocolate/writing with pen and paper 6 size/age of boy with axe 7 number of dogs 8 first aid kit 9 number of umbrellas 10 rope swing

Unit 5 Vocabulary

The rebellious grandmother

Procedure

Give a copy of the worksheet to each pair of students and focus their attention on the word bank at the top of the page.

Tell them to tell the story of the rebellious grandmother in the past, using these words and those written below each picture. Allow students to take notes if they wish.

Encourage them to add as much extra information as possible e.g., where the story took place, the names of the other characters, how the different characters feel at different stages in the story.

As they are telling the story, go around the class helping with any vocabulary they need and correcting. When they have finished, have a couple of the pairs tell the story and compare their versions. Students can then write their stories up for homework as an additional activity.

Unit 5 Grammar 1

Rules around the World

Procedure

Give a copy of the worksheet to each pair of students and tell them to read through the rules and choose a verb form in order to make the rule correct. Encourage them to discuss their answers, giving reasons for their opinions.

Get feedback from the class and tell them the correct answers.

Now have the students work together to make the rules true for their own countries. If you have a mixed nationality class but various students of the same nationality, you might want to re-group them so that they are working with students of the same nationality.

Get feedback from the students about the rules in their countries.

Answers

1 can't 2 shouldn't – stretching generally considered rude 3 have to 4 can't 5 should 6 don't have to 7 don't have to 8 shouldn't 9 shouldn't – the word for *clock* in Chinese is similar to *death* 10 don't have to – you can leave at 14 11 can't 12 shouldn't – they eat with the first three fingers of the right hand

Unit 5 Grammar 2

How long have you ...?

Procedure

Cut out the cards and give one to each student. Tell students they have to ask questions to the other people in the class in order to find out the information given on their card. Remind them that the first question will be in the present and the second in the Present Perfect.

Tell students to stand up and ask their questions to all other members of the class. Students answer using *for* or *since*. Those asking the questions must make a mental or written note in order to work out who has done that thing for the longest or shortest period of time.

When they have finished, get feedback from each member of the class. If you have more than ten students, you can allow those with the same card to consult answers before feedback.

Unit 5 Grammar 3

What did life use to be like before ...?

Procedure

Divide the class into two groups, and give a copy of worksheet A to group A and worksheet B to group B. Tell the students to work together in groups of three or four to complete the sentences saying how things were different before the invention of each thing. Encourage them to give write as many ideas as possible. Go around the class helping with vocabulary.

Now rearrange the class so that a Student A is with a Student B. Tell them to take it in turns to read their sentences to their partners without saying the invention. The listener has to guess the invention from the clues.

Unit 5 Communication
Whose life is this?

Procedure

Divide the class into groups of four to six and give a famous person role card to each student. Now give them a copy of the suggested questions box and tell them to put it on the desk or in a place where everybody can see it.

Tell students that they all represent a famous person. The other students in each group have to ask questions in order to guess who that famous person is, using the suggestions in the box. Tell students that they cannot guess the famous person until they have finished asking the questions.

As a follow-up, have students choose their own famous people for the next class and start the next class by following the same procedure. Alternatively, you could bring in some celebrity magazines, which the students can use to research about their person.

Unit 6 Vocabulary
Around the world quiz

Procedure

Divide the students into small groups of three or four. Give each group a copy of the quiz and tell them to discuss the questions and write their answers on a separate sheet of paper.

When they have finished collect in the answers and give each sheet to a different group so that they can correct the answers. Tell them to give one point for each correct answer.

Go through the questions with the whole class, eliciting answers.

Answers

1 Ottawa 2 Berne 3 Canada 4 Spain 5 Mexico 6 Turkey 7 Iraq 8 Britain 9 Cyprus, Iceland and Malta 10 Italy 11 France 12 New Zealand 13 Poland 14 The Germans (students don't get a point if they put the country 15 Japan

The winners are the group with the most points.

Unit 6 Grammar 1
What will happen to Peter's Bay?

Procedure

Give the students a copy of the top half of the worksheet with the information about Peter's bay and read through the text together as a class, checking that the students understand the situation.

Now divide the class into four groups and give role card A to one group, and B, C, and D to the other groups. Allow the students time to read through the information and then tell them to work within their groups to prepare what they will say at the meeting. Tell them to make predictions using will and the ideas from the role card but suggest that they think of some more ideas of their own too.

Reorganise the students so that you have groups made up of A, B, C and D. If you don't have multiples of four, double up the role cards of C and/or D. Tell the students to have a debate within their groups about the future of Peter's Bay. Allow the students 5–10 minutes to do this.

When they have finished get feedback from the whole class and then tell the students to forget their roles and pretend they are simply villagers. Have a class vote to see whether the project should go ahead or not.

Unit 6 Grammar 2
Too much, too many or not enough?

Procedure

Give a copy of the worksheet to each pair of students. Focus their attention on the first picture and elicit possible sentences to describe what is happening e.g., *The man is too weak to carry the washing machine* or *The man isn't strong enough to carry the washing machine* or *The washing machine is too heavy* or *The washing machine isn't light enough.* Write all the possibilities on the blackboard. Discuss with the students which sentences are most likely in everyday conversation.

Tell the students to make at least two sentences for each of the following pictures in pairs.

When they have finished, get feedback from the whole class.

Now focus their attention on the second half. Tell them to work in groups of three or four to discuss their opinions with regard to the topics given. Encourage them to explain their opinions.

Unit 6 Grammar 3
Guess the *like* question

Procedure

Give each student a copy of the worksheet and tell them to answer the questions by writing a few words in each of the boxes on the bottom half of the sheet. Tell them not to write the answers in order.

When they have finished, demonstrate how to fold the sheet and have them do the same with their own. Now organise the class into pairs and have the students exchange sheets with their partner. Tell the students to look at their partner's sheet and try to guess the questions for each answer. When they guess correctly, they tick the square. Encourage students to do this without looking back at the questions, but if they have difficulty allow them to look back.

Get feedback from the class by asking students about their partner e.g., *Which countries would your partner like to visit?*

UNIT 6 Communication

A perfect holiday!

Procedure

Give a copy of the worksheet to each student and tell them to match the words in the box and the pictures with a partner.

Check the words with the whole class and then tell students to discuss which of these things would be suitable for the people listed at the bottom of the page. Encourage them to give reasons, explaining their choices.

Answers

1 mountain hiking excursions 2 sunbathing 3 museums and galleries 4 busy nightlife 5 romantic restaurants 6 cheap accommodation 7 life pop concerts 8 exotic food 9 all night beach parties 10 funfair 11 water park 12 sightseeing 13 high temperatures 14 theatre 15 shopping 16 café

UNIT 7 Vocabulary

Find the word

Procedure

Give a copy of the worksheet to each student. Tell them to find words that satisfy each clue with their partner. When they have finished get feedback from the whole class.

Answers

1 thumb 2 wrist 3 waist 4 toes 5 shoulders 6 mouth 7 stomach 8 stressed 9 elbow 10 diet 11 ear 12 lips 13 medicine 14 ankle 15 cheeks

UNIT 7 Grammar 1

Advertising promises

Procedure

Give a copy of the worksheet to each pair of students and tell them to name the products being advertised with their partner, using the words from the box. Get feedback from the whole class.

Now tell the students they are going to think of slogans for each advert based on the promised result of using each one. Focus their attention on the example and elicit possible sentences from the class e.g., *If you use Flash, you will have the cleanest clothes in town* or *You won't worry about dirty clothes ever again if you use Flash.* Remind students that the result clause can be negative or positive.

When they have finished get feedback from the whole class and then tell them to think of another product to advertise and a slogan. This can be done in small groups or as a whole class. Encourage them to be as imaginative as possible. As an extension, these can be made into whole radio adverts that can then be performed for the rest of the class.

UNIT 7 Grammar 2

What type of person?

Procedure

Divide the class into two groups, A and B, and give a copy of Student A to group A and Student B to group B.

Tell the students to work with a partner to complete the questions by putting the verb in the correct form.

Now reorganise the class so that one Student A is with one Student B. Tell them to ask and answer each others' questions. Encourage them to ask follow-up questions in order to get extra information.

Now tell the students to think of adjectives to describe their partner's personality based on their answers to the questions. Insist that students use the answers they have already been given to their worksheet questions. Write an example on the board e.g., *My partner is ambitious because she wants to be rich one day.*

Get feedback from the whole class or reorganise the class again so that each student tells another student about their original partner.

UNIT 7 Grammar 3

What's my problem?

Procedure

Tell the students you have an imaginary problem and write *I get angry very often* on the blackboard. Elicit reasons for this problem from the students e.g., *You're stressed* or *you're very sensitive*. Now ask them to give you advice and explain the result e.g., *You should count to ten when you get angry so that you have time to keep calm.* Now ask for another piece or advice and elicit purpose e.g., *Don't do too many things so that you don't get stressed.*

Divide the class into small groups of three or four and give them the cut-up problem cards and tell them to put them face down on the desk. Tell all the students in the group except one to look at a problem card. They have to make sentences for each category without saying the problem. The student who doesn't look has to guess the problem.

When they have finished another student takes the turn of guessing and so on until the cards have finished.

Unit 7 Communication
Stressful situations

Procedure

Give a copy of the worksheet to each pair of students and have them look at the pictures. Tell them to talk about each picture, discussing the reasons for the stress, how much they relate to the situation and ways of avoiding that stress.

Get feedback from the class and then focus their attention on the discussion questions at the bottom of the page. Divide the class into groups and tell each group to choose one of the questions. Tell them to talk about that question and to be prepared to report back to the rest of the class.

Unit 8 Vocabulary
The speed quiz

Procedure

Give a copy of the worksheet to each small group of students and tell them to discuss the questions and choose the correct answer. Take in the papers and redistribute them so that another group corrects the questions of each group. Tell them to give one point for each correct answer.

Answers

1 b 2 b 3 c 4 c 5 a 6 a 7 a 8 b 9 b 10 b

Unit 8 Grammar 1
Passive playtime

Procedure

Divide the class into A and B and give a copy of worksheet A to group A and worksheet B to group B.

Tell the students to write the questions as in the example, working in pairs. Go around the class checking that they have the correct questions.

When they have finished put two Student As with two Student Bs so that you have two teams to take part in the quiz. Tell the students to ask each other the questions, giving one point for a correct answer. Allow students to use dictionaries if they want. The winner is the team with the most points.

Unit 8 Grammar 2
How well do we know each other?

Procedure

Give a copy of the worksheet to each student and tell them to complete the sentences with names of other members of the class. Include yourself if you want. Students should know each other's names by this point but if they don't allow them to get up and ask each other. If the class don't know each other well, tell them to use their imagination

When they have finished tell the students to mingle, asking questions to check if they were right or wrong. Tell them that if they were wrong, they should ask other classmates to try to find somebody who corresponds to the sentence.

Get feedback from the whole class.

Unit 8 Grammar 3
Who did it?

Procedure

Give the students a copy of the first part of the worksheet and read through the instructions with the whole class.

Now give each student a role card. If you have more than ten students, separate them into two groups or double some of the role cards. If you double the role cards, tell the students that some of the activities were being done by more than one person. Make sure you give the role of murderer to a strong student.

Tell the students to mingle with the other students asking: *What were you doing ... ?* Tell them to follow this questions with others in order to find out more information and decide if the person is telling the truth or not. Put examples on the board if you think the students need them e.g., *Who were you with? What was it like?* Tell students to write a name next to each activity in the table given.

When they have finished allow students to discuss with a partner who they think the murderer is, giving reasons. Get feedback from the class and then get the murderer to identify him/herself.

Unit 8 Communication
Discussion time

Procedure

Cut the worksheet in half and give a copy of the top half to each student. Tell the students to listen to the statements that you read out and mark a column for each one according to how much they agree or disagree with each statement.

Read the statements from the second part of the sheet, repeating each one several times and if necessary rephrasing it to make sure that the students understand.

When you have read all ten and the students have filled in the table, organise the class into small groups of three or four. Distribute copies of the statements, and have the students discuss each one, comparing the way in which they had filled out the 'agree–disagree' table.

Get feedback for the whole class.

Unit 9 Vocabulary

What's my job?

Procedure

Give a copy of the first half of the worksheet to each student and tell them to think of questions they could ask using the suggestions in the box (or their own ideas) in order to discover somebody's job. Point out that the answers can only be *yes, no* or *it depends*.

Get feedback from the class, writing any difficult questions on the board and explaining any of the expressions that students don't understand.

Now choose a job yourself (e.g., doctor). Have the students ask you 20 questions in order to discover the job.

Divide the students up into small groups of three or four and give each group a set of role cards. The students take in turns to pick up a job card and the others have to ask 20 questions in order to guess that job. They continue until all the cards have been used.

Unit 9 Grammar 1

Which candidate, which job?

Procedure

Give a copy of the worksheet to each student and read through the job adverts with the whole class.

Tell the students to discuss which of the four candidates is the most suitable for each job and why. Get feedback from the whole class.

Organise the students in groups of four and tell students A and B to take the roles of interviewers, one for each of the two jobs. Students C and D each take the role of a different candidate. Give students a few minutes to think of questions and answers and then Student A interviews C while Student B interviews D and then the candidates change over. Each candidate has to convince the interviewer that he or she is the best for the job.

Unit 9 Grammar 2

Abilities: past, present and future

Procedure

Give a copy of the worksheet to each student and tell them to match the vocabulary in the box with each picture. Get feedback from the whole class.

Now tell the students that they have to talk with a partner about their own abilities in relation to each picture in the past, present and future as in the example. Encourage them to give reasons and explain their statements.

When they have finished, have different students talk about one picture each for the whole class.

Unit 9 Grammar 3

What, where and when?

Procedure

Give each student or pair of students a copy of the worksheet and tell them to work in pairs in order to complete the sentences with the correct form of the verb (passive or active) and solve the anagram.

Get feedback from the class giving one point for each correct solution. The pair with the most points are the winners.

Answers

1 was discovered, Alexander Fleming 2 Abraham Lincoln was 3 The Mona Lisa was stolen 4 Winona Ryder was arrested 5 were written, Mozart 6 William Shakespeare died 7 Lord of the Rings was given 8 was discovered, Marie Curie 9 Drinking alcohol was made 10 Alexander Bell invented 11 The Taj Mahal was built 12 Albert Einstein was 13 Challenger exploded 14 London eye opened 15 were united, Berlin Wall

Unit 9 Communication

Negotiated solutions

Procedure

Divide the students into pairs and give a copy of Student A to one of the pair and Student B to the other. Tell students to read the first situation and check they understand. Now tell them to negotiate a solution. After a few minutes stop them and get feedback about the solutions they reached.

Continue using the same procedure for the other situations. If you don't have much time, students can read all the situations and then choose two of the four situations to roleplay.

Unit 10 Vocabulary
Animal crossword

Procedure

Divide the class into two groups, A and B, and give a copy of worksheet A to group A and of worksheet B to group B.

Have the students check they understand all of the words written in their crossword in pairs, helping them with any problems they might have.

Now rearrange the students so that one Student A is with one Student B. Tell them not to look at each other's paper. Focus the students' attention on the example sentence and tell them to give each other clues for the rest of the words. Write *down* and *across* on the blackboard so that students can identify the direction of the words.

Unit 10 Grammar 1
Phrasal verb question time

Procedure

Divide the class into two groups, A and B, and give a copy of worksheet A to group A and of worksheet B to group B.

Tell the students to work in small groups to match a verb and prepositions and complete the sentences.

Now put a student from group A with a student from group B. Tell them to ask and answer each other's completed questions.

Get feedback from the whole class about the questions.

Answers

Student A

1 grow up 2 pick up 3 come across
4 look up to 5 get on with 6 look after.

Student B

1 grow up 2 take to (x2) 3 come across
4 bring up 5 get on with 6 look after.

Unit 10 Grammar 2
Find the difference

Procedure

Divide the class into pairs and give a copy of worksheet Student A to one of the pair and Student B to the other. Tell the students not to look at each other's paper.

Focus their attention on the example and tell them to describe their pictures in a similar way or ask questions in order to find ten differences. Go round the class as they do this helping with vocabulary and correcting any mistakes.

When they have finished, have each pair look at both pictures together and have various students report back on the differences. Check they are using countable and uncountable nouns correctly.

Answers

The differences are: 1 number of monkeys
2 information board 3 number of tables
4 child eating ice cream (boy/girl) 5 juice in jug
6 number of hamburgers 7 amount of cake
8 rubbish/paper on ground 9 zookeeper's speech
10 weather/clouds

Unit 10 Grammar 3
Noughts and crosses

Procedure

Divide the class up into groups of four and divide each four into two teams of two. If you have odd numbers make some teams of one or three. Give each team a copy of the grid and explain the title 'Noughts and Crosses'. Read through the instructions with the students and check that they understand how to play the game.

Give a copy of the sentences A to one team and sentences B to another team. Each team must decide whether to be noughts or crosses.

Tell the students to take it in turns to choose a number and the other team will read them the sentence. If they decide right or wrong correctly they put the symbol in the square. Now the other team plays.

At the end, the students count how many noughts and crosses they have and add an extra point if they have three in a row. The winner is the team with the most points.

Unit 10 Communication
A danger to animals?

Procedure

Give each student or pair of students a copy of the worksheet. Tell them to match the words to the pictures. Explain the meaning of any of the words that students don't understand.

Now tell the students to discuss the questions with a partner.

When they have finished get feedback from the whole class.

Answers

1 Factory, pollution and smoke 2 Hunting, capture and gun 3 Cut down, farming and roads 4 Kennel, abandon and holidays

Unit 11 Vocabulary
Transport race

Procedure

Give a copy of the worksheet to each pair of students and tell them they have to find a word for each of the clues as quickly as possible. The number of letters for each word is given in brackets. The first pair to finish must shout stop and all the students have to finish writing.

Swap the papers around so that different pairs correct each other's and get answers from the whole class. The winning team is the pair with the most correct answers.

Answers

1 lorry 2 taxi 3 motorbike 4 ride 5 plane 6 coach 7 bus 8 miss 9 ferry 10 van 11 train 12 get off 13 catch 14 bicycle 15 take 17 car

Unit 11 Grammar 1
Already done it?

Procedure

Give a copy of the worksheet to each pair of students and tell them to make sentences to describe the pictures using *just*, *yet* and *already*. Go around the class helping with any vocabulary they might need.

Get feedback from the whole class about the pictures.

Now tell them to discuss the pictures with regard to their own experiences. Some of the pictures like number two they will need to talk about in a time limit such as today *I haven't done the washing up yet today.*

Get feedback from the whole class.

Unit 11 Grammar 2
Find out

Procedure

Cut up the cards and distribute one to each student. Tell the students to read the card and work out what questions they will have to ask in order to discover the information.

Get the students to stand up and mingle with the others asking their questions and making a note (mental or written) of the answers.

Get feedback from the whole class on the answers. If you have more than ten students, you might want to let students with the same card confer before this feedback session.

Unit 11 Grammar 3
Explain that!

Procedure

Divide the students into small groups of three or four and give each group a pile of cards, which they put on the desk face down.

Have one of the students take a card and read it aloud. Tell the rest of the students in the class to think of an explanation for the situation using the Past Perfect. Brainstorm the explanations, encouraging students to elaborate their explanations by asking follow up questions using e.g., where, why, when, etc.

Now tell the students to do the same with the rest of the cards in small groups, with students taking it in turns to take a card, give an explanation and ask questions about that explanation.

Unit 11 Communication
Travel options

Procedure

Divide the students into two groups, A and B, and give a copy of worksheet A to group A and of worksheet B to group B.

Tell the students to look at the missing information and work out questions to ask in order to find that information. You may have to teach the question: *How long does it take?*

Now rearrange the class so that a Student A is working with a Student B and tell them to ask and answer questions in order to complete the information.

Finally, focus the students' attention on the questions at the bottom of the worksheet and have them discuss their answers with their partner. Get feedback from the whole class.

Unit 12 Vocabulary
The money game

Procedure

Arrange the class so that the students are sitting in small groups of three or four, and give a copy of the worksheet, dice and counters to each group.

Tell the students to put their counters on start and shake the dice to see who goes first. Tell them that when they land on a square they have to do one of three things: complete the sentence, answer the question or discuss the statement. If a student can't do one of the tasks, he or she misses the next turn.

Students play the game until one of them reaches finish, consulting any answers they are not sure about with you.

Answers

1 earn 2 win 4 sales 6 India 8 lend 9 cash machine 11 win 12 piggy bank 13 spend 14 Italy 16 withdraw 17 cost 18 wallet 19 save 21 Japan 22 stock exchange 23 borrow

UNIT 12 Grammar 1

Hypothetical questions

Procedure

Arrange the class so that the students are sitting in small groups of three or four, and give each group a pile of question cards, which they put face down on the desk.

Tell the students to take it in turns to take a question card and read the question to the rest of the group, who must give their answers. Students continue until they have answered all the questions.

UNIT 12 Grammar 2

What did you say?

Procedure

Arrange the class so that the students are sitting in pairs and give a copy of worksheet A to one student and worksheet B to the other. Tell the students to ask each other the questions and try to remember the answers. They are not allowed to write anything.

Now rearrange the students so that each one is working with a different partner. Tell them to try to report what their first partner said. Go around the class monitoring and checking that students are using reported speech. This time the one who is listening makes notes of the answer.

Now have students sit with the another student to whose answers they were listening previously in order to check the information that they had heard. They do this by making sentences such as: *Sam told me that your favourite colour is red. Is that right?* Again, monitor the students carefully.

Get feedback from the class about how many students had remembered all the information correctly.

UNIT 12 Grammar 3

Which pair said that?

Procedure

Arrange the students in pairs and give them a copy of the worksheet. Tell the students to put their names at the top and discuss each of the categories in order to find one thing they have in common for each.

When they have finished, collect in the sheets and redistribute them. Tell the students to practise making sentences with both and neither for the information they have been given.

Now have students read out the sentences to the rest of the class. After each pair has finished, allow one or two students from the rest of the class to ask an extra question e.g., *Has either of them got blond hair?* Before writing down the names of two students who they think the information corresponds to.

When all the students have read out the information and students have noted down names for each sheet, reveal the real answers and see if the students guessed correctly.

UNIT 12 Communication

Problems, problems, problems!

Procedure

Arrange the students in pairs and give a copy of worksheet Student A to one and Student B to the other. Tell the students to read through the different situations, consulting any difficult words in a dictionary or with you.

Now tell the students to act out each situation in pairs. Give them a time limit of three or four minutes for each situation and get feedback from the class about how they solved the situation after each one.

DVD worksheets

1 London

Before watching

1 Match the nouns (1–8) with the adjectives (a–h). More than one answer is possible.

1 boutiques	a) asleep
2 people	b) busy
3 neighbourhood	c) empty
4 restaurants	d) famous
5 sights	e) keen
6 streets	f) lively
7 tourists	g) trendy
8 weather	h) wet

While Watching

2 Imagine you are interviewing a Londoner about their city. Watch the film and find the answers to your questions.

1 Is there anything to do early in the morning?
2 How many people come to London to work every day?
3 What places are tourists keen to visit?
4 How often does Big Ben chime?
5 When do the shops open in Oxford Street?
6 What can you find in Covent Garden?
7 Where and when can I see the Changing of the Guard?
8 What time do Londoners have lunch?
9 Can you recommend something typical to eat?
10 What landmarks can I see if I take a boat along the river?
11 What's the weather like?
12 Does Tower Bridge ever open?
13 Are there any nice parks in London?
14 When does the evening rush hour begin?
15 What time do the West End theatres open?
16 What can I do after the pubs close?

After Watching

3 Work with a partner using the information in the film and the questions above to plan a trip to London.

Before Watching

1 Use the prompts to ask your partner questions with *Have you ever...?*

1 go fishing
2 drive a bus
3 go to Paris
4 sit on a deckchair
5 see a cricket match
6 go for a walk in the rain
7 eat a sandwich in the rain
8 listen to a concert on the beach

While Watching

2 In which order do you see people doing the activities in Ex. 1?

3 Complete Cliff's plan with the phrases in the box.

like a mobile hotel	paying	the limit
to lend us	to the south of France	we live in it

I've persuaded London Transport (1) ________ this old bus. We fix it up (2) ________. This year (3) ________, take it (4) ________. Then next year, we'll be ready to take (5) ________. The sky's (5) ________!

4 Order the lines in each verse of the song.

1
a Fun and laughter on a summer holiday, ___
b No more working for a week or two. ___
c No more worries for me and you for a week or two. ___
d We're all going on a summer holiday, _1_

2
a Now let's see if it's true. ___
b We're going where the sea is blue. ___
c We're going where the sun shines brightly. ___
d We've seen it in the movies. ___

3
a Doing things they always wanted to. ___
b Everybody has a summer holiday, ___
c So we're going on a summer holiday ___
d To make our dreams come true for me and you. ___

After Watching

5 Discuss.
Have you ever been on holiday in the rain?
What can you do to have fun when it's raining?

3 Jamie Oliver

Before watching

1 Use a dictionary to find out the meanings of the cooking verbs. Then mime the verbs to your partner and see if they can guess what they are.

1 boil	2 chop	3 cut	4 fry
5 pour	6 put	7 serve	8 slice
9 sprinkle	10 stir	11 stuff	12 wrap

While watching

2 Watch the first part of the film and answer the questions.

1 Who is Jamie Oliver?
2 What's he famous for?
3 Where does he go in this programme?
4 What does he cook there?

3 Complete the instructions from the recipe with verbs from Ex. 1.

1 _________ fennel seeds over the whole fish
2 _________ the herbs inside the fish
3 _________ a layer of herbs on the bottom
4 _________ up your lemons
5 _________ the fish in paper

4 Match the beginnings and endings of these sentences.

1 This is a really fantastic way ...	a) and they're great with fish.
2 Salmon's ideal ...	b) because it's slightly oily.
3 I've got some fennel seeds ...	c) is wet it.
4 So once you've done that, ...	d) is wrap it up.
5 I'm going to ...	e) I've got some nice herbs.
6 And then what you want to do ...	f) of cooking fish.
7 So all you've got to do now ...	g) put a layer of herbs on the bottom.

After watching

5 Jamie Oliver uses informal English. What do the underlined expressions mean?

1 I've got <u>a serious amount</u> of herbs.
2 I'm going to <u>plonk</u> the fish on top of that.
3 Get your lemons and put <u>'em</u> in the middle.
4 Just copy what you <u>done</u> with the herbs, really.
5 Wet it to stop it burning too <u>quick</u>.

6 Think of a recipe you know well and describe it to your partner. Try to use the language on this page.

4 Surviving in the Sahara

Before watching

1 Discuss the guidelines below. Do they offer good or bad advice?

Guidelines for surviving in the desert

1 If you break down, stay with your vehicle.
2 Get in the shade.
3 Take a parachute with you.
4 Create an air space by doubling your parachute.
5 Take the seat out of your vehicle.
6 Keep your mouth shut, and roll your sleeves down.
7 Don't over-ration your water.
8 Make a large V-shaped sign in the sand.
9 Keep your eyes open for scorpions.
10 Use the fuel from the vehicle to make a fire.
11 Take warm clothes such as an Arab *djellabah*.

While watching

2 Watch the first part of the film and decide if these statements are true or false.

1 The Sahara desert is bigger than the whole of Europe.
2 It rains everywhere in the Sahara at least once a year.
3 Ray loves the Sahara.
4 Ray enjoys being on his own.

3 Match the advice in Ex. 1 (1–11) with the reasons (a–k).

a The sand is too hot to sit on.
b You don't want to get stung.
c They're ideal for creating shelter.
d It gets really cold in the desert at night.
e It's got to be inside you if it's going to help you.
f It's an internationally recognised distress signal.
g It will save you a lot of effort in your attempt to attract rescuers.
h You've got to do everything to conserve moisture.
i It helps to make effective insulation from the sun's rays.
j It's the biggest thing you've got, and it's like a huge emergency kit.
k It enables you to think clearly and to make the right decisions about survival.

After watching

4 Choose one of the survival situations below, and agree on a list of guidelines for surviving there. Don't forget to give reasons for your guidelines.

- Lost in the Arctic
- Living in a poor district of a big city with a high crime rate
- Shipwrecked in a small lifeboat with five other people

Before watching

1 Think about relationships between these people. What problems might there be?

stepmother and stepson
father and daughter
mother-in-law and daughter-in-law

While watching

2 Watch the film and answer these questions.

1 Why has Chelsea come to back her parents' home?
2 How do Chelsea and Norman get on?
3 Who is Bill? What don't we see him in this scene?
4 How old is Billy-Ray?

3 Complete what Ethel says with the words in the box.

ahead didn't fun show so surprise

1 Go ________! He's waiting for you.
2 I'm ________ glad you're home.
3 Where's your friend? You did bring your friend, ________ you?
4 Well, this is a great ________!
5 Isn't this ________? Norman, why don't we put Billy in Chelsea's old room?
6 Take him up! ________ him where everything is.

4 Put the sentences into the dialogues.

a

Chelsea: We rented a car that explodes every 40 miles.
Norman: 3
Chelsea: In Boston.
Norman: ___
Chelsea: I don't know. Green, I think.
Ethel: A green one!
Norman: ___
Chelsea: I don't know.
Ethel: Oh, it doesn't matter Norman.
Norman: ___
Chelsea: Well, I guess I should have looked.

1 Of course it doesn't matter. I was just curious.
2 No, what sort of make is it?
3 Rented a car, huh?
4 What sort of car is it ?

b

Billy Ray: I hear you turned 80 today.
Norman: 3
Billy Ray: Yeah. Man, that's really old.
Norman: ___
Billy Ray: Your father's still alive?
Norman: ___

1 Huh! You should meet my father.
2 No, but you should meet him.
3 That what you heard?

After watching

5 What happens next? Choose the most likely option.

1 There is a huge argument and Norman's birthday ends in tears.
2 Chelsea, Bill and Billy Ray spend a lovely holiday at the cottage on Golden Pond.
3 The next day Chelsea and Bill go to Europe to get married, leaving Billy at the cottage.

Before watching

1 Look at page 138 of your Students' Book, and ask your partner questions about the people in the photos. Student A ask questions about Alison and Kathleen. Student B ask questions about Jennifer and Astrid.

While watching

2 Answer the questions.

1 Why did Alison move to Scotland?
2 How often does she visit her family and friends?
3 What's the weather like in Erie?
4 What did Astrid not like about Perth?

3 Complete with the correct form of the verbs in brackets.

1 I ________ (live) in Belfast until 1994.
2 The Albert Clock in Belfast ________ (fall) over.
3 I ________ (go) home about once a month.
4 I ________ (be) born in Erie.
5 Usually it ________ (snow) between October and March.
6 I don't think that I ________ (go) back and live there.
7 It ________ (not/feel) like home to me.
8 I ________ (spend) all of my childhood and my teen years there.

4 Choose the correct forms.

1 The people in Belfast enjoy *to tell* / *telling* jokes.
2 I'd recommend people *to visit* / *visiting* the place where the Titanic was built.
3 I go home about once a month *to visit* / *visiting* my family and friends.
4 My favourite thing about *to live* / *living* in Erie was my friends.
5 There are lots of things you can do, particularly if you love *to be* / *being* in the outdoors.
6 You can go *to swim* / *swimming* on the beaches.
7 *To be* / *Being* able to walk along the coast was just lovely.
8 I would love *to go* / *going* back to Australia.

After watching

4 Use the language on this page to write sentences about you and your home town. Tell a partner.

7 Carry on Doctor

Before watching

1 What do you think of the power of positive thinking? Can it prevent you from becoming ill? Can it help you in life?

While watching

2 Francis Bigger is an unlucky man. Put the eight unfortunate things that happen to him in the correct order.

a A doctor falls and injects him in the bottom with a huge syringe. ___
b He drinks some tea which tastes horrible. ___
c He falls off a stage. _1_
d He gets thrown out of the back of the ambulance when it stops. ___
e He is woken up by a careless cleaner. ___
f A male nurse washes his face in a very rough way. ___
g The nurse wakes him up at 6a.m. ___
h The ambulance driver drives too fast and hurts him. ___

3 Which of Francis' problems (a–h) above do the lines below (1–6) correspond to? Who says them?

1 He's in a hurry!
2 I'll let you know when it's over.
3 Look, I don't want 'washie time'.
4 Nothing can happen to me.
5 That's not what I would call it.
6 This isn't going to hurt.

After watching

4 Imagine you are Francis Bigger. Write a letter to a friend explaining everything that has happened to you since you appeared on stage to talk about *The Bigger Way*. Use the language on this page and on page 139 of your Students' Book.

8 Speed-dating

Before watching

1 How many different ways of meeting people can you think of? Which do you think is the best way of meeting people?

While watching

2 Complete the card with information about Darren and Kavita.

Name	Darren	Kavita
Age	1)	24
Profession	dentist	7)
Residence	Docklands, London	Osterley, West London
Married/Single/Divorced	2)	8)
Reasons for trying speed-dating	3)	9)
Ideal partner	4) She should be ________ -________- ________ , ________, have a good ________ ________ ________, and be from a similar ________ professionally.	10) A guy with an immense ________. Someone she can have a stimulating ________ with. Someone who can make her ________.
Free time	5)	11)
Religion	6)	12)

3 Complete these questions about speed-dating.

1 How long can you speak to each date?
2 Does that give you enough time to decide whether they interest you or not?
3 What are the advantages of speed-dating?
4 What do you do after talking to each date?
5 What mustn't you forget to do?
6 What happens if both people tick yes?

After watching

4 What do you remember about Darren and Kavita?

1 What were they doing while they were introducing themselves?
2 What were they doing when they explained why they were trying speed-dating?
3 What were they doing when we heard them describing their ideal partners?
4 What were they holding while they were talking to each other?

5 Copy the form above in Ex. 2 and use it to interview some of your classmates. Do not take more than three minutes with each person.

Before watching

1 Match the compound nouns (1–5 with a–e) and the verb-noun collocations (6–10 with f–j).

compound nouns			
1	IT	a	line
2	market	b	policy
3	after-sales	c	programme
4	customer care	d	share
5	product	e	skills

verb – noun collocations			
1	make	a	a deal
2	deal in	b	products
3	sell	c	a profit
4	close	d	a sales team
5	motivate	e	retail technology

While watching

2 Answer the questions.

1 How does Steve react when the security camera talks to him?
2 Why is he so nervous?
3 Has the security camera talked to other job candidates before?
4 Does Steve know a lot about the company? Why/Why not?
5 What is the most important part of an interview?
6 Does the security camera help Steve?
7 Why, according to the security camera, is Steve the ideal candidate?
8 What does the company sell?

3 Complete the questions the security camera asks Steve. Watch the film again to check your answers.

1 What do you know about the _________?
2 How much _________ did the company _________ last year?
3 How big is their _________ _________?
4 What do you know about their _________ _________?
5 What about their _________–_________ _________? The _________ _________ _________?
6 They _________ in _________ _________, but exactly what sort of _________ do they _________?
7 Do you feel _________?
8 Did you practice _________ _________ out loud on your own?

After watching

4 Add more ideas to this list.

Useful tips for job interviews

- Be confident
- Believe in yourself
- _________
- Be charming
- _________
- _________
- Encourage people to relax when they're with you
- _________
- Be dynamic, full of energy and ideas
- _________

10 Wolves

Before watching

1 Which fictional characters are described below? What do the verbs in bold mean?

1. The man who goes into a phone box and turns into a super hero.
2. The boy who was brought up by wolves and who danced with a bear called Baloo.
3. The boy who comes across a magic lamp.
4. The boy who grows up in the jungle and becomes king of the animals.
5. The boy who kept making up a story about a hungry wolf.
6. The girl who looked after her grandfather and who got on very well with a boy called Peter.

While watching

2 Complete the sentences with the words in the box. Watch the film. Which action do you not see?

after / away / down / into / on / up

1. A black sheep puts ________ a wolf's head.
2. A wolf dresses ________ as Little Bo Peep.
3. A sheep runs ________ a wolf playing a flute.
4. The sheep lifts ________ the wolf's dress.
5. The sheep runs ________.
6. The wolf falls ________.
7. Little Bo Peep looks ________ her sheep.
8. A werewolf jumps ________ a monster's back.
9. A man turns ________ a wolf.
10. A wolf picks ________ a sheep.

3 Decide whether these statements belong to fact, fiction or to both.

		Fact	Fiction
1	Wolves are frightening, dangerous animals.		
2	Wolves are very intelligent.		
3	Wolves can dress up as humans.		
4	Some people become werewolves at night.		
5	Wolves are found only in remote areas.		
6	Wolves can talk to humans.		
7	Wolves use body language and sound to communicate with other wolves.		
8	Wolves live and hunt in packs.		
9	Wolves often attack and kill humans.		
10	Wolves are nearly extinct.		

After watching

4 Discuss.

Why are people still frightened of wolves?

11 Gill's wild world

Before watching

1 Find out which members of your group have been to the following places.

- The Alps
- The Antarctic
- The Arctic
- Canada
- Cuba
- Fiji
- The Himalayas
- London
- Mongolia
- New York
- New Zealand
- Paris
- Rome
- Russia
- Scotland
- Thailand

While watching

2 Watch the film and say which of the places in Ex. 1 Gill mentions.

3 Imagine you are interviewing Gill. Watch the film to find her answers to these questions.

1 What do you do?
2 Who do you work for?
3 Where have you been most recently?
4 Why don't you use a laptop computer?
5 How many pages do you have to write some weeks?
6 How many people read your articles?
7 How many countries have you been to?
8 Have you ever been to Russia?
9 What's the most amazing place you've ever been to?
10 What did you particularly like about it?
11 What did you like about Fiji?
12 Have you ever had any narrow escapes on your travels?
13 What's the best thing about your job?
14 Is your TV programme always filmed in wild places like Canada and New Zealand?
15 What are you working on at the moment?
16 What's special about Antarctica?

After watching

4 Role play the interview with Gill.

Student A: You interview Gill. Ask her eight of the questions in Ex. 3 as well as any relevant follow up questions.

Student B: You are Gill. Give the fullest possible answers to the questions your partner asks you.

12 The Ladykillers

Before watching

1 Look at the famous fictional criminals. What did they do?

Al Capone   Robin Hood   Bonnie and Clyde

While watching

2 In which order do these things happen?

1 The men argue about what to do.
2 The men try to pick up the money.
3 The men admire the money.
4 Mrs Wilberforce stands on the Professor's scarf.
5 Mrs Wilberforce tells them she's sad to see them go.
6 The strap on Mr Lawson's cello case gets stuck in the door.

3 Mrs Wilberforce told a friend what had happened. Complete her story with one word in each gap. Watch the film again to check your answers.

The gentlemen seemed so (1) ________ when they came home for their last rehearsal and saw the big case that I had brought back from the station for them. I (2) ________ the Professor that I had to give him back his ten shillings because the cab man (3) ________ refused to take it, but he didn't seem interested. Anyway, they took that big case (4) ________, and then I heard them playing that lovely music again.

Later on, they all came down to say goodbye. I told the Major that I had (5) ________ hoping that they would be able to play a concert, and explained that my friends (6) ________ be so disappointed to have missed them. And as for me, I said that I (7) ________ so sad to see them go. Just then that nice Mr Lawson went upstairs to get his cello. I told the Major that I only (8) ________ they had enjoyed their stay as much as I had, and he assured me they had, so I wished him good fortune in his travels. I (9) ________ to the Professor for standing on his scarf, and then they all left. The last one to go was Mr Lawson, who (10) ________ me for the nice tea and everything, and I closed the door. But just a few seconds later the door bell (11) ________, and I opened the door, and there was Mr Lawson (12) ________ on the ground next to his empty cello case, surrounded by lots of banknotes. And he had such a (13) ________ look on his face.

Then, (14) ________, the other gentlemen came running back and Professor Marcus told me that it was alright, that everything (15) ________ under control, and he shut the door in my face! I opened the door to see what was going on, but the Professor just closed the door again and (16) ________ 'goodbye'. He really didn't seem as polite as before. I went up the stairs (17) ________ look in their rooms, and then I came down again. When I opened the front door again, they were all in the car, which was (18) ________ a few yards away. And as I was (19) ________ them, the gentlemen got out of the car and started walking back towards the house.

After watching

4 Put Mr Harvey's reasons for returning to the house into reported speech.

'I tell you, we must do something. She knows. She saw the money. She'll talk. And my picture's on file. And so is Harry's. And so is yours. If they take her down to the gallery, she'll shop us. They've got our fingers and thumbs.'

Mr Harvey told the others that they had to do something. He said that she ...

Teaching notes

1 London

▶ This film has a high vocabulary load. You might want to pre-teach some of the following words and phrases: to make deliveries, roast beef dinner, suburbs, highway to take a ride, lucky, nearby, for a while, market stalls, were first staged here, crowds, having fun

OPTIONAL WARMER

Write 'Sights to see and things to do in London' on the board. Divide you class into two teams. Elicit sights to see and things to do in London from each team.

Before Watching

1 ▶ Ss discuss their answers and giving reasons.

▶ Play the introductory section for Ss to listen for which collocations the narrator uses in the film.

Answers: 1 g) 2 a) 3 f) 4 b) 5 d) 6 c) 7 e) 8 h)

While Watching

2 ▶ Ss read through the questions with a partner.

▶ Watch the film and allow the Ss to make notes.

▶ Watch the film again, pausing for Ss to answer.

▶ Ss write down the answers in full sentences.

Suggested answers:

1 Yes, you could visit some of the city's markets.
2 More than 3 million people come to work in London.
3 Tourists visit famous sights like the Tower of London.
4 It chimes once every quarter hour.
5 All of the shops are open by 10 o'clock.
6 It's a neighbourhood with boutiques and market stalls.
7 You can see it at Buckingham Palace at 11.30a.m.
8 Most Londoners have lunch at about 1p.m..
9 Yes, you might try a traditional roast beef dinner.
10 You can see the Houses of Parliament and St Paul's.
11 It's unpredictable. It can rain any day of the year.
12 Yes, it does. You might see a boat pass through.
13 Yes, of course. There are some lovely green parks.
14 It begins at 5p.m.
15 They open at about 7.30p.m.
16 You can go to a club.

After Watching

3 ▶ Ss practise their roles and then act out the conversation. Then ask the Ss to swap roles and repeat the exercise.

OPTIONAL EXTENSION

Ask the Ss to think of suitable questions that a tourist to their city might ask. Ss act out conversations using their questions.

2 Summer Holiday

OPTIONAL WARMER

Ask the Ss to write what they did during their last summer holiday on their piece of paper, e.g., *Last summer, I went walking in the mountains*. Ask them not to let anyone see what they have written. Take in the pieces of paper, read them out and see if the Ss can guess who wrote what.

Before watching

1 ▶ Elicit the correct questions from the prompts by asking pairs of Ss to model a question and an answer.

▶ Put the Ss into pairs and have them practise asking answering the questions.

▶ Ask Ss to report anything interesting they discovered.

While watching

2 ▶ Play the introduction to the film as Ss order the activities. Ss compare answers in pairs.

▶ Play the introduction again, pausing the film every time they see one of the actions.

▶ Play the film through all the way to the end, so Ss can see what happens.

Answers: 8, 4, 6, 1, 7, 5, 2, 3

3 ▶ Give the Ss a short time to try and complete the task based on what they can remember of the film.

▶ Watch the first part again for Ss to check the answers.

Answers: 1 to lend us 2 like a mobile hotel 3 we live in it 4 to the south of France 5 paying passengers 6 the limit

4 ▶ Watch the last part of the film as Ss order the lines.

▶ Play the section again for Ss to check their answers.

Answers:
1 d, b, a, c
2 c, b, d, a
3 b, a, c, d

After watching

5 ▶ Ss discuss the questions in pairs.

▶ Discuss the questions with the whole class.

OPTIONAL EXTENSION

Ss discuss and write about their best summer holiday.

3 Jamie Oliver

OPTIONAL WARMER

Form groups and tell them they have to agree on the ideal meal (a starter, a main course, a dessert, and a drink).

Before watching

1 ▶ Ask the Ss to look up the meanings of the verbs.

▶ Form pairs and demonstrate how to use mime to indicate one of the verbs. Allow them time to mime the other verbs.

While watching

2 ▶ Read through the questions with the Ss and ask if they can remember any answers from Lesson 3.1.

▶ Watch the introduction to the film without pausing and elicit the answers to Ex. 2.

Answers:
1 He's one of the most popular chefs on British TV.
2 For his recipes, restaurants and informal style.
3 He goes to the south-west of England.
4 He cooks a salmon with fresh herbs.

3 ▶ Ask the Ss to read through the questions, thinking about what might fit into the gaps.

▶ Give Ss a short time to complete the collocations in Ex. 3, watching the rest of the film.

▶ Watch the rest of the film again, pausing where necessary to check the answers.

Answers: 1 sprinkle 2 stuff 3 put 4 slice 5 wrap

4 ▶ Give the Ss time to read through the questions.

▶ Ss match the beginnings and the endings of the sentences using what they remember from the film.

▶ Ss watch the film again, matching up the sentences.

▶ Watch the film again for Ss to check their answers.

Answers: 1 f 2 b 3 a 4 e 5 g 6 d 7 c

After watching

5 ▶ Ask the Ss to look at the sentences in Ex 5 and think about what the underlined expressions might mean.

▶ Elicit the answers from the Ss.

Answers: 1 a lot of 2 put 3 them 4 did 5 quickly

6 ▶ Ss prepare the vocabulary they need for their recipes.

▶ Form pairs and have them describe their recipes.

OPTIONAL EXTENSION

Ss write the recipe they described.

4 Surviving in the Sahara

OPTIONAL WARMER

Write on the board *One of the most beautiful and stunning places on Earth*. Describe a place that you think is beautiful and stunning, and then ask the Ss to describe places that they find beautiful and stunning.

Before watching

1 ▶ Ask the Ss to read the guidelines in Ex. 1. Elicit the meaning of any difficult vocabulary from the Ss.

▶ Ss discuss which guidelines offer good or bad advice, working in pairs.

Answer: They all offer good advice.

While watching

2 ▶ Ask the Ss to read the statements in Ex. 2, and decide if they are true or false.

▶ Watch the first part of the film for Ss to check their answers.

Answers: 1 true 2 false 3 true 4 true

3 ▶ Form groups of three and ask the Ss to read through the reasons for the advice (a–k), checking any unknown vocabulary.

▶ Ss then match the guidelines in Ex 1 with these reasons.

▶ Watch the rest of the film, pausing where necessary, for Ss to check their answers.

Answers: 1 j 2 k 3 c 4 i 5 a 6 h 7 e 8 f 9 b 10 g 11 d

After watching

4 ▶ Form groups, have them choose one of the survival situations, and give them a time limit to come up with a list of guidelines and their corresponding reasons. Encourage them to use language from this unit.

▶ When the Ss have finished, form new groups with Ss from different groups and have them report their guidelines to the others.

▶ Ss discuss which of the situations is the most difficult to survive with the whole class.

OPTIONAL EXTENSION

Ask the Ss to write sentences comparing life in the Sahara desert with life in their home town.

5 On Golden Pond

OPTIONAL WARMER

Write the following sentences on the board; *I always get on really well with ... I usually get on well with ..., but we sometimes have arguments. I don't get on very well with ... .*

Ss complete them with the name of someone in their lives.

Before watching

1 ▶ Put Ss in pairs and ask them to think about the following relationships; mother-in-law and daughter-in-law and father and daughter.

▶ Ss discuss the relationships, highlighting any problems or tensions that could occur.

While watching

2 ▶ Ss read the questions and check if they can remember any answers from watching the film the first time.

▶ Watch the film while Ss write their answers.

▶ Elicit the answers from the whole class.

Answers:
1 Because it's Norman's 80th birthday.
2 They don't get on very well.
3 Bill is Chelsea's fiancé, he's parking the car.
4 He turned 13 two weeks ago.

3 ▶ Elicit who wants the occasion to go well (Ethel).

▶ Give the Ss time to read and complete the task.

▶ Watch the film again for Ss to check their answers.

Answers: 1 a 2 e 3 b 4 f 5 c 6 d

4 ▶ Put the Ss into pairs and give them time to think about the order of the sentences.

▶ Play the film again for Ss to check their answers.

Answers: a) 3, 1, 2 b) 3, 1, 2

After watching

5 ▶ Discuss what the Ss think happens next.

Answer: 3

▶ Discuss if they think the film has a happy ending.

Answer: Norman and Billy Ray learn to communicate and trust each other. Norman learns to trust his daughter and communicate with her.

OPTIONAL EXTENSION

Ss prepare a short talk about a film they have seen. Encourage them to choose a film that deals with relationships.

6 Around the world

OPTIONAL WARMER

Write the following prompts on the board, and ask the Ss to write answers which are true for them.

1 This is something I really enjoy doing.
2 This is a place I recommend you to visit.
3 This is a place where I'd like to live.
4 This is the place where I was born.
5 This is something I don't like.
6 This is my favourite place in the whole world.

Form pairs. Ss should take turns to say one of their answers, and then guess which prompt their partner's answer corresponds to.

Before watching

1 ▶ Form pairs, and ask the Ss to look at the sections about the people on page 138 of their Students' Book.

▶ Ss ask their partner questions about the four women. Elicit some questions that can be asked.

While watching

2 ▶ Ask the Ss to read the questions in Ex. 2.

▶ Watch the film, pausing for Ss to find the answers.

Answers:
1 to go to university
2 about once a month
3 hot and sunny in summer, very cold in winter
4 Sometimes, it's too hot.

3 ▶ Give the Ss time to choose the correct form of the verbs.

▶ Watch the film, for Ss to check their answers.

Answers: 1 lived 2 is falling 3 go 4 was 5 snows 6 'll go 7 doesn't feel 8 spent

4 ▶ Give Ss a few minutes to think about the verb forms.

▶ Watch the film, pausing to check Ss' answers.

Answers: 1 telling 2 to visit 3 to visit 4 living 5 being 6 swimming 7 Being 8 to go

After watching

5 ▶ Introduce the topic and elicit useful phrases for the activity, e.g., *I was born ..., I lived there for ... years.*

▶ Give the Ss a time limit to write some sentences.

▶ Form pairs. Ss discuss each other's sentences.

OPTIONAL EXTENSION

Ss prepare an interview similar to those they have seen in the film. Have them interview each other.

7 Carry on Doctor

OPTIONAL WARMER

Write the following phrases on the board: *the blinds, the hoovering, an accident, a sip of tea, a syringe, a thermometer under someone's tongue, someone's face, to hospital in an ambulance*. Ask the Ss if they can remember the verbs which follow these phrases on page 139 of their Students' Books. (open the blinds, do the hoovering, have an accident, take a sip of tea, prepare a syringe, put a thermometer under someone's tongue, wash someone's face, go to hospital in an ambulance.)

Before watching

1► Freeze the film on the first scene and ask Ss to read out what is written on the banner and on the blackboard at the back:

- Think the Bigger Way! • Think power!
- Think positive! • Think Bigger!

► Explain that 'Bigger' is the name of the speaker on the stage, and elicit the Ss' opinions with regard to the questions in Ex. 1.

While watching

2► Form pairs and ask the Ss to order the sentences in Ex. 2. Play the film through once for Ss watch.

► Watch the film again without pausing to check Ss' answers.

Answers: 1 c 2 h 3 d 4 g 5 b 6 f 7 e 8 a

3► Give the Ss a short time to read through the sentences in Ex. 3, and to guess which problems they correspond to and who said each one. Explain that there is not a sentence for every situation in Ex. 2.

► Ss watch the film again, pausing where necessary, to check their answers.

► You might mention at this stage that the doctor's name in the film is *Doctor Kilmore*, and see if anyone can explain the pun.

Answers: 1 g (the nurse) 2 d (an ambulance man) 3 g (Francis) 4 g (Francis) 5 f (Francis) 6 c (Francis) 7 – b (Francis) 8 a (the doctor)

After watching

4► Tell Ss that they should write an informal letter, and that they should use the language both on this page and on page 139 of their Students' Book.

OPTIONAL EXTENSION

Ask the Ss to prepare an anecdote about something that went wrong in their lives. In the next class, form groups and have them tell each other their anecdotes.

8 Speed-dating

OPTIONAL WARMER

Write statements with personal information about yourself on the board, e.g., *I'm 30 years old.*

Elicit the questions which might produce the answers on the board.

Before watching

1► Ask the Ss to look at the questions in Ex. 1, and discuss the different ways of meeting people.

► If nobody mentions speed-dating, remind them of what they saw on page 140 of their Ss' book.

While watching

2► Give the Ss time to study the card.

► Watch the film for Ss write in their answers.

► Elicit the answers, pausing the video if necessary.

Answers: 1 27 2 Single 3 You're not under any pressure. 4 down-to-earth, pretty, sense of humour, background 5 At weekends, he visits his parents. 6 Hindu 7 IT consultant 8 Single 9 Her recent introductions and relationships have not been successful. It's a great way of meeting new people. It's exciting to meet different people in one night. 10 Intellect, conversation, laugh 11 She likes chilling in bars, eating out and going to parks. 12 Hindu

3► Give the Ss time to answer the questions in Ex. 3.

► Play the film again for Ss to find the answers.

Answers: 1 three minutes 2 It's enough time to get a good idea. 3 It's a great way of meeting a lot of new people in a short time. 4 You complete a card with the other person's name. 5 tick *yes* or *no* 6 The organisers exchange the people's email addresses.

After watching

4► Ss work in pairs, answering the questions.

► Elicit the Ss answers.

► Play the film again for Ss' to check their answers.

Answers:
1 They were driving home. 2 They were getting ready to go out, and ironing. 3 They were walking with friends in the street. 4 They were holding pens.

5► Tell Ss that they are going to interview their class.

► Give them time to interview 3 classmates.

OPTIONAL EXTENSION

Ask the Ss to write a short piece about either how they or a friend met their partner (husband, wife, boyfriend, girlfriend).

9 The interview

OPTIONAL WARMER

Tell the Ss that they are the managers of a school where you have applied for a job, and they are going to interview you. Form small groups, and give them a few minutes to come up with suitable questions. Act out the interview, and then ask if you've got the job.

Before watching

1 ▶ Give the Ss a short time to study the words.

▶ Ss work in pairs, matching the words.

▶ Elicit the answers from the Ss.

Answers: 1 e 2 d 3 b 4 c 5 a 6 h 7 j 8 g 9 f 10 i

While watching

2 ▶ Give the Ss a short time to read the questions.

▶ Play the film without pausing and elicit full answers.

▶ Rewind and replay any scenes if necessary.

Suggested answers: 1 He doesn't believe it and refuses to speak to the camera. 2 He's going to a job interview and he's wondering whether he's good enough. 3 Yes, to shop-assistants, taxi-drivers and school teachers. 4 No. He doesn't know what they sell. He's been thinking about bonuses and promotion. 5 According to the camera, it's the first impression. 6 Yes and no. It gives him lots of advice but it makes him feel even less confident and more nervous. 7 He has years of experience, is excellent at closing deals, can motivate a sales team and is constantly improving his computer skills. 8 security cameras

3 ▶ Allow Ss time to complete the questions.

▶ Ss compare their answers with a partner.

▶ Watch the film again to check the answers.

Answers: 1 job 2 profit make 3 market share 4 main competitors 5 after-sales policy customer care programme 6 deal retail technology products sell 7 positive 8 answering questions

After watching

4 ▶ Elicit which tips the camera told Steve (all of them).

▶ Ss add as many tips as they can.

▶ When they have finished, Ss compare their ideas.

OPTIONAL EXTENSION

Tell Ss they are going to role-play a job interview.

Ss prepare the interview.

Ss act out their interviews.

10 Wolves

OPTIONAL WARMER

Write on the board *What are you frightened of?* Discuss with the whole class, ensuring that wolves, werewolves, and horror films come up in the discussion.

Before watching

1 ▶ Ask the Ss to read the descriptions, and elicit who they correspond to.

▶ Elicit the meanings of the phrasal verbs.

▶ If you have time, ask the Ss to continue the guessing game by inventing some descriptions of their own.

Answers: 1 Superman, becomes 2 Mowgli from the Jungle Book, was raised 3 Aladdin, finds 4 Tarzan, changes from boy to man 5 the boy who cried 'wolf', created 6 Heidi, cared for, had a good relationship with

While watching

2 ▶ Give the Ss a short time to read the sentences in Ex. 2 and to choose the best words for the gaps.

▶ Elicit the correct answers.

▶ Watch the film without pausing to check which action is not included.

Answers: 1 on 2 up 3 after 4 up 5 away 6 down 7 after (not included in the film) 8 on 9 into 10 up

3 ▶ Form pairs and give the Ss a short time to decide if the sentences in Ex. 3 correspond to fact, fiction or to both.

▶ Play the film again, pausing where necessary, to check the answers.

Answers: 1 both 2 both 3 fiction 4 fiction 5 fact 6 fiction 7 both 8 both 9 fiction 10 fact

After watching

4 ▶ Discuss the question with the whole class.

▶ Elicit the theory given in the film, replaying the last section, if necessary. (Perhaps man's fear of wolves lies in the past. In the long, cold winters, people and wolves competed for the same food.)

OPTIONAL EXTENSION

Ask each student to find out at least one more fact about wolves. In the next class, collate all the new facts on the board. Ask the Ss to use all the new information, and the information from this unit to write a text about wolves.

11 Gill's wild world

OPTIONAL WARMER

Prepare a list of 10 geography questions before your class. Tell the Ss you are going to read some clues about some places in the world. They should listen and then guess the places you are describing.

Before watching

1 ▶ Elicit the questions the Ss should ask each other, e.g., *Have you ever been to...? When did you go there?* etc.

▶ Give Ss enough time to find out the information.

While watching

1 ▶ Watch the film and elicit the places Gill mentions.

▶ Ask Ss to check their answers in pairs.

Answers: The Antarctic, The Arctic, Canada, Fiji, The Himalayas, Mongolia, New York, New Zealand, Russia and Thailand.

2 ▶ Explain that you will want the Ss to role-play an interview, but they must find out the information.

▶ Read the questions, helping with vocabulary.

▶ Watch the film again, pausing where necessary, and eliciting the answers to the questions.

Suggested answers:

1 I'm a travel writer and TV programme maker.
2 I work for newspapers and TV programmes.
3 I've just got back from Antarctica.
4 Because I prefer travelling light.
5 Sometimes I have eight pages to write every week.
6 Sometimes two million people read my articles.
7 I've been to about 70 countries.
8 No, I haven't been to Russia yet.
9 The most amazing place I've ever been to is Canada.
10 I loved the open spaces, and the scenery was stunning.
11 It has some of the friendliest people I've ever met.
12 One time I was nearly eaten by a shark in Thailand.
13 the excitement of going to new places
14 No, it's filmed in all sorts of places.
15 At the moment I'm working on a trip to Antarctica.
16 It's the coldest, driest and windiest place on earth.

After watching

4 ▶ Ss agree on who is going to play each role.

▶ Give them a few minutes to prepare the interview.

▶ Ask the Ss to swap roles after the first interview.

OPTIONAL EXTENSION

Ask the Ss which of the places in Ex. 1 they would most like to visit and why.

12 The Ladykillers

OPTIONAL WARMER

Discuss the following questions with the whole class. What would you do if a friend of yours confessed he/she was a thief? What would you do if you overheard a gang of criminals planning a bank robbery? What would you say if someone invited you to take part in a bank robbery?

Before watching

1 ▶ Ask the Ss to look at the list of famous criminals.

▶ Ss work in pairs, discussing what the criminals did.

Answers: Al Capone sold alcohol illegally during prohibition in the 1930s in Chicago. Robin Hood stole money from the rich and gave it to the poor in Sherwood Forest, Nottingham. Bonnie and Clyde were fictional bank robbers in the USA. Nick Leeson was the 'rogue trader' who went to prison for committing fraud while working for Baring's Bank.

While watching

2 ▶ Ss guess the order the things happened.

▶ Play the film for Ss to check their answers.

Answers: 3, 5, 4, 6, 2, 1

3 ▶ Form pairs and give them enough time to try to complete the text in Ex. 3.

▶ Watch the film again, to elicit the answers.

Answers: 1 happy 2 told 3 had 4 upstairs 5 been 6 would 7 was 8 hoped 9 apologised 10 thanked 11 rang 12 kneeling 13 guilty 14 suddenly 15 was 16 said 17 to 18 parked 19 watching

After watching

4 ▶ Ask the Ss to transform Mr Harvey's speech to reported speech. You may wish to play the film again.

▶ Give them time, and then elicit the correct answer.

Suggested answer: Mr Harvey told the others that they had to do something. He said that she knew, and that she had seen the money. He said that she would talk and that his picture was on file and so were Harry's and Mr Lawson's. He claimed that if they took her down to the gallery, she would shop them, and said that they had their fingers and thumbs.

OPTIONAL EXTENSION

Ask Ss to role-play a conversation back at the house. Ss can act their conversations out. N.B. The film ends as Mrs. Wilberforce foils the attempts to kill her and ends up with the money.

Test 1 Units 1-3

Grammar

likes and dislikes

1 Fill in the missing words to complete the following sentences.

I really <u>**hate**</u> getting up early in the morning but it is necessary.

1. I can't ______ waiting for a long time in the traffic.
2. I'm quite keen ______ going to the cinema.
3. He really ______ like meeting too many people because he's shy.
4. Trish absolutely ______ cooking. She thinks it's the best thing in the world.
5. We don't ______ what we do tonight. It makes no difference to us.
6. I quite ______ this singer's voice but I don't usually buy his records.

3 points

Present Simple and Adverbs of Frequency

2 Put the words in the correct order to make sentences. Remember to begin the sentence with a capital letter.

always early work Jeanette finishes.

<u>Jeanette always finishes work early.</u>

1. like don't swimming I go because never I it.

   ____

2. often uncle in visit France we our.

   ____

3. clubbing absolutely Tina usually because loves she goes it.

   ____

4. sometimes you play do golf?

   ____

5. ever bed to late we go hardly.

   ____

6. weekends does lie-in Jim at have always a?

   ____

3 points

Present Continuous

3 Complete the sentences with the correct form of the verb in brackets. Choose either Present Simple or Present Continuous.

She **prefers** (prefer) listening to music to reading.

1 I sometimes ________ (watch) a film on TV.

2 At the moment I ________ (work) as a shop assistant but I will stop when I go back to university in October.

3 I ________ (study) now, but I think I'll go to the gym later.

4 My friends and I often ________ (have) a picnic on Saturdays.

5 I ________ (not understand) what you are saying.

6 We ________ (have) a very interesting conversation right now.

3 points

so and *neither*

4 Agree or disagree with what A says using *so*, *neither* or a short sentence.

A: I have got the new Eminem CD.

(agree) **B:** **So have I**.

1 **A:** I won a prize for the best speech last year.
(disagree) **B:** ______________ .

2 **A:** I'm really into James Brown's music.
(agree) **B:** ______________ .

3 **A:** I love going to pop concerts.
(agree) **B:** ______________ .

4 **A:** I didn't go to that meeting.
(disagree) **B:** ______________ .

5 **A:** I don't like this disco.
(agree) **B:** ______________ .

6 **A:** I haven't got many records.
(disagree) **B:** ______________ .

3 points

Past Simple and Present Perfect Simple

5 Complete the gaps with the correct form of the verb in brackets.

I have travelled (travel) a lot since I was at university. I (1) ________ (enjoy) seeing new places for many years and last summer I (2) ________ (have) a memorable holiday. My wife and I (3) ________ (go) to Montpellier in the south of France. (4) ________ you ________ (ever be) there? I don't think I (5) ________ (see) such an interesting place for a very long time. In fact, it was my brother who (6) ________ (recommend) it to me. Believe it or not, he (7) ________ (visit) this city seven times! I can see why. The beaches are lovely and the architecture of the old city centre is superb.

We (8) ________ (eat) some delicious food and, on our last night, we (9) ________ (see) an incredible performance by acrobats in the famous Comedy Square. I (10) ________ (watch) a lot of shows in my life but very few as good as that one. However, I don't think I'll do the same as my brother because there are many other beautiful and exotic places that we also want to visit.

5 points

defining relative clauses

6 Fill the blanks by selecting the correct option in the following sentences.

Diana is the person *which/who* called you on the phone the other day.

1 Las Vegas is a place *where/which* you can spend a lot of money.

2 Derek is the man *who/which* won last year's Christmas lottery.

3 On this map you can see the little town *who/where* I was born.

4 This is the CD player *who/which* I bought last week.

5 Mustafa is the Turkish friend *which/who* visited us two years ago.

6 Here is the computer *which/where* isn't working.

3 points

going to (future plans) and Present Continuous (future arrangements)

7 Complete the sentences with the correct form of the verbs in brackets.

Sheila **is going to work** (work) as an electronic engineer when she finishes her studies.

1 I have already spoken to Patrick. We ________ (have) dinner at his house tonight.

2 Carlos and Susana accepted our invitation. They ________ (come) to our party on Saturday for sure.

3 In the future, when I get more experience, I ________ (start) my own business.

4 I'm sorry but I don't have time to help you tonight. I ________ (go) to a nice restaurant with my boyfriend because it's his birthday.

5 Are you ________ (buy) a house some time in the future?

6 I feel very thirsty so I ________ (have) something to drink.

7 I've already phoned Karim, Sharon and the others. We ________ (go) to the theatre tonight.

8 My daughter has just passed her final exams so we ________ (celebrate). I hope she has no plans as it'll be a nice surprise for her.

9 Nadia told me that she ________ (fly) to New York next year. That's if she saves enough money!

10 I've started cooking dinner. We ________ (eat) lamb tonight.

5 points

Total: 25 points

Pronunciation

1 Write the words in the correct column.

brush put cushion run ugly full push does cut bull lucky bush

/ʊ/	/ʌ/
pull	*cup*
________	________
________	________
________	________
________	________
________	________
________	________

3 points

2 Put the Past Simple form of the verbs in the correct column depending on the pronunciation of the ending.

performed started watched stopped listened learned needed washed wanted played ended worked

/t/	/d/	/id/
walked	*believed*	*sounded*
________	________	________
________	________	________
________	________	________

4 points

3 Underline the silent letter in the words.

ba<u>l</u>let <u>k</u>nock recei<u>p</u>t

1 answer 4 doubt 7 writing

2 literature 5 debut 8 listen

3 honest 6 knowledge 9 island

3 points

Total: 10 points

Vocabulary

1 Complete the sentences with the correct verb.

I have a three-hour break at lunchtime, so when I feel tired I often **have** a nap.

1 On Sundays we normally ________ in bed late.
2 On hot summer nights I find it difficult to ________ asleep.
3 When we don't want to cook we sometimes ________ a take-away pizza.
4 The first thing I do when I arrive at work is ________ my emails.
5 I usually ________ a shower at about half past six in the evening.
6 My mother always knocks on my bedroom door to ________ me up in the morning.

3 points

2a Fill in the missing letters to complete the words.

I work very hard so I always need some time for relaxation

1 We are looking for e _ _ r _ _ t _ c professionals who can work hard.
2 My friend Gordon is a good artist. He is extremely _ma _ _na _ _v _ .
3 Donna is studying nuclear physics so she obviously has a very high level of i _ _ e _ l _ _en _ e .
4 t _ r _ _ n _ s _ is a problem that we can all suffer from when we work too hard.

2 points

b Complete the sentences below with a suitable noun.

I would really love to learn to speak another **language** because I enjoy travelling abroad.

1 My sister is a journalist and she is writing an interesting ________ for a newspaper at the moment.
2 I become very nervous when I have to make a ________ in public.
3 I believe that this writer won a ________ for this fantastic novel.
4 She scored over 80% so she passed the exam with ________ .

2 points

3 Complete the sentences with either a sense verb or an adjective.

We love going to this restaurant because their lamb **tastes** absolutely delicious.

1 The perfume which you're wearing ________ great.
2 Those cakes in the window ________ so mouth-watering that I think I'm going to buy one.
3 The noise which they are making in the kitchen ________ horrible.
4 I'm not going back to that restaurant again. Their vegetables were really ________ .
5 He is a top-class chef who makes some very ________ meals.
6 Your hands ________ very cold.

3 points

Total: 10 points

Reading

1 Read about the famous British rock group *The Kinks.*

The Kinks are a group from London which became big in the mid-1960s. They have been together since 1963. Only *The Rolling Stones* have been together as an active rock and roll band for a longer time – they formed one year before in 1962.
The original band was Ray Davies (lead singer and rhythm guitar), his brother Dave (lead guitar and vocals), Mick Avory (drums) and Pete Quaife (bass). They were first called *The Ravens* but later they changed their name to *The Kinks*. However, they did much more than writing and playing nice pop songs. As a songwriter, Ray Davies has always been intelligent and very observant about everyday life. He uses many different styles of music. His brother Dave has also been a fine guitar player from the beginning. Their first style of music was a hard-rock style, like in their hit 'You Really Got Me' (1964). Today many people think that this song is the first example of heavy metal.
During a BBC interview at the beginning of their career, the presenter of the programme asked Dave, 'Why does the group liked having long hair?' He answered, 'Girls like men to have long hair these days. The same interviewer then asked Dave's brother, 'What do you need to have a successful hit record?' Ray replied, 'It has to be original, honest and be exactly what the kids want'. The presenter of the show liked the honesty and friendliness of the group.
The Kinks were part of a 'British rock invasion' with other famous groups like *The Who*, *The Beatles* and *The Rolling Stones* but they never copied their ideas about music or their style from other bands; they basically 'did their own thing'. Ray wrote funny songs such as 'A Well-Respected Man' and 'Dedicated Follower of Fashion' and in the late 1960s the group tried using Indian music and other different styles. At this time the group suffered its worst experiences because they did not enjoy the same success as before. There were some bad feelings among the members of the group because of personal and musical differences. But things got better and in the 1970s *The Kinks* were very popular when they toured the USA.
In the 1970s and 1980s, many younger groups got their ideas from the band's energetic sound and good songs; groups like *The Jam*, *Madness* and *The Pretenders*. In fact, *The Pretenders'* first hit single 'Stop Your Sobbing' was a copy of an old Kinks song. *The Kinks* changed from having a small number of fans in the late 1960s to being very big rock stars during the 1970s and 1980s.
On the day before they entered the Rock and Roll Hall of Fame, Ray said that the best thing for himself and the group was the support of their fans. He really wanted to thank his fans for accepting all the members of *The Kinks* as people and for believing in them.

2 Are the following sentences true or false?

The Kinks started as a band before the Rolling Stones. <u>*false*</u>

1 The band is still active today.
2 The group was called *The Kinks* in the beginning.
3 Nearly all their songs sounded the same or similar.
4 They weren't friendly to the TV presenter who wanted to interview them.
5 The words of Ray's songs were not always very serious.
6 The group never had any problems selling records or with each other.
7 Their tours of the USA in the 1970s were successful.
8 Many younger groups were influenced by *The Kinks*.

8 points

2 Answer the questions.

What two types of music are mentioned in connection with the song 'You Really Got Me'?

<u>Hard rock and heavy metal.</u>

1 What qualities made *The Kinks* a really special group in the beginning?
2 In the interview, why did *The Kinks* say they like to have long hair?
3 According to Ray, what was necessary to make a special hit record?
4 What two things caused some of the problems among members of the group in the late 1960s?
5 What image did The Kinks have in the 1960s and what was their 'new' image during the 1970s and 1980s?
6 For what two reasons does Ray express his thanks to his fans?

12 points

Total: 20 points

Listening

1 Are the following sentences true or false?

All four friends had coffee after the meal. *true*

1. The speaker doesn't live far from the new café.
2. The food was the only thing that he liked there.
3. You can order not only English food but also foreign food there.
4. The speaker is a vegetarian.
5. There were four people sitting at the table including the speaker.
6. The group of friends left immediately after finishing their meal.
7. The meal was very expensive.
8. The speaker thought that the waiter was a nice person.

8 points

2 Answer the questions.

When did the speaker first try the café?

Last Saturday evening

1. Where exactly is this new café?
2. Name two of the three things that made the place more like a restaurant than a café.
3. What did the speaker order for his main course?
4. What did Paula and Nick have for their main course?
5. What did the speaker have for dessert?
6. What is the speaker going to do in the future?

12 points

Total: 20 points

Writing

1 Choose ONE of the following and write a text of about 150–175 words.

1. Describe a famous department store which you know in as much detail as possible.
2. Describe the best concert you have ever been to. (Don't forget to use the Past Simple when you are expressing actions which finished in the past).
3. Diet is a very important part of people's lives. Do you agree or disagree? Support your opinion and ideas with examples.

15 points

Test 2 Units 4-6

Grammar

comparatives

1 Rewrite these sentences without changing the meaning.

The black horse is more beautiful than the white one.

The white horse is not as beautiful as the black one.

1 Brian is heavier than Gary.

____

2 Reading a book is more interesting than watching TV.

____

3 Your story is not as good as Anne's story.

____

4 Salads are healthier than fast food.

____

5 Her car is not as expensive as my van.

____

6 An argument is not as bad as a fight.

____

(3 points)

superlatives

2 Choose the correct word in *italics*.

Angela is the most interesting person *of* / *in* in the class.

1 This one is the *best* / *better* of all the books which are on the table.

2 Sydney is the *most modern* / *modernest* city I've ever seen.

3 This has been the biggest surprise *in/of* the day.

4 Simon is the *older* / *oldest* of the three brothers.

5 The Taj Mahal is one of the *most nice* / *nicest* buildings in the world.

6 Canary Warf is *the highest* / *most highest* building in London.

(3 points)

indirect questions

3 Put the words into the correct order to form indirect questions.

concert know you starts the when do?

Do you know when the concert starts?

1 you can tell me who can I contact ?

2 winning are do if they you know ?

3 know bottles do in many you fridge how the are ?

4 me animal the what the tell world you dangerous is can most in ?

5 tell is the what can time me you ?

6 time you what know finishes do the exam ?

(3 points)

should, *can* and *have to*

4 Complete the sentences with the correct form of the verbs (*should, shouldn't, have to, don't have to, can* or *can't*).

At the moment I'm doing a special summer course in a health farm in order to feel younger and healthier. The rules are strict here. For example, we have to go to bed no later than 10p.m. and get up early in the morning. We (1) ________ eat junk food and the doctors here say that we (2) ________ have different types of vegetables with every meal, although this is not an obligation. There is a fantastic gym where we (3) ________ do all kinds of exercises but we all know that we (4) ________ use the gym too much. We (5) ________ join in all the health activities available if we don't want to, but we (6) ________ take part in at least three per day. This is a rule.

3 points

Present Perfect Simple with *for* and *since*

5 Choose the correct word in *italics*.

Terry has been a university student since *2002/four years*.

1 We have been married for *seven months/ last September*.

2 I haven't seen a decent film for *last year/ages*.

3 Linda has worked as a civil engineer since she *graduated/eleven years*.

4 They have been here since *two hours/10a.m.*

5 Jim has supported West Ham United for *when he was born/his entire life*.

6 Sheena has collected classical music for *about six months/about May*.

3 points

used to

6 Complete the sentences using the prompts. Use *used to* or *didn't use to*.

Before the TV was invented, people used to go to the cinema more. (go/cinema)

1 Before the invention of the aeroplane, people ________ . (fly/balloon)

2 Before the Internet was invented, people ________ . (send/emails)

3 Before the invention of the car, people ________ . (use/other means of transport)

4 Before the first ever umbrella, people ________ . (stay/dry when it rained)

2 points

will

7 Choose the correct form of the verb in italics to complete the sentences.

Don't worry. I promise you that there *will/won't* be any problems.

1 In the future we *are doing the shopping/will do the shopping* by Internet or telephone.

2 I think Sergio García *wins/will win* the next British Open.

3 Sometimes my computer *doesn't/won't* work well and that is annoying.

4 Paul *will/won't* get the job because he's very inexperienced.

5 *I'll have/I'm having* roast lamb for the main course, please.

6 We shouldn't go to that country next winter. *It's/It'll be* too cold then.

3 points

too, enough and *very*

8 Rewrite the sentences using *too*, *enough* or *very* without changing the meaning.

I don't have enough money to buy this car.

This car is too expensive.

1 Eileen is too short to be a model.

____

2 I don't like this programme. It's too boring.

____

3 We don't want to go to that place. It isn't near enough.

____

4 They have asked me for too many qualifications for this job so I won't get it.

____

5 Sean isn't fast enough to win this race.

____

6 This hobby takes too much time so I'm not going to continue.

____

3 points

uses of *like*

9 Answer the questions.

What is Jeremy like?

He's kind and friendly.

1 What would you like to study in the future?

____

2 What does your girlfriend look like?

____

3 What do you like doing on holiday?

____

4 What is your new boss like?

____

2 points

Total: 25 points

Pronunciation

1 Underline the stressed words in each sentence.

This is the most interesting book I've ever read.

1 She is the most beautiful girl in the world.

2 That is the most frightening story I've ever heard.

3 The Nile is the longest river on the planet.

4 This is the hardest job I've ever done.

2 Do you pronounce the *t* at the end of *shouldn't* and *can't* in these sentences?

You shouldn't act in this way. *Yes*

1 We can't go tonight because we're busy.

2 You shouldn't enter this competition.

3 You can't invent stories like that.

4 You can't play until you finish your homework.

5 They shouldn't ignore his advice.

6 You shouldn't talk so loudly.

3 Put the following words in the correct column.

bowl bomb got gold stop hole smoke road role what rock watch

/əʊ/	/ɒ/
won't	*wait*
________	________
________	________
________	________
________	________
________	________
________	________

3 points

Total: 10 points

Vocabulary

1 Answer the following questions.

What do we use to look at ourselves in the bathroom? A mirror

1 How do you describe a person who gives a lot of things to other people? ________

2 What do we use to dig a hole in the ground? ________

3 How do you describe a person who has a lot of natural ability? ________

4 What is used for cutting down trees? ________

5 How do you describe a person who isn't frightened of anything? ________

6 What do we use to cut paper? ________

7 What type of person is motivated by success, power and social status? ________

8 What instrument, which uses batteries, do we use to see in the dark? ________

4 points

2a Describe the following people referring to their ages.

A sixteen-year-old boy. Teenager

1 A woman who retired twenty years ago. ________

2 A very small child who is learning to walk and talk. ________

3 A fifty-year-old man. ________

b Complete the sentences with the correct word.

Eating healthily means not eating junk food.

1 George is lucky because he ________ a good salary.

2 It's very sad when you lose ________ with old school friends.

3 If a person smokes forty cigarettes a day, they are a ________ smoker.

3 points

3 Rewrite the definitions correctly.

We use a washing machine to clean carpets.

We use a vacuum cleaner to clean carpets.

1 We use CD walkman to watch DVD's.

____

2 We use a dishwasher to wash clothes.

____

3 We use a cooker to keep food cold and fresh.

____

4 We use an answerphone to listen to different programmes and music.

____

5 We use a hairspray to dry our hair.

____

6 We use an oven to keep frozen food.

____

3 points

Total: 10 points

Test 2 Units 4-6

Reading

1 Read the text about holidays in Bulgaria.

For holiday-makers who wish to try something new without spending too much money, Bulgaria is a very interesting country. It is a country which has changed very quickly over the last decade and today we can see a modern and progressive country. It has become a very popular holiday destination for British tourists thanks to the diversity of the country; it has dramatic mountains, popular beaches by the Black Sea, castles and palaces as well as some impressive Roman ruins. The food is delicious and not very expensive and the coffee is excellent. But the biggest thing which attracts more tourists is the wonderful hospitality of the Bulgarians.

Sofia is a very interesting capital city with an unusual mix of different architectural styles. A lot of Sofia was destroyed but it was rebuilt after World War Two. However, one or two 14th century buildings survived the war. A large mountain called Mount Vitosha can be seen from many streets in the city and this is a popular place for skiing and trekking. The mountain can be easily reached by local bus. Another popular city to visit is Varna because it has lovely beaches, but these can be busy during the summer months.

About 8% of the population is of Turkish origin and this can be seen in Bulgaria's typical meals and traditional music. There are many colourful festivals in different regions of the country that are exciting to watch.

The weather in Bulgaria is temperate with cold, wet winters and hot, dry summers. Spring is probably the best time to visit as the weather is mild and lots of cultural events take place.

The typical diet in this country is meat, potatoes and beans, and meals almost always come with salads. You can also find kebabs and pizzas in many fast-food restaurants at very good prices.

As I have mentioned, the Bulgarian people are extremely friendly and open. Their hospitality towards foreigners is excellent. It is also interesting to watch how Bulgarians communicate, in particular the fact that they nod their heads to say *no* and they shake their heads to say *yes*. This can be very confusing at first but people adapt to it after a while.

All things considered, Bulgaria is really an experience I will never forget.

2 Underline the correct endings to the sentences.

Bulgaria has changed
a) only a little. b) a reasonable amount.
c) a lot in recent years.

1 The thing which brings most people to Bulgaria is
a) the Roman ruins. b) the coffee. c) the people.

2 Sofia
a) didn't suffer damage during the war.
b) suffered a lot of damage.
c) suffered only a little damage.

3 You can get a local bus to Mount Vitosha from Sofia, it's
a) not difficult. b) quite expensive. c) very slow.

4 The Turkish origins of Bulgaria are evident in its music and
a) food. b) politics. c) architecture.

5 The writer thinks the weather in Bulgaria is best in
a) summer. b) winter. c) spring.

6 Meals in Bulgaria are usually served with
a) meat. b) salad. c) potatoes

6 points

2 Answer the questions.

What type of country is Bulgaria today?

A modern and progressive country.

1 Which types of building attract tourists to Bulgaria?

____

2 Why is summer not the best time to go to Varna?

____

3 Why does the writer prefer spring to visit Bulgaria?

____

4 What non-traditional food can be found in Bulgaria?

____

5 What does the writer like about Bulgarian people?

____

6 Apart from the language, what is the biggest communication problem that foreign visitors have with Bulgarians?

____

7 How does the writer describe her visit to Bulgaria at the end of the text?

____

14 points

Total: 20 points

Listening

1 Choose the correct answer.

Tanya was originally from
a) The Bahamas. b) Jamaica. c) Barbados.

1 In the beginning, she
a) found life impossible.
b) was determined to succeed.
c) thought that life was easy.

2 She
a) often wrote to her friends in Barbados.
b) lost touch with her friends in Barbados.
c) sometimes visited her friends in Barbados.

3 She married Robert
a) before her accounting course.
b) during her accounting course.
c) after her accounting course.

4 She has two children;
a) one teenager and one toddler.
b) both are teenagers.
c) two toddlers.

5 Tanya's relations with her colleagues are
a) good. b) indifferent. c) bad.

6 Tanya's salary is
a) very high. b) OK, but not great. c) very low.

6 points

2 Answer the questions.

What is Tanya's job? She is an accounts manager.

1 What type of company does she work for?

____

2 Name two types of work she did when she arrived?

____

3 What did she do when she had enough money?

____

4 What was she determined to do?

____

5 Name two things that Tanya does in her free time.

____

6 What advice does she give?

____

7 What type of person can succeed in this situation?

____

14 points

Total: 20 points

Writing

1 Choose one of the following and write a text of about 150–175 words.

1 What has been the biggest challenge in your life? Have you achieved this goal?

2 Describe how you have changed as a person during the different stages of your life from being a small child to being an adult.

3 Write about an interesting travel experience which you have had. If you have never been abroad, you can write about a visit to a different part of your own country.

15 points

Test 3 Units 7-9

Grammar

First Conditional

1 Choose the correct word in *italics*.

If I finish work before 7pm today, I <u>will call</u> / *call* you.

1 You'll get lost if you *take / will take* this road.

2 You *don't / won't* win this match if you play like you did last week.

3 If you *listen / will listen* to that loud music every day, you'll go deaf.

4 We'll lose this customer if we *won't / don't* apologise for our mistake.

5 If they *hurry up / don't hurry up*, they'll miss the train.

6 If you eat any more ice cream, you *will feel / you are feeling* bad tomorrow.

(3 points)

gerunds and infinitives

2 Complete the sentences with the correct form of the verb in brackets.

We can't afford <u>to buy</u> (buy) a car like that.

1 I considered ________ (leave) my job but I finally thought it was better to stay.

2 They decided ________ (not join) the tennis club.

3 We should leave early to avoid ________ (be) caught in the traffic.

4 Lyn hopes ________ (get) good exam results this year.

5 I haven't finish ________ (eat) my lunch yet.

6 Tom enjoys ________ (play) cricket.

(3 points)

purpose, reason and result

3 Choose the correct word in *italics*.

I always try to look after myself <u>so</u>/*because* I normally don't have too many health problems. Going on a good diet, for example, is very important (1) *so that/for that* your body gets all the vitamins and proteins that it needs. Sleeping at least seven hours a day (2) *for to/to* help your mind and body to get enough rest is also recommended. Doing physical exercise is a good idea too but don't do too much (3) *so that not to/in order not to* put excessive strain on your muscles. I strongly advise you to take this advice seriously (4) *so that / because* good health should be a priority in life.

(2 points)

Present Simple Passive

4 Put the words in the correct order to make sentences.

of restaurant lot is delicious a in food prepared this.

<u>A lot of delicious food is prepared in this restaurant.</u>

1 two house in milk consumed this day

litres of are every.

____

2 mechanic a is car year my a inspected by twice.

____

3 in telephones Japan made mobile are these.

____

4 watched by this million is people programme four.

____

5 officers building by police protected that is two.

____

6 her visited Ruth friends is of by many.

____

(3 points)

questions

5 Write the questions for the answers.

My name is Mario.

What is your name?

1 I went to the cinema with Stephanie.

Who ________________________ ?

2 I would like the small one, please.

Which ________________________ ?

3 There are sixty students in the room.

How many ________________________ ?

4 Because I was hungry.

Why ________________________ all the biscuits?

5 You can find this type of architecture in Russia.

Where ________________________ ?

6 I like going to the cinema on Saturdays.

When ________________________ ?

7 I came to work by train yesterday.

How ________________________ ?

8 I will finish the job next week.

When ________________________ ?

4 points

Past Continuous and Past Simple

6 Complete the sentences with the correct form of the verb in brackets (Past Continuous or the Past Simple).

It was very busy in our office yesterday because we had (have) a lot of work to finish before the end of the day. While I (1) ________ (prepare) an important document, my colleague (2) ________ (type) some new contracts on her computer. Suddenly my boss (3) ________ (interrupt) me because he (4) ________ (want) me to make a couple of urgent phone calls to China for him. Then an urgent fax (5) ________ (arrive) when I (6) ________ (speak) on the telephone. I was worried about the enormous amount of work I had to complete but in the end everything was okay.

3 points

can/could/be able to

7 Rewrite the sentences correctly, using *can*, *could* or *be able to*.

Jeremy can to speak a lot of languages.

Jeremy can speak a lot of languages.

1 Next year she will can use more computer programmes than now.

____

2 Three years ago I can't understand German but now I speak quite well.

____

3 I am not able to swim very well when I was a small child but now I can.

____

4 My baby daughter can walk quite well in a few months time.

____

5 They don't can run very fast.

____

6 He could afford to buy that computer because it was too expensive.

____

7 We be able to travel more in the future.

____

8 I couldn't play golf at all so I get bored when people talk about it.

____

4 points

Past Simple Passive

8 Rewrite these active sentences in the Past Simple Passive.

The police arrested the robber.

The robber was arrested by the police.

1 They offered Sheila a job in a hotel.

____

2 They built this museum in 1826.

____

3 John Lennon wrote the song 'Imagine'.

____

4 They told us that we had to go to a meeting.

____

5 Steven Spielberg directed 'Schindler's List'.

____

6 They gave Derek a form to fill in.

____

3 points

Total: 25 points

Pronunciation

1 Underline the stressed syllable in each of the words.

reserved ambitious chatty

1 beautiful	4 stomachache	7 overweight
2 hard-working	5 well-built	8 unattractive
3 consider	6 handsome	9 reliable

3 points

2 Put the words into the correct column.

were strong learn was word bird dog wash

/ʊ/	/ʌ/
doll	*third*
______	______
______	______
______	______
______	______

4 points

3 Underline the vowel stress on the following words.

salary experience qualifications

1 secretary	4 interviewee	7 factory
2 interviewer	5 bonus	8 progress
3 receptionist	6 mistake	9 research

3 points

Total: 10 points

Vocabulary

1 Which word in each group is different?

beautiful/handsome/unattractive/good-looking

Unattractive is different because it's negative.

1 skinny/slim/overweight/fat

2 thumb/nose/eye/mouth

3 organised/motivated/hard-working/unreliable

3 points

2a Rewrite the sentences using the correct verb.

The amount of traffic during the rush hour has been improving recently.

The amount of traffic during the rush hour has been rising recently.

1 My eyesight is getting better, I think I will have to see an optician soon.

____

2 The quality of telecommunication products has gone up considerably during these last years.

____

3 Customer service has fallen since I last came to this department store.

____

4 The number of students in this university is deteriorating.

____

2 points

b Complete the sentences with the correct preposition.

I was going out with my ex–boyfriend Peter when my sister got married.

1 I can't put ________ with his lateness anymore.

2 It took me a very long time to get ________ my father's death.

3 My ex–wife and I split ________ because we had completely different interests in life.

4 I really like the new girl in the office so I think I'll ask her ________ .

2 points

3 Complete the sentences with the correct form of *do* or *make*.

The police officer made a big mistake when he arrested the wrong person.

1 We have ________ some research before we can begin this project.

2 This company closed down because it was not ________ much money.

3 The jury hasn't ________ any decision yet about the final verdict.

4 Yesterday the man ________ a strong complaint about his food being cold.

5 Can you please ________ me a big favour and look after my dog for a while?

6 What were you ________ when the thief entered the shop?

3 points

Total: 10 points

Reading

1 Read the text about Concorde.

The story of Concorde began when Britain worked with France in order to develop a supersonic passenger jet. Both countries wanted to be the first to develop this type of aircraft so they signed the Anglo-French Supersonic Aircraft Agreement to build the Concorde. The Americans also tried to develop a similar jet during the 1960s. However, people from environmental groups really didn't like the noise-pollution, damage to the atmosphere and the costs of a project of this type, which were very high. The U.S. congress finally decided to stop giving money for an American supersonic passenger jet in 1971.

By this time, the British and French had completed the Concorde but it was very disappointing. In the 1960s, people thought that supersonic flying was the future of commercial air-travel, nearly all the biggest airlines wanted to buy this plane. There were orders for more than 270 of the jets, but high petrol costs and problems with environmental groups reduced the number of orders. The Concorde was finally only bought by two airlines – Air France and British Airways. The production of the plane ended in 1979 and only 16 concordes were ever made.

However, the Concorde was still a great achievement of design and engineering with a top speed of 1,490 mph (2,385 khp) and a normal flying speed of 1,354 mph (2,165 kph). It flew at 60,000 feet (18,300m), it could fly a distance of 3,740 miles (nearly 6000 km) and it was powered by four very large engines. There were nine people working on it and it could carry 100 passengers. The plane was extremely powerful but first-time passengers were surprised by the smooth and comfortable ride.

For nearly 25 years, the Concorde enjoyed lots of success and flew to such destinations as Japan, as well as offering a famous trip round the world in 1986, which cost $20,800 per person. It could cross the Atlantic Ocean in about three and a half hours, less than half the time of regular aeroplane. The plane was very popular with celebrities, sports stars and rich people.

Unfortunately, there was a terrible accident in which 113 people were killed. This completely changed the success of Concorde. On 25th July, 2000, an Air France Concorde crashed in Gonesse, outside Paris, shortly after take-off and it was discovered that this disaster was caused by technical problems. The Concorde jets were immediately taken out of service and their future looked uncertain. Concorde made its last flight on October 24th, 2004.

This was the end of the world's most famous jet but maybe not the end of supersonic airlines. It seems incredible but the Americans are now working on a hypersonic project to design and build a jet that can fly at 4,800 mph (7680 kph)!

2 Are the sentences true or false?

Only two European countries were involved in the project to build a supersonic jet. *true*

1. The USA has had a lot of success with supersonic passenger jet planes.
2. More than 200 Concorde jets were sold to several different airlines.
3. Economic and environmental reasons made the number of sales go down.
4. It could fly for over 3,000 miles.
5. Nine people used to work on each Concorde jet.
6. Concorde lost a lot of money over nearly twenty-five years of service.
7. The accident happened at the airport.
8. The world may see more supersonic passenger jets in the future.

8 points

3 Answer the questions.

In what two ways was the Concorde a fantastic invention?

design and engineering

1. Why did the British and French decide to work together on the Concorde project?

   ______

2. What two things did environmental groups not like about the American supersonic jet?

   ______

3. How did first-time passengers feel about flying in such a powerful jet?

   ______

4. What kind of people enjoyed flying with Concorde?

   ______

5. What was the reason for the terrible plane crash in July, 2000?

   ______

6. What is the future for supersonic air travel?

   ______

12 points

Total: 20 points

Listening

1 Listen to the recording. Are the sentences true or false?

The speaker's company sells TVs and DVDs. *true*

1 The incident happened on a Tuesday evening.

2 On the day of the crime, he left his office at about 6p.m.

3 They went to the supermarket by car.

4 The speaker was attacked by one of the criminals.

5 The check-out area is a place where people pay for their products in a supermarket.

6 Some people ran after the two men when they left.

7 The speaker tried to help the police with their investigations.

8 The two thieves were short and well-built.

8 points

2 Answer the questions.

What was the speaker's previous job and what is his present job?

He was previously a sales rep but now he is a regional sales manager.

1 What does the speaker like about his new job?

2 What was the weather like when he left the office?

3 Why were he and his wife in a hurry?

4 Why did the speaker run inside the supermarket?

5 What happened to him when he fell?

6 What crime were the two men found guilty of and what was their punishment?

12 points

Total: 20 points

Writing

1 Choose ONE of the following and write a text of about 150–175 words.

1 Do you think that most people think too much about their physical appearance?

2 Do you like travelling by plane?

3 Tell the story of your first ever job interview and how you felt.

15 points

100 points

Test 4 Units 10-12

Grammar

countable/uncountable nouns

1 Complete the sentences with *a few*, *a little*, *many* or *much*.

How much information do you have?

1 During my first year in England I only had ______ friends but now I have a lot.

2 We don't have ______ milk in the fridge so we'll have to buy some more.

3 How ______ cats has she got?

4 How many biscuits have we got left? Only ______ .

5 I only have ______ money so I can't afford to buy this furniture at the moment.

6 They don't have ______ tickets left so you'll have to hurry up and buy one.

(3 points)

the definite article (*the*)

2 Complete the sentences with *the* or nothing *(-)*.

I like __-__ hamsters very much. They make good pets.

1 Here's ______ book I bought the other day.

2 Sometimes, ______ people can be very resistant to change.

3 I love eating ______ Chinese food.

4 Janet is ______ tallest girl in the class.

5 Do you remember ______ TV programme about wild animals?

6 Nowadays ______ carpenters are very well-paid.

(3 points)

Present Perfect Simple with *just*, *yet* and *already*.

3 Correct the sentences.

We haven't eaten our dinner already.

We haven't eaten our dinner yet.

1 Mr Thomson can see you now. He has already finished his telephone conversation.

____

____

2 I haven't seen the new Robert de Niro film already.

____

____

3 Have you prepared those documents already? The boss is becoming impatient.

____

____

4 Why are you looking so tired? I have already run eight kilometres.

____

____

5 Relax. I've just finished the report. In fact, I finished it two days ago.

____

____

6 Wait a moment. You haven't just signed these papers.

____

____

(3 points)

verbs with two objects

4 Put the words in the correct order to make sentences.

already boss promotion me my offered new a has

My new boss has already offered me a promotion.

1 me twenty lend can pounds you ?

____

2 story very told she a me interesting .

____

3 tomorrow you the send will papers I .

____

4 has wife cake my birthday my me on promised a .

____

5 money of bank the owes lot he a .

____

6 please, a water bring of glass me can you ?

____

3 points

Past Perfect Simple

5 Complete the text using either the Past Perfect Simple or the Past Simple of the verbs in brackets.

I saw (see) an incredible show when I was in London last year. I (1) ________ (be) there many times before because I have relatives living there, but this visit (2) ________ (be) really special. I ________ (have) the chance to see one of the best jugglers in the world. When I (4) ________ (get) to Covent Garden (a square in the city), the show (5) ________ (start) but I only missed a few minutes. The juggler was juggling with seven balls and balancing a stick on his nose at the same time. By the time the show (6) ________ (finish) I was late for the theatre but that didn't matter.

3 points

Second Conditional

6 Put the verbs in brackets into the correct form to make Second Conditional sentences.

If I felt (feel) hungry, I would eat something right now.

1 He ________ (earn) more money, if he found a better job.

2 If they ________ (can act) better, they would be on TV.

3 If I ________ (know) how to cook, I'd have a better diet.

4 I ________ (take) my umbrella if it rained.

5 If I ________ (move) to a new city, I would try to find some new friends.

6 She ________ (buy) a new car if she had enough money.

3 points

reported speech

7 Rewrite the sentences in reported speech.

Alex: I'm reading a very interesting book.

Alex told me that he was reading a very interesting book.

1 Jenny: I have worked very hard.

Jenny said ______________________

2 Tony: I went to the theatre to see a new play.

Tony told ______________________

3 Esther: I can sing quite well.

Esther told ______________________

4 Jack: The government will win the elections.

Jack said ______________________

5 Anne-Marie: I like going out with my boyfriend.

Anne-Marie said ______________________

6 Tim: Watching TV is boring.

Tim told ______________________

7 Jill: I have spoken to them.

Jill said ______________________

8 Colin: I bought your tickets for the concert.

Colin told ______________________

4 points

both, neither and *either*

8 Choose the correct word in *italics*.

I don't like *either/neither* of these books.

1 *Both/Neither* of my brothers love tennis. They play it nearly every day.

2 *Neither/Either* boy will pass this exam because they haven't studied.

3 I'm really hungry so I'm going to eat *either/both* of these sandwiches.

4 Tonight we can go to *either/both* the cinema or the theatre.

5 *Either/Neither* Erica nor James spent much money at the shops.

6 Which one would you like? I really don't mind. *Neither/Either* of them would be fine.

5 points

Total: 25 points

Pronunciation

1 Underline the stressed words in these sentences.

Did you have to put up with any bad behaviour from the children?

1 How long did it take you to get over losing your last girlfriend?

2 When you were younger, who did you go out with?

3 Do you think I should ask her out for dinner?

4 Why did Peter and Mary split up?

4 points

2 Put the words in the correct column.

yet judo jump young yes jungle

/dʒ/	/j/
job	*yellow*
________	________
________	________
________	________
________	________
________	________
________	________

3 points

3. Underline the stressed words in these sentences.

She ate both cakes that were on the plate.

1 Neither of my sisters are working yet.

2 You can choose either the red one or the blue one.

3 Both of my dogs are black.

3 points

Total: 10 points

Vocabulary

1a Complete the sentences with the correct preposition.

When I was cleaning out my garage, I came across some interesting old books.

1 When Tom's parents are not home, his grandmother looks ______ him.

2 I was brought ______ on a farm, so I really love the countryside.

3 I picked ______ a little German on holiday last summer.

4 We really look up ______ our maths teacher because she is very clever.

b Complete the sentences with the correct form of the verb.

John will appeal to a tribunal because he thinks that his company's decision to sack him is unfair.

1 Our holiday next year will ______ on our financial situation.

2 I'm sorry but I don't ______ with you. I think this idea would cause problems.

3 Dorothy ______ a lot of money on clothes the other day.

4 I've ______ for a job in the new sports centre but a lot of other people are also interested.

4 points

2 Answer the questions.

On which type of holiday do you go to the mountains to do a popular winter sport? A skiing holiday

1 On which type of holiday do you expect to see beautiful and interesting things? ______________

2 On which type of holiday are you closest to nature? ______________

3 On which type of holiday can you go sunbathing every day? ______________

3 points

3 Complete the sentences.

Most people bow before their king or queen.

1 When you meet a person in some countries, it is common to ______ them on both cheeks.

2 To say *hello* or *goodbye* when you are not near someone, people normally ______ .

3 In business situations and social situations, westerner people normally ______ hands.

3 points

4 Answer the questions.

What do you leave a taxi driver or a waiter/waitress when you are happy with the service? A tip

1 What do you pay when you borrow money from a bank? ______________

2 What do we call the money that you receive when you are too old to work? ______________

3 What do we call the money that we pay to the government? ______________

4 What verb do we use when we want to take money out of the bank? ______________

5 What do we earn every month for the work that we do? ______________

6 What verb has the opposite meaning of *to spend*? ______________

3 points

Total: 10 points

Reading

1 Read the following text about Kenya.

Welcome to Kenya, the land of discovery. Of all the countries in Africa, none can offer the amazing different kinds of scenery found in Kenya. It also has lots of different kinds of wild animals and birds. This is a country where big cats and large mammals like antelope, giraffes and hyenas still run free in their natural habitat. You can even see the migration of wildebeest, zebras and gazelles, which starts around July each year; I can strongly recommend this.

We are a family-owned safari tour operator and both of our directors were born and brought up here. Working as a team with all our staff, we pay particular attention to detail and offer a personalised service. Our objective is to work with each customer, family and group in an individual way. We want you to work with us, discussing your interests, style of travel, questions related to time and money and any other things that would influence your trip, so that we can prepare a programme that is ideal for you, your family or your group. Travelling to Africa is expensive; but our tours offer the best value for your money.

Our vehicles are 7-seater safari minibuses with a slide-open roof that is perfect for watching wild animals and sight-seeing. The buses are well-maintained to offer a high level of comfort and safety and are fully equipped with first-aid kits, as well as guide books on the wildlife and birds of East Africa.

We know for a fact that the success of your safari will depend on your driver/guide. It is because of this that we have a great team of carefully selected drivers and guides who are well-trained and experienced with a great knowledge of wildlife and animal behaviour. They speak English, Spanish and French so the choice is yours. The accommodation that you choose will depend on your budget and there are several types available, ranging from five star hotels and luxury tent-camps to basic camping for those who want to 'rough it'. In case of emergency we provide free membership with the Flying Doctors' Society of Africa to all our customers who are on safari with us. This means that you can use the Flying Doctors' Service including evacuation to a good hospital with one telephone call.

If you are interested in taking a holiday with us, the best source of information is someone who has been there recently. Many of our past customers have allowed us to pass their email contacts to others in order to share their experiences and give them an opportunity to hear the inside story. One last thing, if you feel that what we offer does not match what you want to do, and you are worried about wasting your money, please send us an email telling us your ideas and we will work together to design your dream safari.

2 Are the sentences true or false?

The scenery in Kenya is very nice but also very similar all over the country. *false*

1 Wild animals are not put in zoos here.
2 The directors of the company are Kenyan.
3 The safari tours offered are interesting but not very flexible.
4 Travelling to Africa is not expensive.
5 It is possible to open the roof of the minibuses.
6 Only expensive luxury accommodation is available.
7 Customers have to pay extra for medical services while on safari.
8 It is a good idea to have contact with other people who have been on a safari before deciding to go.

8 points

Total: 20 points

3 Answer the questions.

Which three things does the writer say are different in Kenya?

The scenery, wild animals and birds

1 What does the writer recommend us to watch?

____

2 What does this safari tour company particularly concentrate on to keep its clients happy?

____

3 What things should the tourist speak about with the company before agreeing on a travel plan?

____

4 What can be used in an immediate medical emergency before any doctor can arrive?

____

5 What does the writer mean exactly by the expression to *rough it*?

____

6 Which qualities should a good safari driver/ guide have?

____

12 points

Listening

1 Choose the correct answer.

The speaker is from

a) Orlando. b) Ohio. c) Oklahoma.

1 She was in Britain for

a) two weeks. b) three weeks. c) four weeks.

2 She travelled around the country by

a) coach. b) car. c) train.

3 The speaker stayed in London for

a) one day. b) a few days. c) two weeks.

4 After London, her next stop was in

a) Cardiff. b) Stratford-upon-Avon. c) Cambridge.

5 Whose house was in Stratford-upon-Avon?

a) Sean Connery's b) The Queen's c) Shakespeare's

6 What famous place did she visit in Liverpool?

a) Anfield Stadium b) The Beatles Museum

c) The History Museum

7 She loves the city of York for its

a) people. b) mountains. c) historical architecture.

8 When she discovered that Britain didn't have a lot of nice beaches or sunny weather, she

a) was very disappointed.
b) was quite disappointed. c) didn't mind.

8 points

2 Answer the questions.

Which types of accommodation did the speaker use?
Hotels and Bed and Breakfasts

1 What did she find incredible when she first arrived?

____

2 What place did she like best in London?

____

3 What things did she like about people from Liverpool?

____

4 What impressed her about Yorkshire?

____

5 How does she say 'that's not important'?

____

6 Which places will she visit next year?

____

12 points

Total: 20 points

Writing

1 Choose ONE of the following and write a text of about 150–175.

1 Many species of animals are in danger of extinction. How can we protect them?

2 Tell the story of the funniest travelling experience you have ever had.

3 Are you happy with the quality of education at schools and universities in your country? What things would you like to change?

15 points

Test 1

Grammar

1 likes and dislikes
1 stand 2 on 3 doesn't 4 loves 5 mind 6 like

2 Present Simple and Adverbs of Frequency
1 I never go swimming because I don't like it. 2 We often visit our uncle in France. 3 Tina usually goes clubbing because she absolutely loves it. 4 Do you sometimes play golf? 5 We hardly ever go to bed late. 6 Does Jim always have a lie-in at weekends?

3 Present Continuous
1 watch 2 am working 3 am studying 4 have 5 do not/don't understand 6 are having

4 *so* and *neither*
1 I didn't. 2 So am I. 3 So do I. 4 I did. 5 Neither do I. 6 I have.

5 Past Simple and Present Perfect Simple
1 have enjoyed 2 had 3 went 4 Have/ever been 5 have seen 6 recommended 7 has visited 8 ate 9 saw 10 have watched

6 defining relative causes
1 where 2 who 3 where 4 which 5 who 6 which

7 *going to* (future plans) and Present Continuous (future arrangements)
1 are/'re having 2 are/'re coming 3 am/'m going to start 4 am/'m going 5 going to buy 6 am/'m going to have 7 are/'re going 8 are/'re going to celebrate 9 is/'s going to fly 10 are/'re eating

Pronunciation

1

/ʊ/	/ʌ/
put	*brush*
cushion	*run*
full	*ugly*
push	*does*
bull	*cut*
bush	*lucky*

2

/t/	/d/	/id/
watched	*performed*	*started*
stopped	*listened*	*needed*
washed	*learned*	*wanted*
worked	*played*	*ended*

3

1 answer 2 literature 3 honest 4 doubt 5 debut
6 knowledge 7 writing 8 listen 9 island

Vocabulary

1

1 stay 2 fall 3 get 4 check 5 have 6 wake

2a

1 energetic 2 imaginative 3 intelligence 4 tiredness

b

1 article 2 speech 3 prize 4 distinction

3

1 smells 2 look 3 sounds 4 disgusting 5 tasty 6 feel

Reading

2

1 true 2 false 3 false 4 false 5 true 6 false 7 true 8 true

3

1 They had an intelligent and observant songwriter, a variety in musical styles and a good guitarist.
2 Because it attracted girls.
3 The song had to be original, sincere and be what the kids want.
4 They were selling fewer records and there were personal and musical differences among them.
5 In the 1960s they were cult heroes but in the seventies they were very big rock stars.
6 For accepting The Kinks as people and for believing in them.

Listening

Tapescript
There are so many places to eat in my town nowadays. For example, there's a new café which is very near to my house. It's in front of the old cinema in Gibson Street. I wanted to try it so last Saturday evening I went there with three of my friends. It's probably one of the best cafés I've ever been to. The quality of the food, the service and the interior design were great. It was more like a restaurant than a simple café.
There was a lot of variety. It was possible to order Italian and Indian dishes as well as more traditional English food. I ordered a steak which was absolutely delicious. They served it with chips, onions and tomatoes. My friend Paula had lamb with boiled potatoes and so did Nick. There were some vegetarian options on the menu so Anne selected a Quiche Lorraine. I was the only one who had dessert – a chocolate-flavoured ice-cream which I liked a lot. Everybody had a cup of coffee and we stayed and chatted for a while before we paid the bill. The price was very reasonable. The waiter who served our table was Portuguese and he was very friendly. He told us some interesting things about his country. We had a great time and I'm certainly going to recommend this place to everyone in the future.

1

1 true 2 false 3 true 4 false 5 true 6 false 7 false 8 true

2

1 In front of the old cinema in Gibson Street.
2 The three things are: The quality of the food, the service and the interior design.
3 A steak served with chips, onions and tomatoes.
4 Lamb with boiled potatoes.
5 A chocolate-flavoured ice-cream.
6 He is going to recommend the new café to everyone.

Test 2

Grammar

1 comparatives
1 Gary is not as heavy as Brian.
2 Watching TV is not as interesting as reading a book.
3 Anne's story is better than your story.
4 Fast food is not as healthy as salads.
5 My van is more expensive than her car.
6 A fight is worse than an argument.

2 superlatives
1 best 2 most modern 3 of 4 oldest 5 nicest 6 highest

3 indirect questions
1 Can you tell me who I can contact?
2 Do you know if they are winning?
3 Do you know how many bottles are in the fridge?
4 Can you tell me what the most dangerous animal in the world is?
5 Can you tell me what the time is?
6 Do you know what time the exam finishes?

4 *should*, *can* and *have to*
1 can't 2 should 3 can 4 shouldn't 5 don't have to
6 have to

5 Present Perfect with *for* or *since*
1 seven months 2 ages 3 she graduated 4 10a.m.
5 his entire life 6 about six months

6 *used to*
1 people used to fly in balloons.
2 people didn't use to send emails.
3 people used to use other means of transport.
4 people didn't use to stay dry when it rained.

7 *will*
1 will do the shopping 2 will win 3 doesn't 4 won't
5 I'll have 6 It'll be

8 *too*, *enough* and *very*
1 Aileen isn't tall enough to be a model.
2 It isn't interesting enough.
3 It is too far.
4 I don't have enough qualifications to get this job.
5 Sean is too slow to win this race.
6 I don't have enough time to continue this hobby.

8 uses of *like*
Suggested answers only
1 I would like to study medicine.
2 She has blonde hair and blue eyes.
3 I like visiting interesting places.
4 He is determined and ambitious.

Pronunciation

1
1 She is the most <u>beautiful</u> <u>girl</u> in the <u>world</u>.
2 That is the most <u>frightening</u> <u>story</u> I've ever <u>heard</u>.
3 The Nile is the <u>longest</u> <u>river</u> on the <u>planet</u>.
4 This is the <u>hardest</u> <u>job</u> I've ever <u>done</u>.

2
1 No 2 Yes 3 Yes 4 No 5 Yes 6 No

3

/ʌʊ/	/ɒ/
bowl	*bomb*
gold	*got*
hole	*stop*
smoke	*what*
road	*rock*
role	*watch*

Vocabulary

1
1 generous 2 a spade 3 talented 4 an axe 5 brave
6 scissors 7 ambitious 8 a torch

2a
1 old/elderly 2 a toddler 3 middle-aged

b
1 earns 2 touch 3 heavy

3
1 No, we use a DVD player to watch DVDs.
2 No, we use a washing machine to wash clothes.
3 No, we use a fridge to keep food cold and fresh.
4 No, we use a radio to listen to different programmes and music.
5 No, we use a hairdryer to dry our hair.
6 No, we use a freezer to keep frozen food.

Reading

2
1 c) 2 b) 3 a) 4 a) 5 a) 6 c)

3
1 castles and palaces
2 There are too many people on the beaches.
3 The weather is good (pleasant) and there are more cultural events.
4 pizzas and kebabs
5 They are extremely pleasant and open and show excellent hospitality.
6 They nod to say *no* and shake their heads to say *yes*.
7 An experience which she will never forget.

Listening

Tapescript
Tanya Coles is a thirty-three-year-old accounts department manager from Barbados who has lived in West London for fifteen years. She works for a company which makes industrial products and is married with two children. Life for her in London, however, hasn't always been easy.
'When I first arrived here I was only a teenager and life was difficult because I had to work hard to survive. I had to do all kinds of different jobs including cleaning, nannying and factory work before I had enough money to get a place of my own. In those early days it was sometimes hard to cope with life and I also lost touch with nearly all my friends who live back in Barbados. However, I was determined to succeed and I used to push myself hard to achieve my goals. I often had to rely on my mental strength as a person.
Little by little, life became better as I got to know more people and I could finally study for a diploma in accounting. Shortly after I graduated, I got married to Robert and we now have two lovely kids: Roger, who is nearly a teenager, and Bertha, who is just a toddler.
I have worked in my present job for four years now and I get on really well with nearly all my colleagues. I earn a reasonable salary although it's not as much as it should be and I still find time to study and improve my professional skills. I have to look after my children too, of course, but I don't mind because I really like doing it.
I'm now much happier than I was fifteen years ago. The advice that I can give to someone who is starting a new life in a different country is that you shouldn't feel too sad when things go badly. You should think positively and see it as a challenge and, if you are brave and ambitious enough, you will have a great chance to be successful.'

1
1 b) 2 b) 3 c) 4 b) 5 a) 6 b)

2
1 A company that makes industrial products.
2 Cleaning, nannying and factory work.
3 She got a place of her own.
4 Her mental strength as a person.
5 Study, improve her professional skills and look after her children.
6 They shouldn't feel too sad when things go badly. They should think positively and see it as a challenge.
7 You have to be brave and ambitious.

Test 3

1 First Conditional

1 take **2** won't **3** listen **4** don't **5** don't hurry up **6** will feel

2 gerunds and infinitives

1 leaving **2** not to join **3** being **4** to get **5** eating **6** playing

3 purpose, reason and result

1 so that **2** to **3** in order not to **4** because

4 Present Simple Passive

1. Two litres of milk are consumed every day in this house/in this house every day.
2. My car is inspected by a mechanic twice a year./My car is inspected twice a year by a mechanic.
3. These mobile telephones are made in Japan.
4. This television programme is watched by four million people.
5. That building is protected by two police officers.
6. Ruth is visited by many of her friends.

5 questions

1. did you go to the cinema with
2. one would you like
3. students are (there) in the room
4. did you eat
5. can you find this type of architecture
6. do you like going to the cinema
7. did you come to work yesterday
8. will you finish the job

6 Past Continuous and Past Simple

1 was preparing **2** was typing **3** interrupted **4** wanted
5 arrived **6** was speaking

7 can/could/be able to

1. Next year she will be able to use more computer programmes than now.
2. Three years ago I couldn't understand German but now I speak quite well.
3. I couldn't swim very well when I was a small child but now I can.
4. My baby daughter will be able to walk quite well in a few months time.
5. They can't run very fast.
6. He couldn't afford to buy that computer because it was too expensive.
7. We will be able to travel more in the future.
8. I can't play golf at all so I get bored when people talk about it.

8 Past Simple Passive

1. Sheila was offered a job in a hotel.
2. This museum was built in 1826.
3. The song "Imagine" was written by John Lennon.
4. We were told that we had to go to a meeting.
5. 'Schindler's List' was directed by Steven Spielberg.
6. Derek was given a form to fill in.

Pronunciation

1

1 beautiful **2** hard-working **3** consider **4** stomachache
5 well-built **6** handsome **7** overweight **8** unattractive
9 reliable

2

/ɒ/	/ɜː/
strong	*were*
was	*learn*
dog	*word*
wash	*bird*

3

secretary	interviewer	receptionist
interviewee	bonus	mistake
factory	progress	research

Vocabulary

1

1. Slim is an attractive characteristic but the others are not.
2. A thumb is on our hand while the other words are parts of the face.
3. Unreliable is a negative adjective while the others are positive.

2a

1. My eyesight is getting worse.
2. The quality of telecommunication products has risen considerably during these last years.
3. Customer service has deteriorated since I last came to this department store.
4. The number of students in this university is going down.

b

1 up **2** over **3** up **4** out

3

1 to do **2** making **3** made **4** made **5** do **6** doing

Reading

2

1 false **2** false **3** true **4** true **5** true **6** false **7** false
8 true

3

1. They wanted to make the world's first supersonic passenger jet.
2. Noise pollution and damage to the atmosphere
3. They felt surprised because it was a comfortable ride.
4. Celebrities, world-class athletes and the rich
5. Technical problems
6. Uncertain; in fact, it will probably disappear.

Listening

Tapescript

The incident happened about the time when I was promoted from sales rep to regional sales manager. I work for a company which sells televisions, DVDs and other electronic products. I decided to take this new job because I wanted extra responsibility and a better salary. Anyway, it all occurred one Friday evening after work. When I left the office at about 7p.m., it was raining. I had to meet my wife and then drive to the local supermarket in order to do the shopping for the weekend. We were hoping to avoid the rush hour because we were in a hurry and wanted to get to the supermarket before they closed. Finally we arrived and, as soon as we went into the supermarket, we heard shouts and screams from the other side of the store. I ran to see what was happening but I fell over. I immediately got up but I realised that I had a sprained ankle so I couldn't walk fast. I walked to the check-out area, where customers pay for their things. I saw two armed men who were wearing masks. One of them was shouting 'Give me the money from all the cash registers'. They got the money and then left and nobody followed them.
I decided to help the police by telling them what I had seen but I couldn't help them very much. I only observed that the two men looked young and were both tall and well-built. They had masks on so I didn't see their faces. Well, the good news is that the following day the two thieves were arrested and, a few months later, they were found guilty of armed robbery and given a long prison sentence.

1

1 false **2** false **3** true **4** false **5** true **6** false **7** true
8 false

2

1. Extra responsibility and a better salary
2. It was raining
3. They wanted to get to the supermarket before it closed.
4. He heard shouts and screams and wanted to see what was happening.
5. He had a sprained ankle.
6. They were found guilty of armed robbery and received a long prison sentence.

Test 4

Grammar

1 countable/uncountable nouns

1 a few 2 much 3 many 4 a few 5 a little 6 many

2 the definite article (*the*)

1 the 2 – 3 – 4 the 5 the 6 –

3 Present Perfect Simple with *just*, *yet* and *already*

1 Mr. Thomson can see you now. He has just finished his telephone conversation.
2 I haven't seen the new Robert de Niro film yet.
3 Have you prepared those documents yet? The boss is becoming impatient.
4 Why are you looking so tired? I have just run eight kilometres.
5 Relax. I've already finished the report. In fact, I finished it two days ago.
6 Wait a moment. You haven't signed these papers yet.

4 verbs with two objects

1 Can you lend me twenty pounds?
2 She told me a very interesting story.
3 I will send you the papers tomorrow.
4 My wife has promised me a cake on my birthday.
5 He owes the bank a lot of money.
6 Can you bring me a glass of water, please?

5 Past Perfect Simple

1 had been 2 was 3 had 4 got 5 had started
6 had finished

6 Second Conditional

1 would earn 2 could act 3 knew 4 would take 5 moved
6 would buy

7 reported speech

1 Jenny said that she had worked very hard.
2 Tony told me that he had gone to the theatre to see a new play.
3 Esther told me that she could sing quite well.
4 Jack said that the liberals would win the elections.
5 Anne-Marie said that she liked going out with her boyfriend.
6 Tim told me that watching TV was boring.
7 Jill said that she had spoken to them.
8 Colin told me that he had bought my tickets for the concert.

8 *both*, *neither* and *either*

1 Both 2 Neither 3 both 4 either 5 Neither 6 Either

Pronunciation

1

1 How long did it take you to get over losing your last girlfriend?
2 When you were younger, who did you go out with?
3 Do you think I should ask her out for dinner?
4 Why did Peter and Mary split up?

2

/dʒ/	/j/
judo	*yet*
jump	*young*
jungle	*yes*

3

1 Neither of my sisters are working yet.
2 You can choose either the red one or the blue one.
3 Both of my dogs are boxers.

Vocabulary

1a

1 after 2 up 3 up 4 to

b

1 depend 2 agree 3 spent 4 applied

2

1 A sightseeing holiday 2 A camping holiday 3 A beach holiday

3

1 kiss 2 wave 3 shake

4

1 Interest 2 A pension 3 Tax(es) 4 To withdraw
5 A salary 6 To save

Reading

2

1 true 2 true 3 false 4 false 5 true 6 false 7 false
8 true

3

1 The annual migration of wildebeest, zebras and gazelles
2 Detailed and personalised service
3 Interests, style of travel, money, time factors and anything else that may influence the trip
4 A first aid kit
5 This means to sacrifice comfort in order to get the cheapest possible accommodation.
6 He or she should be well-trained, experienced, know a lot about animals and speak different languages

Listening

Tapescript

I've just got back home to Ohio and I think I have just had the best holiday of my life. I did a three-week tour of the UK travelling around the country by coach and staying in hotels and bed and breakfasts in more than ten different towns. It was amazing! As soon as I got off the plane at Heathrow, I couldn't believe the number of different accents and foreign languages I was hearing. London is so cosmopolitan! I stayed there for a few days and did the typical sight seeing tours. You know... Buckingham Palace, Big Ben and all that. But do you know what I enjoyed most? Shopping in Harrods. I had never seen anything like that place before.
After London, we stayed in Cambridge for a day or two to look at the university and other buildings. Then we got on the coach again to go to Wales, which has a lovely capital city. What was its name again? Cardiff, that's right.
The next stop was Stratford-upon-Avon, where we visited Shakespeare's house and, after that, we were off to Liverpool to see the Beatles museum. I loved the people in this city. They were so sincere and their accents were so sweet! We also had the opportunity to admire the city of York, with its beautiful historical architecture and the mountains and countryside in the county of Yorkshire were wonderful too. After that, it was back to London and home again. The only thing you British don't have a lot of is nice beaches and good weather but that's no big deal because we don't either in my part of The States. And do you know what? I've already booked my ticket for another tour next year, this time it's Ireland and Scotland.

1

1 b) 2 a) 3 b) 4 c) 5 c) 6 b) 7 c) 8 c)

2

1 The different accents and foreign languages
2 Harrods. She went shopping there.
3 Their sincerity and their sweet accents
4 The mountains and the countryside
5 That's no big deal.
6 Ireland and Scotland

Notes

Notes

Pearson Education Limited,
Edinburgh Gate, Harlow
Essex, CM20 2JE, England
and Associated Companies throughout the world

www.longman.com

First published 2005

Designed by Pentacor

Illustrated by J. Luis Pardo, Pablo Torrecilla, and Pablo Velarde.

Set in Meta Plus Book 9.5pt
Printed in Spain
by Mateu Cromo

ISBN 0582 84191 7